PrestaShop for Developers

Alex Manfield

PrestaShop for Developers

Copyright © 2012 Alex Manfield

Cover by: Tsou Lee

This book contains proprietary information protected by copyright. No part of this book may be reproduced or transmitted in any form or by any means, electronic or mechanical, including photocopying and recording for any purpose other than the purchaser's personal use without the written permission of the Author.

No patent liability is assumed with respect to the use of the information contained herein. Although every precaution has been taken in the preparation of this book, the publisher and author assume no responsibility for errors or omissions. Nor is any liability assumed for damages resulting from the use of the information contained herein.

ISBN-13: 978-1468122343
ISBN-10: 1468122347

Printed in USA

revision: may 2012
www.levaweb.com

Warning and Disclaimer

Every effort has been made to make this book as complete and as accurate as possible, but no warranty or fitness is implied. The information provided is on an "as is" basis. The author and the publisher shall have neither liability nor responsibility to any person or entity with respect to any loss or damages arising from the information contained in this book.

Trademarks

PrestaShop and all other registered trademarks mentioned in this book belong to their respective owners. Use of a term in this book should not be regarded as affecting the validity of any trademark

Intro

PrestaShop is Open Source eCommerce software. This book is about PrestaShop with the hope that the material contained here could be useful to the community. The idea was to include in a single place most of the information needed to develop under PrestaShop but I'm aware that this book can just scratch the surface leaving to the reader the option to further develop the matter involved in this type of software.
Each one of us has his own way to code and here you'll find my personal way of doing things as I've experienced myself. Most of the code has been edited from the web and tested on Apache server before publishing. If you have any comments please let me know, I'll be glad to learn and update this book in the next revision.

The Open Source concept allows developers to build their applications and to access and modify the source code. To better understand the internals of PrestaShop we need to go through several concepts and technologies. You will probably don't need to have a degree in IT to understand them , just dedicate some time to digest and assimilate them. To help in this process you'll find Tutorials and tools (most of them freeware) which I used while developing with PrestaShop , I hope you'll enjoy them.
The latest version of PrestaShop at the time this book was written is 1.4.4 and version 1.5 was coming out. All references in this book are made to version 1.4.4 except when stated differently. Updates to the new version (currently 1.4.6.2) are described in a dedicated chapter at the end of this book. The trademark PrestaShop has been shorted in this book as PShop. Code references are usually marked with the keyword [code] to facilitate their search. The browser used in this book is Mozilla FireFox 8 under Windows 7 . Terms like Theme and Template have the same meaning in this book.

Credits

This book include code which is public domain or released under the GPL license and code snippets to facilitate the reader to grasp the concepts. Credits to the respective authors are indicated in square brackets in each chapter and at the end of this book.

Audience

If you do minor development in PrestaShop with PHP but you're not very comfortable with OOP and the core modules of this eCommerce solution then this book could help you . It's not intended to be the 'ultimate' resource for veterans but a tool to get answers to common questions and to enable you to write and debug your own code. For each topic this book is written trying to keep in mind a practical approach.
For those not very familiar with basic PHP they can jump to the PHP tutorial before visit the first chapter.

PrestaShop Links

The main official websites of PrestaShop are listed below :

www.prestashop.com
www.prestashop.com/wiki
http://addons.prestashop.com

Acknowledgments

The people from PrestaShop and their enthusiasm for their software together with the web community are the ones who really shaped this book. In particular many thanks to PrestaShop Wiki for the chapter related to *SEO and Marketing* as well as to the people of w3school.com for their contributions to the chapter about the *Programming's Tools*.

Table of Contents

PrestaShop Architecture	8
System Configuration	24
Database	42
Classes	68
PShop Programming Tools	100
Modules	133
Themes	155
SEO & Marketing	200
Step by Step Tutorials	219
NuSphere PhpED	278
Developer's Tools	300
PShop Upgrades	315
Index	321

PrestaShop Architecture

Overview	8
Folder Structure and files	9
FO & BO	10
MVC	11
Cache systems	13
XAMPP	14
Tokens	18
Credits	23

Overview

```
pshop144
   admin32
      ajaxfilemanager
      autoupgrade
      backups
      import
      tabs
      themes
   cache
   classes
   config
   controllers
   css
   docs
   download
   img
   js
   localization
   log
   mails
   modules
   override
   themes
   tools
   translations
   upload
   webservice
```

PShop is a multilingual and multi shop open source eCommerce solution. With PShop you (the administrator) can upload products with their related images to the database and manage orders, invoices, customers, employees (people who help you to manage the shop), manufacturers, suppliers, shipments and more.. (see PShop web site for the complete list of features).

You can sell products which need to be shipped as well as downloadable products (the download link will be sent to the customer automatically after payment). Modules and Themes (also called templates) add functionality to your shop and help you to manage different appearance. They are described in more details later in their respective chapters.

How to install PrestaShop: you require a web server which can be remote or installed in your PC. PrestaShop is written in PHP so you'll need a web server compatible with it and a MySQL backend database. In the chapter dedicated to the Tutorials you'll get more info on this.

Once you make sure that you have installed PHP and MySQL then simply unzip the file in an empty folder of your PC and upload it to the server (under Developer's Tools you'll find some useful info on how to do that). Before pointing your browser to the main entry point of PShop (index.php) you need two more things :

1. Install XAMPP
2. Setup a new database (see XAMPP)

Both the above points are discussed later in this chapter.
Finally point your browser to the URL where you've uploaded your shop and follow the instructions.

- Few basic concepts are required to go smoothly through this book :

- Front Office (FO) : is the part of your shop visible to the visitor (visitor or customer are used here with the same meaning)
- Back Office (BO) : is the control panel of your shop where the administrator configure it and is normally not accessible to your customers.
- Cache [1.1] is a component that transparently stores data so that future requests for that data can be served faster. This can be configured both in PShop and in your browser and , as a developer, you need to be careful to disable it if you want to debug your code effectively (see later in this chapter).
- Module : a software able to add functionality to the standard installation of PShop
- Theme : a software (template) able to change the appearance of your shop

Folder Structure and files

Once you have downloaded the latest revision from PrestaShop website, you have to unpack it into an empty folder from where you'll get the folder structure as below (see the Intro about which versions of PShop are discussed in this book) .

In the root (/PShop144) you'll get important files related to the FO including:

- Index.php : this is the entry point to the FO , means that any call at this file will run a feature of the FO. PShop uses the MVC pattern discussed later in this chapter and related to this file
- Authentication.php : the authentication page of the FO where your visitors are registered
- contact-form.php : this file is used to display (through its controller) contact information about your shop.
- footer.php : this file is included into index.php to display footer

PrestaShop for Developers © Alex Manfield

Administrator : this folder has to be renamed for security reasons and in the root contain files related to the BO like login.php (the administrator login) and the file index.php which is the entry point to the BO.

Administrator/Tabs : contains important files related to the BO like AdminProducts.php and AdminCategories.php able to process categories and products by extending the class AdminTab defined in Admintab.php

FO & BO

PShop , like a real shop, has a front office (FO) and a back office (BO). The front office is the place visited by your customers where they can browse through the products , place an order, pay for it and check the status of their orders. The status is available in a separate menu which become visible after their register on your shop. Many modules are available to help the visitor to navigate through your shop.
The BO is the place where the administrator configure the shop, here for instance you can choose the theme and modules you want to use . Some of the important Tabs are discussed below :

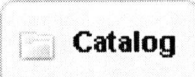
In Catalog you can load your products, configure special offers and discounts, define categories and sub-categories, insert manufacturers and suppliers and check for stock movements.

In Customers you can insert new customers or just check who has been registered on your shop or grouping them together. Customers are usually limited to the FO (if you want them to load and manage their products you may want to see the module MyProducts at www.levaweb.com)

Order processing , status, invoices, delivery slips, customer messages can all be managed here

Payment gateways , currencies, taxes and vouchers are managed here

 Carriers, countries, zones, price ranges and weight ranges are managed here

 Statistics about your shop and visitors are grouped here. Note that the information displayed here is linked to the tab Orders.

 When you click Modules PShop will scan the folder / modules and display them. Some modules can be configured under this tab, others do not have configurable options and simply run as is. All modules can be installed, uninstalled, enabled or disabled. In this tab you can also select the active theme (template) of your shop.

 Employees are people helping you to run the shop. Here you can define a profile and its related permissions then add employees to that. This way they can access the BO with limited privileges defined by the administrator (you). Here you can also manage BO tabs and the customer service.

Under Preferences you can configure many options including contact 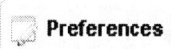 informations, themes (linked to Modules), emails, products, images, performance, measurements units, search options.

 In Tools you can manage languages and translations, bulk data import (see later), DB backup, define CMS pages, manage multi-stores, webservice (accessing your shop from 3rd party tools – see later) and upgrade your shop.

MVC

The MVC architecture is widely used in PShop and in the web in order to build a structured system by dividing it into functional areas. There could be many variants but the basic functionality could be represented as in the following :

- Model : manage the data and could be a class handling a specific task like getting the orders for a specific customer
- View : display data through a user interface (GUI) ie. where the registered visitor query the system for his orders
- Controller : the logic which process the request from the View and pass it over to the Model

Let's take an example from the PShop code :

```
[code   /PShop144/index.php]
require(dirname(__FILE__).'/config/config.inc.php');
ControllerFactory::getController('IndexControll
er')->run();
```

The first line 'require..' initialize constants and variables, the second 'ControllerFactory..' run the controller (IndexController) which in turn will display to the user (View) the homepage of the shop (index.tpl) through the public function run() :

```
[code   /PShop144/classes/FrontController.php]
     public function run()
     {
           $this->init();
           $this->preProcess();
           $this->displayHeader();
           $this->process();
           $this->displayContent();
           $this->displayFooter();
     }
```

The public function init() will check if the customer is registered and will load (if any) his products in the cart (Model) :

```
[code   /PShop144/classes/FrontController.php >
function init()]
if ((int)$cookie->id_cart)
           {
                 $cart = new Cart((int)$cookie->id_cart);
```

```
            if ($cart->OrderExists())
                unset($cookie->id_cart,
$cart);
```

Cache systems

As briefly discussed above the cache system in PShop is used to manage pages which are frequently called to avoid recompilation and improve performance. This can be based in memory or files. These options can be enabled or disabled in the BO > Preferences > Performance . When you're debugging your code it's advisable to disable the cache and force recompile for Smarty (the template engine) if you want to see your modified pages on screen.
CCC (combine, compress and cache) is an other option to improve the performance of CSS, HTML and JavaScript files.

In your browser is probably running an other cache system therefore,

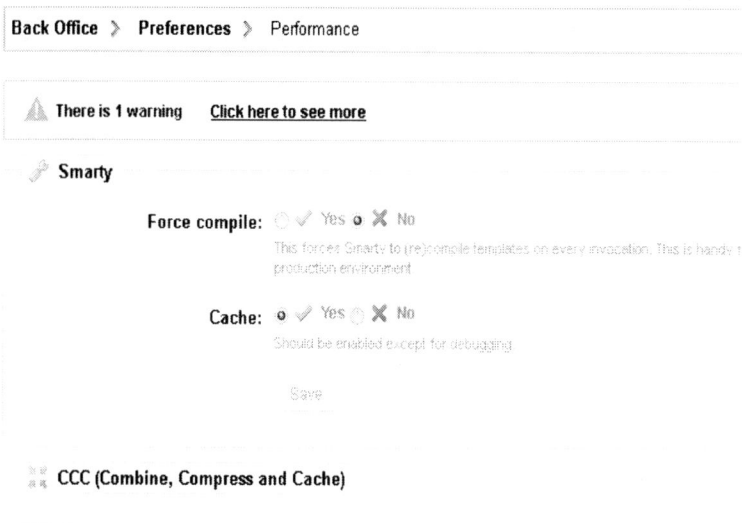

for debugging, you may want to disable it. I normally use FireFox and below is described how to disable the cache in this browser :

1. run FireFox
2. type about:config in the address bar
3. to get closer type 'cache' in the search bar
4. locate the row 'network.http.use-cache' and double-click it to make it 'false'

XAMPP

"XAMPP is an easy to install Apache distribution containing MySQL, PHP and Perl. XAMPP is really very easy to install and to use - just download, extract and start." [1.5]

XAMPP is not exactly part of PShop architecture but since you'll probably want to type and test some PHP code I thought that putting it at the end of this chapter would have made sense.

PHP is a server side script and you cannot run it without a web server which support it therefore either you install a web server on your PC or you upload the PHP files on your remote web server. One more advantage of using XAMPP is that you can debug your code or even a complex application like PShop by stepping through the code like we'll see later in the Tutorials.

On XAMPP official website you'll find versions for both Windows and Mac, let's see how to setup XAMPP and how to use it with PShop. I'll assume you run your code on Windows but the procedure will be mostly the same with Mac.

1. download XAMPP from the official website
2. install it on your PC
3. run or configure it as below

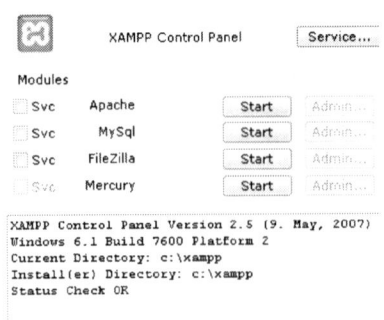

Run the server

XAMPP control panel will open by dbl-Click its icon on your desktop.

If you want XAMPP to run as a Windows Service check the box on the left of each line, otherwise just click Start on the first two lines (I usually start with MySQL then Apache). A Windows service is a program which runs in the background without user intervention and usually is loaded at boot time [1.6].

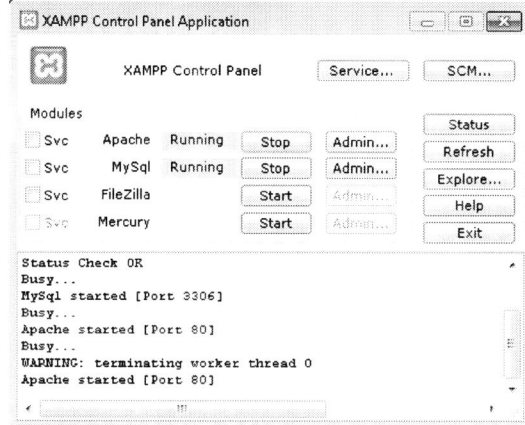

The control panel will now display the new status as below.

To test the web server simply type the following in your browser : http://localhost/xampp and you should get the Welcome page of XAMPP.
(If not see below)

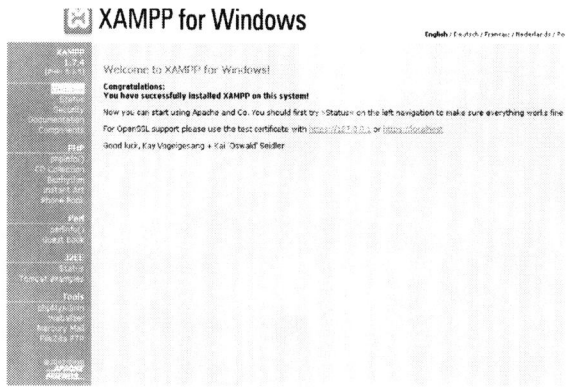

Access PHP version

From XAMPP control panel click on : phpinfo()

Change the port number

In case you're not getting XAMPP control panel, you may have an internal conflict with other web server installed on your PC.
If you have only one web server then you'll probably want to keep the default port (80). In case you have more web server (like IIS or JBoss) on the same system using the same port then you can change it to a different value. Edit file httpd.conf as below:

find "Listen 80" and change this port number to the port that you'll be using on your webserver. For this example, we'll use 7777. Now use "find" once again to look for "ServerName" , few lines below at the end of your server name, change port 80 to 7777. To test your Apache server just type in your browser the following line: http://localhost:8888 It is important that you allow network access to the server through your firewall in order to have a functioning server.

Run a PHP script

PHP scripts are usually files ending with .php like index.php. Type the following code in your text editor :

```
[code test.php]
<?php

echo ("Hi , welcome to XAMPP');
?>
```

All PHP files to be executed should be saved into the folder \htdocs (or its sub-folders). If you installed XAMPP on Windows you should be able to save the above file in : C:\xampp\htdocs\test.php .
To run test.php just make sure XAMPP is running (Apache) then type in your browser : http://localhost/ test.php and you should get "Hi , welcome to XAMPP"

Minimum PHP version Error

In case you get the following error "Minimum Php version required is 5.1.0. Recommended Php version is 5.2.x." but you already have PHP 5.3 (or higher) installed , the following original file should be changed as below :

```
[code install/welcome.php - ORIGINAL]

if (version_compare(phpversion(),'5.1.0') < 0 ||
version_compare(phpversion(),'5.3.0') >= 0) {
if(empty($mod_strings['LBL_MINIMUM_PHP_VERSION'])){
$mod_strings['LBL_MINIMUM_PHP_VERSION'] = 'Minimum Php version required is 5.1.0. Recommended Php version is 5.2.x.';
```

}

[code install/welcome.php - CHANGED]

if (version_compare(phpversion(),' 5.1.0') < 0 || version_compare(phpversion(),' 5.4.1') >= 0) {
if(empty($mod_strings['LBL_MINIMUM_PHP_VERSION'])){

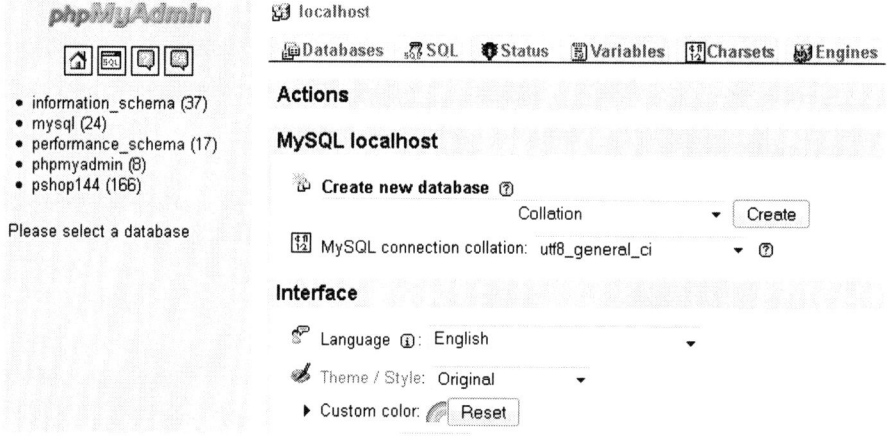

$mod_strings['LBL_MINIMUM_PHP_VERSION'] = 'Minimum Php version required is 5.1.0. Recommended Php version is 5.2.x.' ;
}

Just a little increment in the version number from 5.3.1 to 5.4.1

Access MySQL database

From XAMPP control panel click on phpMyAdmin and you'll get the following page on your browser :

From this page (left panel) you can select a database and update/ delete/ add new tables to it. You can also create a database for PShop. To do this just type PShop144 in the textbox "Create new database" and click "Create".

Tokens

Tokens require some understanding of PHP , therefore for those not much confident about OOP (Object Oriented Programming) it's probably better to have a look first at the PHP Tutorial at the end of this book. Tokens are visible is many pages of PShop , for instance when you click BO > Stats you'll get something like the following line in the address bar of your browser :

http://www.mysite.com/PShop/admin/index.php?tab=AdminStats&token=5a84847838a8592c6ed9d9dbf4ca70a4

Let's see now how pages are processed in PShop by using simple HTML and PHP code samples.
First we'll grasp the concept with few examples then we'll see how it is implemented in PShop.

PShop uses several forms to interact with the user and these forms are usually able to query the database or display data accordingly. Data gathered from the user is usually processed by HTML with POST (data sent through the address bar of your browser is hidden) and GET (data sent is visible in the address bar) methods , let's see an example as below :

```
[code  test.htm - <body> write the code here in your html file</body>]
<form name="input" action="form_action.php" method="post">
Username: <input type="text" name="user" />
<input type="submit" value="Submit" />
</form>
```

By executing the code above you'll get an input textbox with a submit button beside it. After submitting the form the execution will be passed to the file form_action.php
In PHP usually this approach is not used because in this way we need to maintain two files for each form and this can be confusing with large projects. Instead we can have the same page to process the data input and this is done with the help of a PHP server variable called

$_SERVER , see the code below :

```
[code   test.php  -  <body>  write  the  code  here  in
your html file</body>]
<form name="input" method="post" action="<?php echo
$_SERVER['PHP_SELF']; ?>" >
Username: <input type="text" name="user" />
<input type="submit" value="Submit" />
</form>
```

Note that we've included in the code the PHP tags <?php and ?> the extension of the file has become test.php. The first line "?php echo $_SERVER['PHP_SELF'].." will redirect the execution to the same file (test.php) since the filename of the caller is saved in the server variable PHP_SELF.

Now we need to process the input in the same page and this can be done as below :

```
[code   test.php]
<?php
if(isset($_POST['submit']))    // this line will
check if the page has been submitted
{
    $name = $_POST['name'];
    echo "the page has been submitted";  // here we
process the input from the user
}
?>
<form name=" input"   method=" post"   action=" <?php echo
$_SERVER[ 'PHP_SELF' ]; ?>" >
    <input type=" text"  name=" name" ><br>
    <input type=" submit"  name=" submit"
value=" Submit" ><br>
</form>
```

The code above need now to be secured against hackers which could execute an external script by changing the URL in the address bar of the browser or simply to avoid multiple refreshes of the page while it's processing on the server. First we need to protect the variable PHP_SELF then we'll apply a token to the page to make sure that the page is submitted only once. Just replace the line <form method ..> with the following :

```
[code]
<form name="input" action="<?php echo htmlenti-
ties($_SERVER['PHP_SELF']); ?>" method="post">
```

The function htmlentities() is used to encode HTML commands (entities) so that an attempt to change the URL (to execute a malicious script) will fail.

Finally to make sure the page is submitted only once we can generate a token and check if the same is read back when the page is submitted , to do this we save the token in a server variable called $_SESSION which we enable with the call session_start() :

```
[code  test.php]
<?php
session_start();

if (isset($_POST['submit']))   // this will check if the page has been submitted
{
   If(isset($_SESSION['mytoken']) && $_POST['mytoken'] == $_SESSION['mytoken'])
   // the line above will check if 'mytoken' exist and if it is the same as the one created before submitting the page
    {
       $myname = htmlentities($_POST['name']);
       Echo "my name is: $myname <br>";   // here you process data input
    }
}

$mytoken = $_SESSION ['mytoken']= md5(uniqid(mt_rand(),true));
?>
<form name="input"  method="post" action="<?php
```

```
echo $_SERVER['PHP_SELF']; ?>">
    <input type="hidden" name="mytoken" value="<?=$mytoken; ?>">
    <input type="text" name="name"><br>
    <input type="submit" name="submit" value="Submit"><br>
</form>
```

In the above code MD5 (hash algorithm) is encoding a random number and saving it to $mytoken.
If you run the above test.php you'll see the HTML source below in your browser :

```
[code test.php - as seen by the browser]
<form name=" input"  method=" post" action=" /PShop/test.php" >
    <input type=" hidden" name=" mytoken" value=" ed454f9d0db241181fe182bb97a56c8a" >
    <input type=" text" name=" name" ><br>
    <input type=" submit" name=" submit" value=" Submit" ><br>
</form>
```

The function htmlentities() can further be replaced by a custom function (checkname) which will check the data input for a name (ie will not contain numbers). The final code will be as below:

```
[code test.php]
<?php
session_start();

if (isset($_POST['submit']))   // this will check if the page has been submitted
{
  If(isset($_SESSION['mytoken']) && $_POST['mytoken'] == $_SESSION['mytoken'])
   // the line above will check if 'mytoken' exist and if it is the same as the one created before submitting the page
    {
      $myname = checkname($_POST[ 'name']);
```

```
        Echo "my name is: $myname <br>";   // here you
process data input
   }
}
function checkname ($var1)
{
 return preg_replace('/[^a-zA-Z0-9]/','',$var1);
}
$mytoken = $_SESSION [ 'mytoken' ]= md5(uniqid(mt_
rand(),true));
?>
<form name=" input"   method=" post"  action=" <?php echo
$_SERVER[ 'PHP_SELF' ]; ?>" >
   <input type=" hidden"  name=" mytoken"
value=" <?=$mytoken; ?>" >
   <input type=" text"  name=" name" ><br>
   <input type=" submit"  name=" submit"
value=" Submit" ><br>
</form>
```

The function preg_replace will do a search & replace on the string $var1.

Now let's open the code below and see how tokens works in PShop when we run /PShop/admin/login.php :

```
[code /admin/login.php]
/* Cookie creation and redirection */
if (Tools::isSubmit( 'Submit' ))
{
       /* Check fields validity */
       $passwd = trim(Tools::getValue( 'passwd' ));
// ...

/* Redirect to admin panel */
if (isset($_GET[ 'redirect' ]))
$url = strval($_GET[ 'redirect' ].(isset($_GET[ 'token' ]) ?
( '&token=' .$_GET[ 'token' ]) : '' ));
```

The variable $url contain the URL of the redirected page and If we look into the static class Tools we'll find the variable $_POST (and $_GET) as expected :

[code /classes/Tools.php]
```
    public static function isSubmit($submit)
    {
    return (
isset($_POST[$submit]) OR isset($_POST[$submit.'_x']) OR isset($_POST[$submit.'_y'])
OR isset($_GET[$submit]) OR isset($_GET[$submit.'_x']) OR isset($_GET[$submit.'_y'])
        );
    }
```

Tokens are generated in the class Tools by the function getToken (Tools::getToken) called by AuthController.php (line 310). The part related to HTML (which will render the page to the browser) is defined in admin/login.php approx. starting at line 100 using the PHP function echo().

Credits

[1.1] http://en.wikipedia.org/wiki/Cache
[1.2] http://en.wikipedia.org/wiki/Model-view-controller
[1.3] http://php-html.net/tutorials/model-view-controller-in-php/
[1.4] www.apachefriends.org
[1.5] http://en.wikipedia.org/wiki/Windows_service
[1.6] http://www.html-form-guide.com/php-form/php-form-action-self.html

System Configuration

Homepage logo	25
Flash movie	25
Favicon	25
Page Title	26
Orders and Stats	27
Copyright bottom line	27
Email notifications	27
Contact Form	28
Information Blocks	29
Vouchers and Coupons	29
Carriers	31
Preferences	33
Tools	37
Configure BO for your customers	39
Credits	41

In this chapter we'll se how to do basic configuration PShop through the BO or by changing some original code. I would suggest to install XAMPP on your PC and install PShop in a sub-folder of the htdocs. For the purpose of this book we'll use the following PShop root : C:\xampp\htdocs\pshop144

If you do not want to install XAMPP you can test your scripts by uploading them on your remote server. (see Developer's Tools later in this book).

Homepage logo

The logo of the shop can be changed in BO > Modules > Themes
If you want to change the position of the logo then you may have a look at how to create Themes later in this book. The large image at the center of the homepage is called homepage logo and can be changed in BO > Modules > Home text editor . To avoid any confusion with the logo of your shop we'll call it 'homepage image'

Flash movie

You can insert a Flash movie directly in the homepage text editor : BO > Modules > Home text editor
For instance if you save your file in : C:\xampp\htdocs\pshop144\mymovie.swf then you can click the icon "Insert embedded media" and type the following URL : http://localhost/pshop144/Movie1.swf
Your movie will be displayed right below the homepage image providing you've installed the Flash player in your system.

Favicon

This is the small icon associated which your website and displayed in your browser. As per the homepage logo this icon can be changed in BO > Modules > Themes

Page Title

Page title is important especially for improving your SEO (see later). It's advisable to have a meaningful page title to improve the page ranking of your shop. This title can be changed as below :

```
[code classes/Tools.php  Original]
$metaTags['meta_title'] = $defaultValue.' - '.Configuration::get('PS_SHOP_NAME');
```

```
[code classes/Tools.php  Changed]
$metaTags['meta_title'] = $defaultValue.' - ');
```

You may also delete the line commented below :

```
[code classes/Tools.php  ORIGINAL]
public static function completeMetaTags($metaTags, $defaultValue)
    {
        global $cookie;

        if ($metaTags[ 'meta_title' ] == NULL)
            $metaTags[ 'meta_title' ] = $defaultValue.' - '.Configuration::get( 'PS_SHOP_NAME' );  // you may delete this line and the one above
        if ($metaTags[ 'meta_description' ] == NULL)
            $metaTags[ 'meta_description' ] = Configuration::get( 'PS_META_DESCRIPTION' , (int)($cookie->id_lang)) ? Configuration::get( 'PS_META_DESCRIPTION' , (int)($cookie->id_lang)) : '' ;
        if ($metaTags[ 'meta_keywords' ] == NULL)
            $metaTags[ 'meta_keywords' ] = Configuration::get( 'PS_META_KEYWORDS' , (int)($cookie->id_lang)) ? Configuration::get( 'PS_META_KEYWORDS' , (int)($cookie->id_lang)) : '' ;
        return $metaTags;
    }
```

You can also change the page title for each product page, to do this goto BO > Catalog and select a product for edit. In the first Tab 'Info' you'll get a link just before the short description : 'Click here to improve product's rank in search engines (SEO)' where you can change title, description, keywords and friendly URL.

Orders and Stats

In the BO there is the tab Stats where you can check the site traffic and other useful informations.
In particular if we click on the left-menu 'Sales and Orders' , we get the orders displayed on the right panel . If we place an order in the FO and this is not displayed then goto BO > Orders , select the order and make sure to update it ie. check its status as 'Payment accepted'. This way it will be displayed in Stats providing the Calendar (on the left panel) is selected for the proper date range.

Copyright bottom line

In PShop 1.4 the copyright info in the footer has been moved to *modules/blockcms/blockcms.tpl*
In general you can search and comment the variable : $display_poweredby

Email notifications

A useful function implemented in PShop is the email notification which is sent automatically by PShop (usually to the admin) when a customer place an order. This and other options are described below and you can setup them in BO > Modules > Mail Alerts > Configure > Send to this emails

- Gives the customer the option of receiving a notification for an available product if this one is out of stock.
- Receive a notification if a new order is made (admin)
- Receive a notification if the quantity of a product is below the

alert threshold (admin)

Contact Form

When a customer want to send a message to the shop administrator (merchant) they are usually directed to the contact form embedded in PShop.

1. Contact form : it can be customized in BO > Employees > Contacts
2. Contact name : to have it in the subject of the email , you can edit the file below :

```
[code pshop144/contact-form.php   - ORIGINAL]
if (Mail::Send(intval($cookie->id_lang), 'contact' ,
 'Message from contact form' , array( '{email}' => $_
POST[ 'from' ], '{message}' => stripslashes($message)),
$contact->email))
```

```
[code pshop144/contact-form.php   - MODIFIED]
if (Mail::Send(intval($cookie->id_lang), 'contact' , $con-
tact->name, array( '{email}' => $_POST[ 'from' ], '{mes-
sage}' => stripslashes($message)), $contact->email))
```

3. Email message : you can change it in *pshop144/mails/xx/contact.html* where xx is the default language used.
4. Remove logo from emails: this can be done by comment out the line below with // :

```
[code pshop144/classes/Mail.php   - ORIGINAL]
$templateVars['{shop_logo}'] = (file_exists(_PS_
IMG_DIR_.'logo_mail.jpg')) ? $message->attach(new
Swift_Message_Image(new Swift_File(_PS_IMG_
DIR_.'logo_mail.jpg'))) : ((file_exists(_PS_IMG_
```

```
DIR_.'logo.jpg')) ? $message->attach(new Swift_Mes-
sage_Image(new Swift_File(_PS_IMG_DIR_.'logo.
jpg'))) : '');
```

Otherwise you can just replace the above *.jpg files with you own logo

Information Blocks

These blocks can be configured in BO > Modules

1. User info block : adds a block that displays information about the customer.
2. The 'Info Block' allow the user to login and is usually displayed top-right of the standard theme. It doesn't have the option to add links but 'Link Block' does.
3. Link Block : contain links like Terms of Use and Secure Payments
4. Permanent links block : adds a block that displays permanent links such as sitemap, contact, etc.
5. This block is usually displayed in the footer of your shop in the standard theme
6. CMS Block : adds a block with several CMS links. CMS pages are pages created by the user such as 'Privacy' or 'Terms of Use' ..
7. My Account block : displays a block with links relative to user account.
8. Block advertising : adds a block to display an advertisement. By default this include the picture of a monitor displayed on the bottom-left of the standard theme

Vouchers and Coupons

"A voucher is a bond which is worth a certain monetary value and which may be spent only for specific reasons or on specific goods." [2.1]
"In marketing, a coupon is a ticket or document that can be exchanged

for a financial discount or rebate when purchasing a product." [2.2]
A Coupon is essentially the same as a Voucher and in PShop can be a code your customer need to enter before paying the order.

One way to use vouchers could be to create groups of customers say Bronze, Silver and Gold depending on their loyalty to your shop. This is

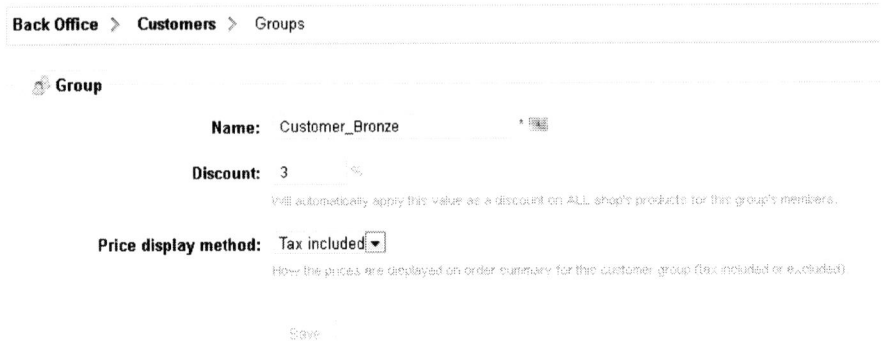

not strictly necessary as you can always assign vouchers to individual customers but it's probably easier to manage groups rather than single customers.

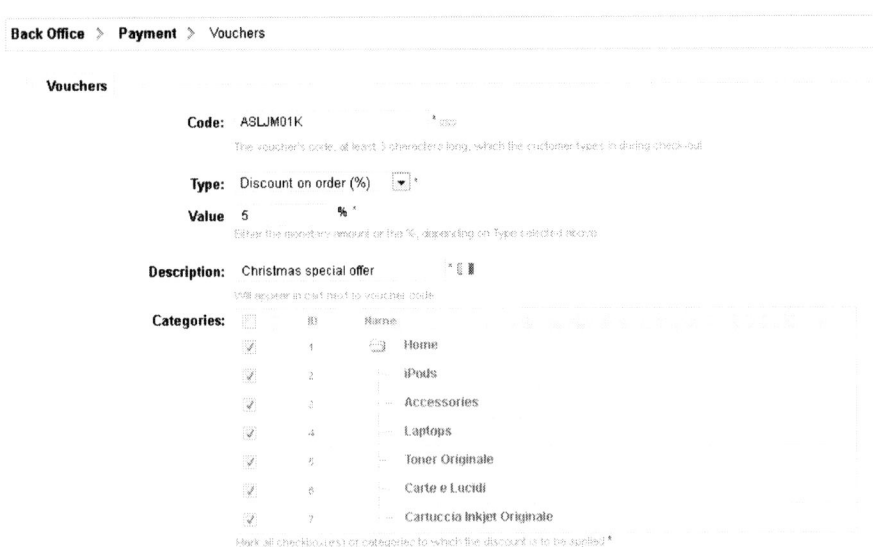

When you create a group you can also assign a default discount to all customers belonging to it. Therefore a voucher assigned to that group will add a discount to the existing one , ie. if the group's discount is 3% and the voucher gives an additional 5% the total discount for the customer will be 8%.
Bronze customers have less orders and therefore less discount compared to Gold customers.
You can access groups in BO > Customers > Groups as indicated below :

Now you can assign vouchers to a particular group of customers .
Goto BO > Payments > Vouchers and click *New* as below :

In PShop you have many options to define your vouchers including starting and ending date, customers with valid voucher, max quantity available for your voucher and the applicable categories of products.

Vouchers can be very effective on increasing your sales and later in a dedicated chapter we'll see how much they can impact your shop from a marketing perspective.

Carriers

The shipping costs of the product(s) are added to the total amount and there is a dedicated Tab in the BO which is designed to manage them : BO > Shipping
In the main window you'll be able to setup global handling charges and fees for a selected carrier, then you can setup more details as in the following links :

- Carriers : here you can define some useful info including name and logo of the carrier, geographical zones of activity

Back Office > Shipping

Handling

- Handling charges: 2 € (tax excl.)
- Free shipping starts at: 0 €
- Free shipping starts at: 0 kg

Save

and customer's group (see vouchers)
- Countries: where the carrier is active
- Price Ranges : assign price ranges to your carriers
- Weight Ranges : as above for weight ranges

If you need more flexibility on calculating the shipping fees you could have a look at the article "Carrier modules: functions, creation and configuration" posted on PrestaShop Blog [2.3]
Later in a dedicated chapter we'll see some hints on how shipping charges can be adjusted to better please your customers.

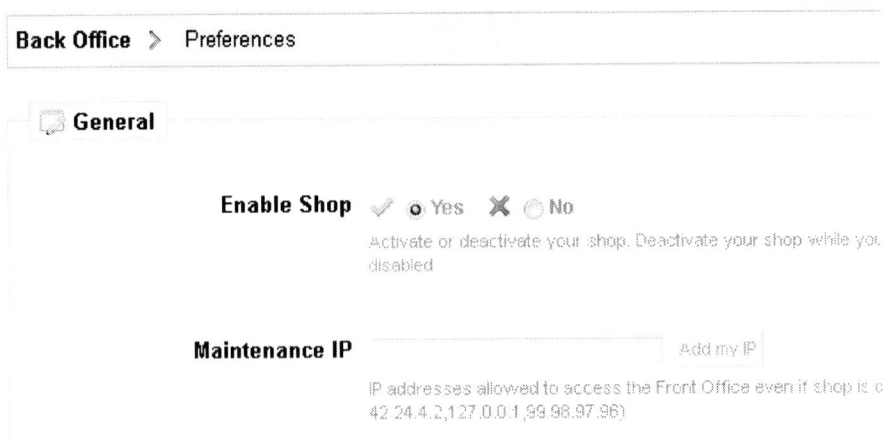

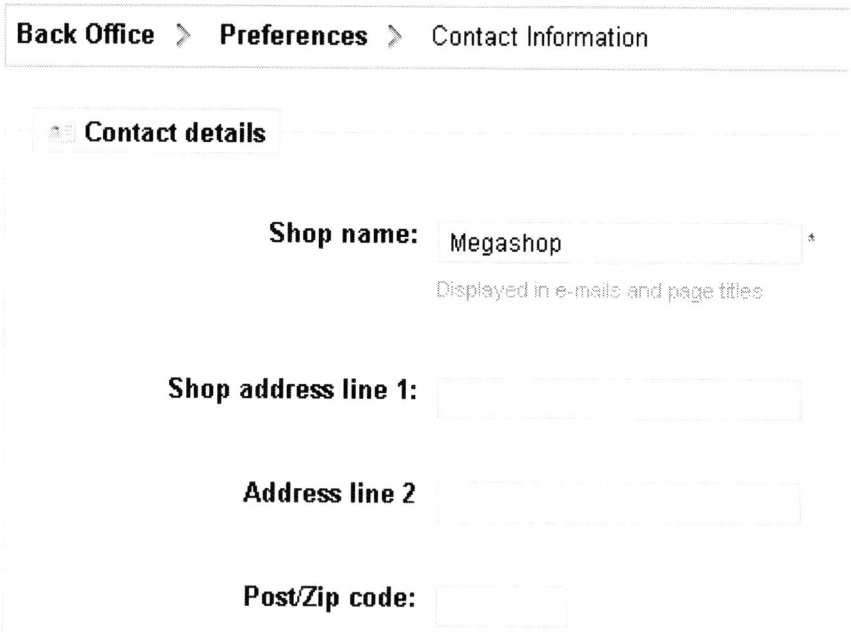

Back Office > **Preferences** > Contact Information

Contact details

Shop name: Megashop *

Displayed in e-mails and page titles

Shop address line 1:

Address line 2

Post/Zip code:

Preferences

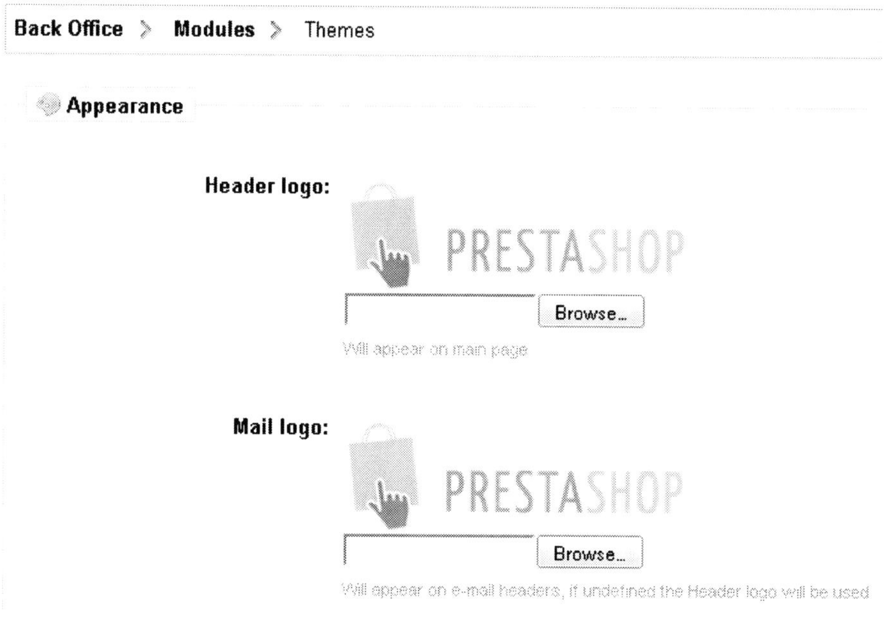

Back Office > **Modules** > Themes

Appearance

Header logo:

[Browse...]

Will appear on main page

Mail logo:

[Browse...]

Will appear on e-mail headers, if undefined the Header logo will be used

PShop has several options which can be setup in order to customize your shop. These can be setup in BO > Preferences. The main options on the first page include the following :

- Enable Shop : can be used for maintenance purpose
- Enable SSL : encryption for secure payments and customer data processing
- Order process page : can be normal (5 steps) or fast (one page checkout)

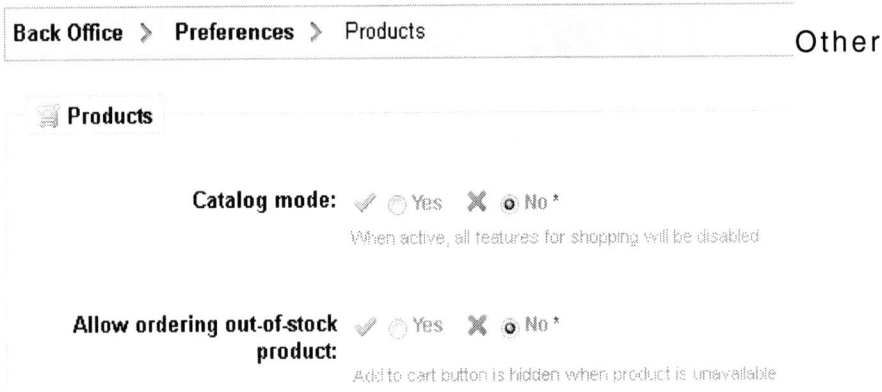

Other options can be displayed in the following links :

Contact Information : here you can define your contact info

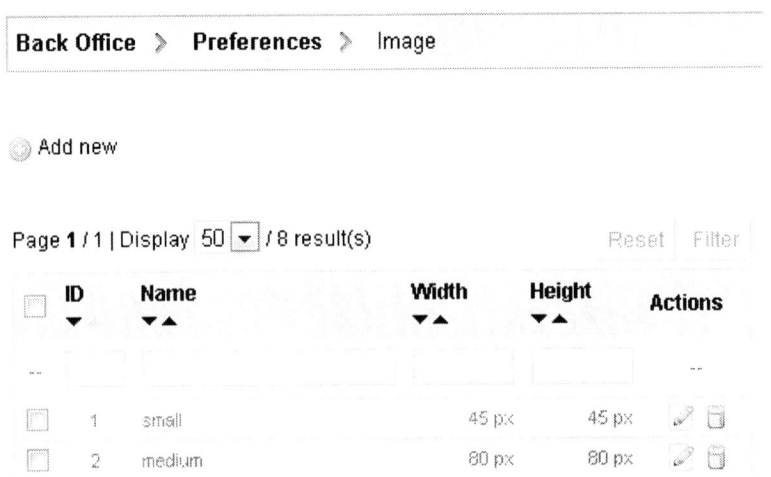

System Configuration - Pag. 34

Appearance : link back to Modules > Themes

Back Office > Preferences > Database

Be VERY CAREFUL with these settings, as changes may cause your PrestaShop online store to config/settings.inc.php file.

Database

Server: localhost
IP or server name, 'localhost' will work in most cases

Products : display several options including :

- Catalog Mode : the customer will not be able to buy as pricing will be disabled on all products

Back Office > Preferences > Localization

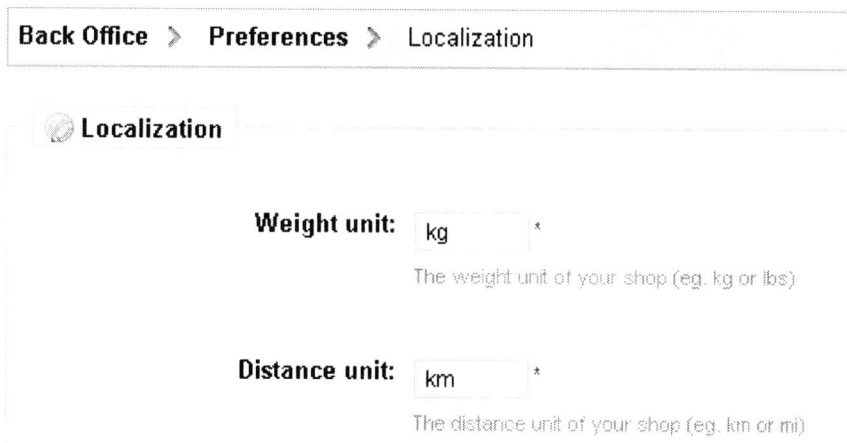

- Minimum purchase amount
- Products per page
- Maximum size of product pictures

Search

Ajax search ✓ ● Yes ✗ ○ No
Enable the ajax search for your visitors.
With the ajax search, the first 10 products matc

Instant search: ✓ ○ Yes ✗ ● No
Enable the instant search for your visitors.
With the instant search, the results will appear

Images : here you can setup image sizes for your shop and even store your images in the new image system which is optimized for

Options

(?) The following features are only available if you enable the Geolocation by IP feature.

Geolocation behavior for restricted countries: Visitors can't see your catalog

Geolocation behavior for undefined countries: Visitors can't see your catalog

Select countries that can access your store:
☐ Name
☑ Afghanistan
☑ Aland Islands

performance (useful if you have lot of images to deal with).

Database : here you can define the database engine for you tables and its name and password. (see the dedicated chapter for more details on the database)

Localization : here you can setup units of measurement or import localization packs including taxes, currency, language and units of measurement.

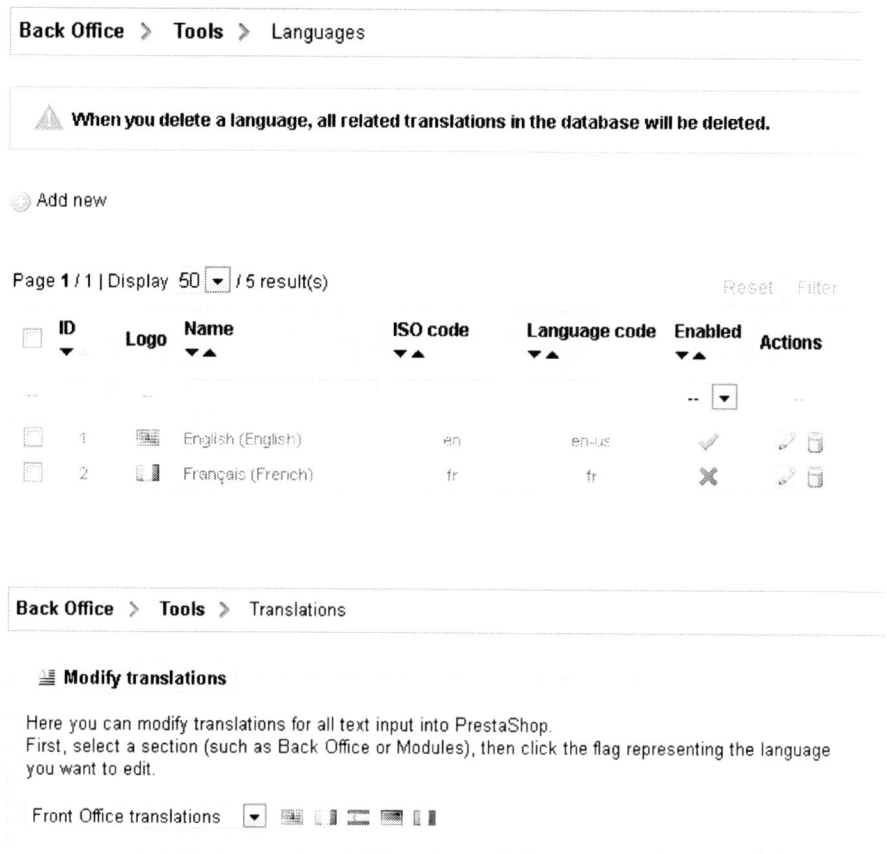

Search : this option can be used to improve the search performance by indexing your products and setting search weights

Performance : this has been discussed in the cache system
Geolocation : here you can define which countries can access your shop (by IP identification)

Tools

There are many tools available to the administrator including :

Languages : here you get a list off all languages installed in your

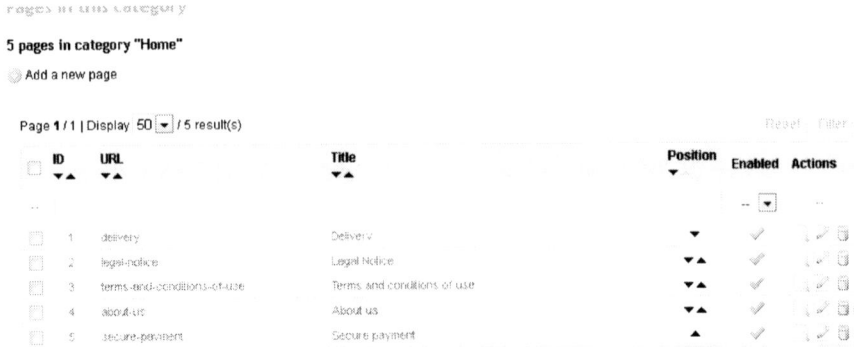

shop. They can be enabled or disabled and you can define the default language for your shop.

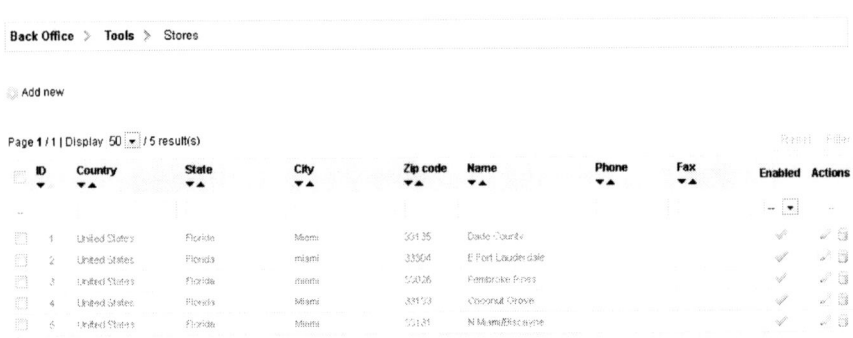

Translations : once you've defined the language you can translate your shop for that language . This include FO, BO, Error messages and more... With this option you ca also import on the server a language pack.

Import : this option allows to import data in the database and will be discussed in a separate chapter

Backup : this option is useful to backup your database. Alternatively you can also do it directly from the phpMyAdmin interface which control the MySQL database in most servers.

CMS : here you can create pages to be added in your CMS module and displayed in the FO.

Stores : being a multi-shop eCommerce, PShop can manage multiple stores from a single control panel. For each store you can change status, address, picture

Webservice : as for the option Import, this option too will be discussed in a separate chapter

Upgrade : this (new) option allows you to upgrade the shop to the new release.

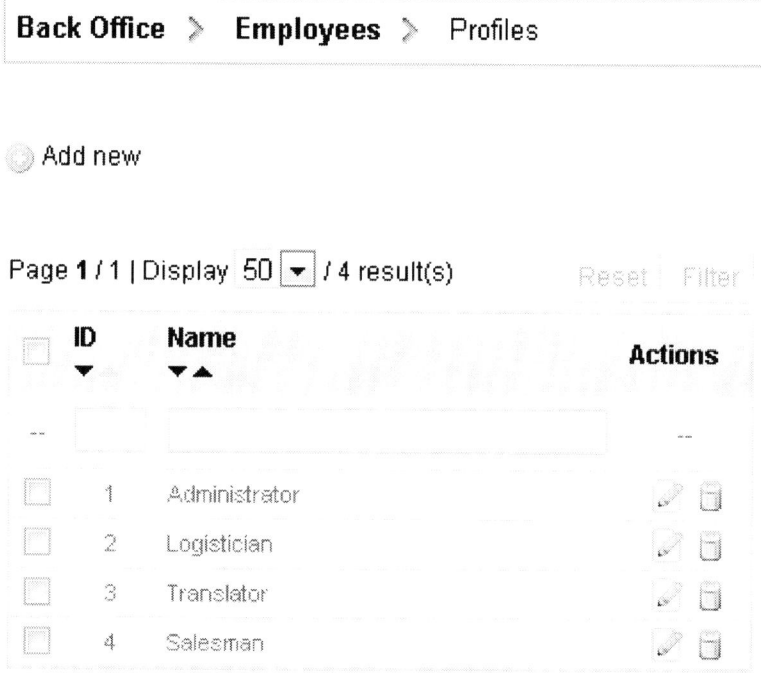

Configure BO for your customers

The BO can be accessed by different users: the administrator (you) who first installed the shop and usually called super-admin, the administrator(s) or employees who usually help you to run the shop and sometimes the customer to whom you've installed the shop or the end user.

Back Office > Employees > Permissions

Logistician	View	Add	Edit	Delete	All
Search	✓	☐	☐	☐	☐
Home	✓	☐	☐	☐	☐
Catalog	✓	✓	✓	✓	✓
» Tracking	☐	☐	☐	☐	☐

In most cases the super-admin and the admin are the same person , let's consider a typical scenario : you have installed an empty shop

Back Office > Employees

Employees

Last name:	bob *
First name:	Trump *
Password:	*
	Leave blank if you do not want to change your password
E-mail address:	bob00@gmail.com *

to your customer which in turn need to populate it with products. In this case you need to give your customer a limited access to the BO since you want to make sure they can manage their products without changing sensitive configuration data in the shop which may damage its structure and functionality.
Customers which can access the BO are called Employees. In the BO you can setup permissions for them :

1. BO > Employees > Profiles : here you have a list of default profiles which you can rename or modify:

2. For each profile you can assign different permissions

3. Finally each profile can be assigned to an employee : *BO > Employees > New* there you can enter name, password, email and assign a profile to the employee.

Credits

[2.1] http://en.wikipedia.org/wiki/Voucher
[2.2] http://en.wikipedia.org/wiki/Coupon
[2.3] http://www.prestashop.com/blog/article/8867

Database

Structure	43
Database Design Tools	47
SQL queries	55
Data Import	56
Web Service	59
SQL Injection	64
Credits	67

In this chapter we'll see how to manage the back-end database of PShop through the BO or by changing some code. As for the previous chapter I would suggest to install XAMPP on your PC and install PShop in a sub-folder of the htdocs. For the purpose of this book we'll use the following PShop root: C:\xampp\htdocs\pshop144

If you do not want to install XAMPP you can test your scripts by uploading them on your remote server. (see Developer's Tools later in this book)

Structure

When you installed PShop you had the option to prefix the system tables with a keyword (by default **ps_**). This is useful in case you want to share the database with other applications. Some Hosting companies provide packages with a limited number of databases and if you run many applications on the same server you can optimize the usage of each database by sharing it with multiple applications.

The name given to the tables is self-explaining ie. *ps_carrier* deal with carriers whereas *ps_cms* with cms pages.

Many tables have the suffix **_lang** which defines the content in the available languages of your shop. For instance the table ps_order_message has associated the table ps_order_message_lang and both are related by the common field *id_ order_message* . The table ps_order_message_lang (see picture below) contain also the index id_lang used to identify the same message (stored in the field *message*) in the available languages defined in BO (see Tools).

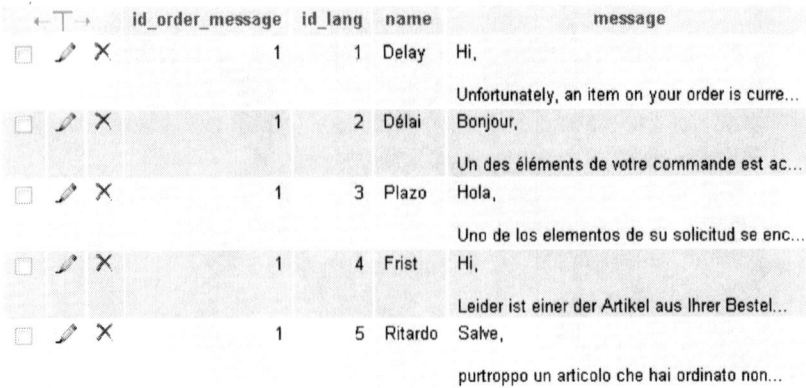

One interesting table is the ps_configuration which store configuration data like PS_SHOP_NAME or PS_TAX , MA_MERCHANT_MAILS (containing the admin email) , plus a number of user-defined variables saved by the developer (see chapter Modules).

If you want to export any table just click on Export on the top of the phpMyAdmin window :

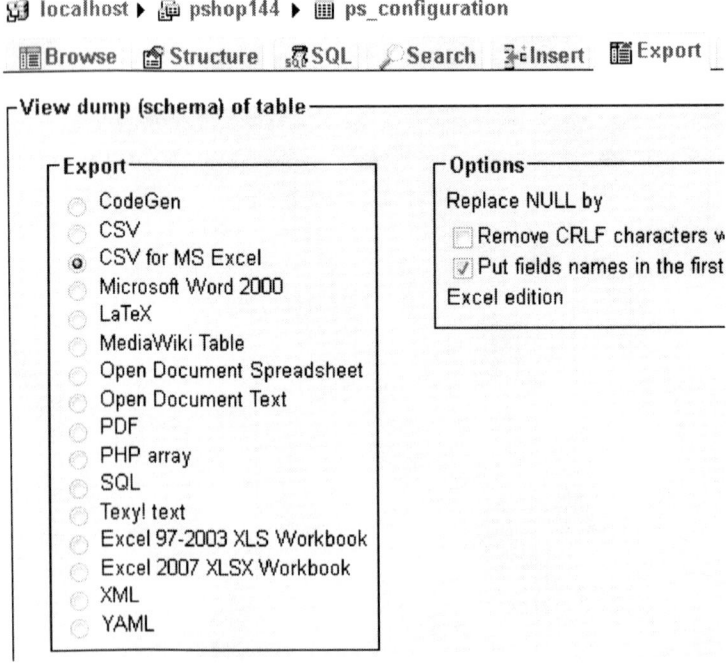

You can also create a simple query and export it (see Tutorials for more details) :

1. click on SQL tab then GO
2. at the bottom of the window click Export

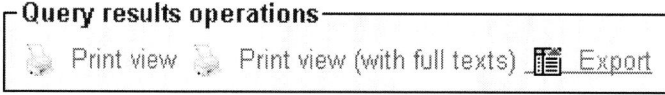

If you want to change the structure of any table (be careful with PShop core tables) just click on Structure on the top of the phpMyAdmin window:

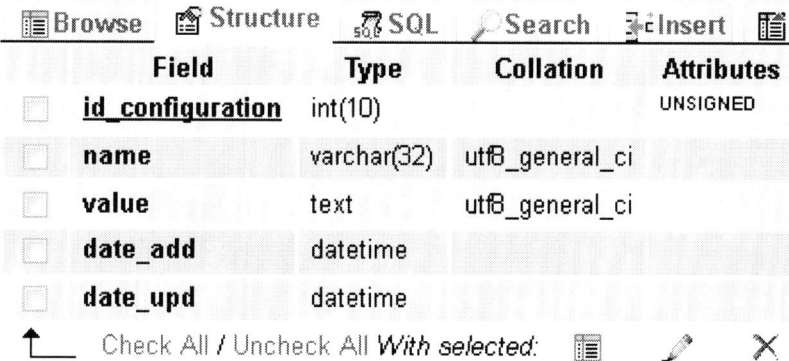

Following are some important concepts about the database management system (DBMS) . MySQL support many storage engines but the most relevant are MyISAM and InnoDB.

Forein keys

A foreign key is a field in a relational table that matches a candidate key of another table. The foreign key can be used to cross-reference tables. [3.1]

For instance in PShop the field *id_order_message* which is common between the two tables *ps_order_message* and *ps_order_message_lang* is a foreign key

Database Locking

The locking mechanism defines how access and updates to the database are controlled. For instance when an object is locked for updating (ie. a table), other processes cannot modify it until the update has completed.
This mechanism affects how many different applications can update the information in the databases well as the queries launched on that data. In fact queries may be accessing data that could have been altered or updated. Both SQL statements (see Tutorial) INSERT and UPDATE require locking therefore in a database multiple applications accessing the same data can have a significant impact.

Locking mechanisms are supported by different storage engines at different levels: table locking, block locking and row locking. Table locking is most commonly supported and is the locking provided in MyISAM tables. The entire table during an update will be locked. This will limit the number of applications that are updating a specific table and can affect heavily used databases because it introduces delays into the update process.
Page level locking locks data according to the page size that is being uploaded. This is not an issue while updating data across a range of locations within the database , but adding a large number of rows involves locking the final page size of the data structure and can introduce significant delays.
Row level locking provides a good compromise since only individual rows within a table are locked. This means that many applications can be updating different rows of the same table without triggering a lock issue. InnoDB supports row level locking.

Indexing

Indexing can dramatically speed up the performance when searching data from the database. This is done differently depending on the storage engine.

Transactions

Transactions provide a safe data exchange during the update or insert process. Data is effectively added to the database only when other conditions in the application execution have completed successfully. For instance you insert your card in the Cash Point to retrieve money but the transaction is registered only when the debit in your account and the cash delivery is completed successfully.

MyISAM

The MyISAM engine is the default engine in most MySQL installations and is a derivative of the original ISAM engine type supported in the early versions of the MySQL system. The engine provides the best combination of performance and functionality, although it lacks transaction capabilities and uses table-level locking. The max database size is defined as 256TB.

InnoDB

The InnoDB Engine supports all of the database functionality of MyISAM engine and also adds full transaction capabilities (with full ACID (Atomicity, Consistency, Isolation, and Durability) compliance) and row level locking of data.

In the InnoDB system caching and indexing structure are cached in memory as well as being stored on disk. This enables very fast recovery, and works even on very large data sets. By supporting row level locking, you can add data to an InnoDB table without locking the table with a resulting speeds up for the data recovery and storage. The max database size is defined as 64TB.

Database Design Tools

A version of the database diagram for PShop can be found at *doc.prestashop.com* . However if you want to keep it always updated it's probably better to generate it yourself and there are free tools able to do it like the two described here: MySQL Workbench and Tod for MySQL. The schema of a database is structure described in a formal language supported by the DBMS [3.2]. The process of getting the schema of your database is also called Reverse Engineering by some tools.

MySQL Workbench

1. Download MySQL Workbench from the official site :

http://dev.mysql.com/downloads

2. Click on *Create EER module from existing Database*
3. Click Next on the window below

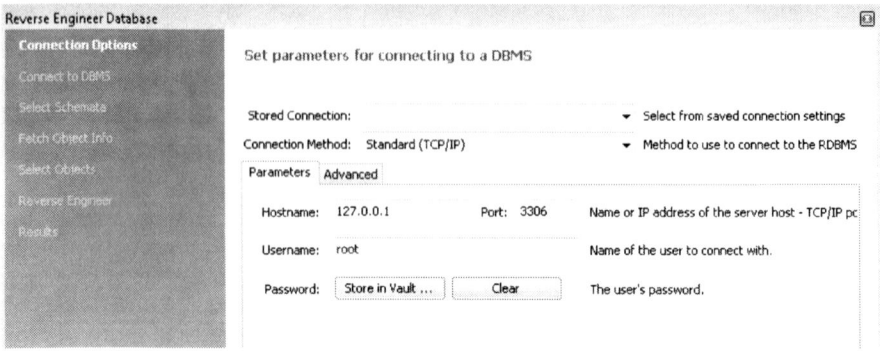

The tool will connect to your database showing the results as below :

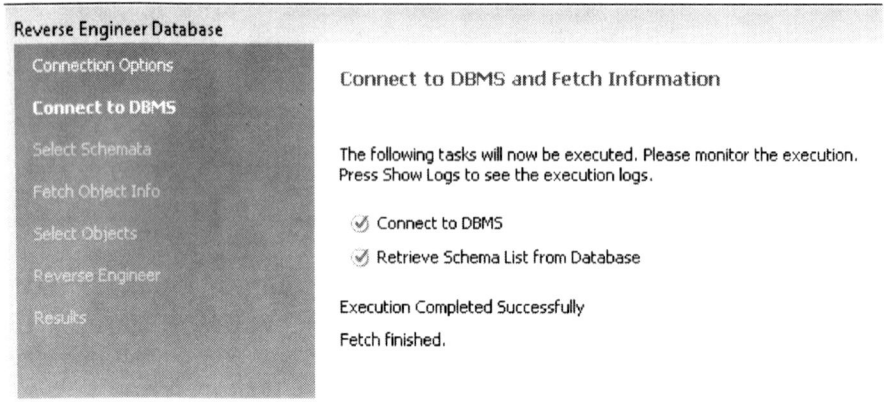

Click Next , select the database and again next for the following windows then you'll get the database diagram :

Database - Pag. 48

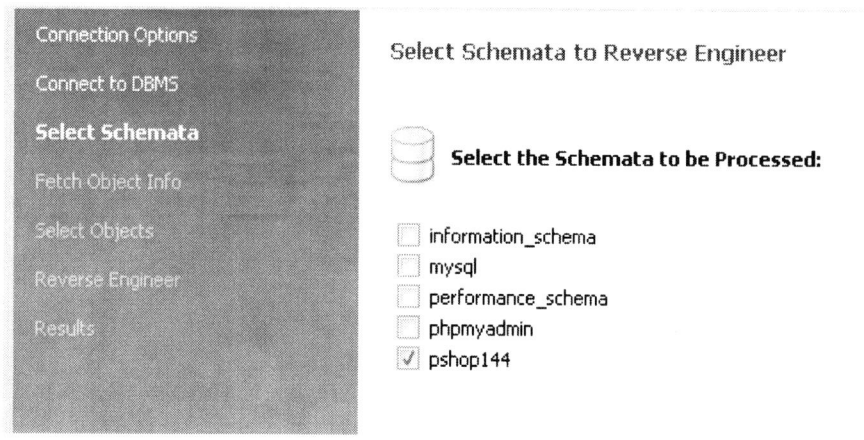

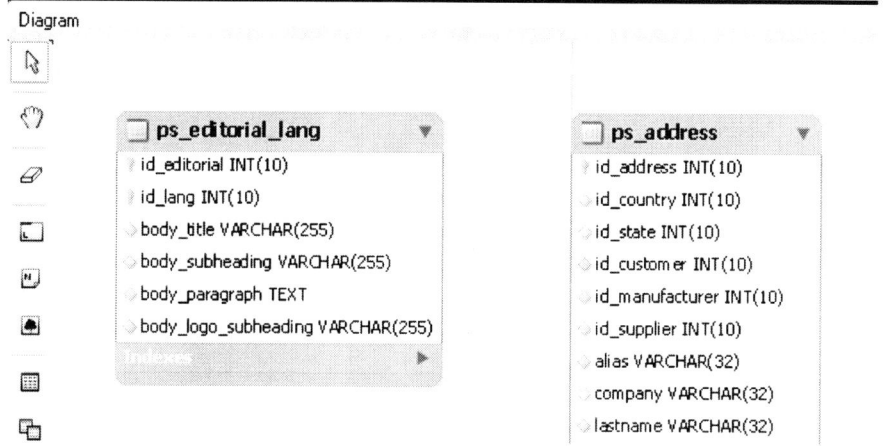

Tod for MySQL

1. download the software from *http://www.quest.com/downloads/*
2. run it and follow the default options as below :

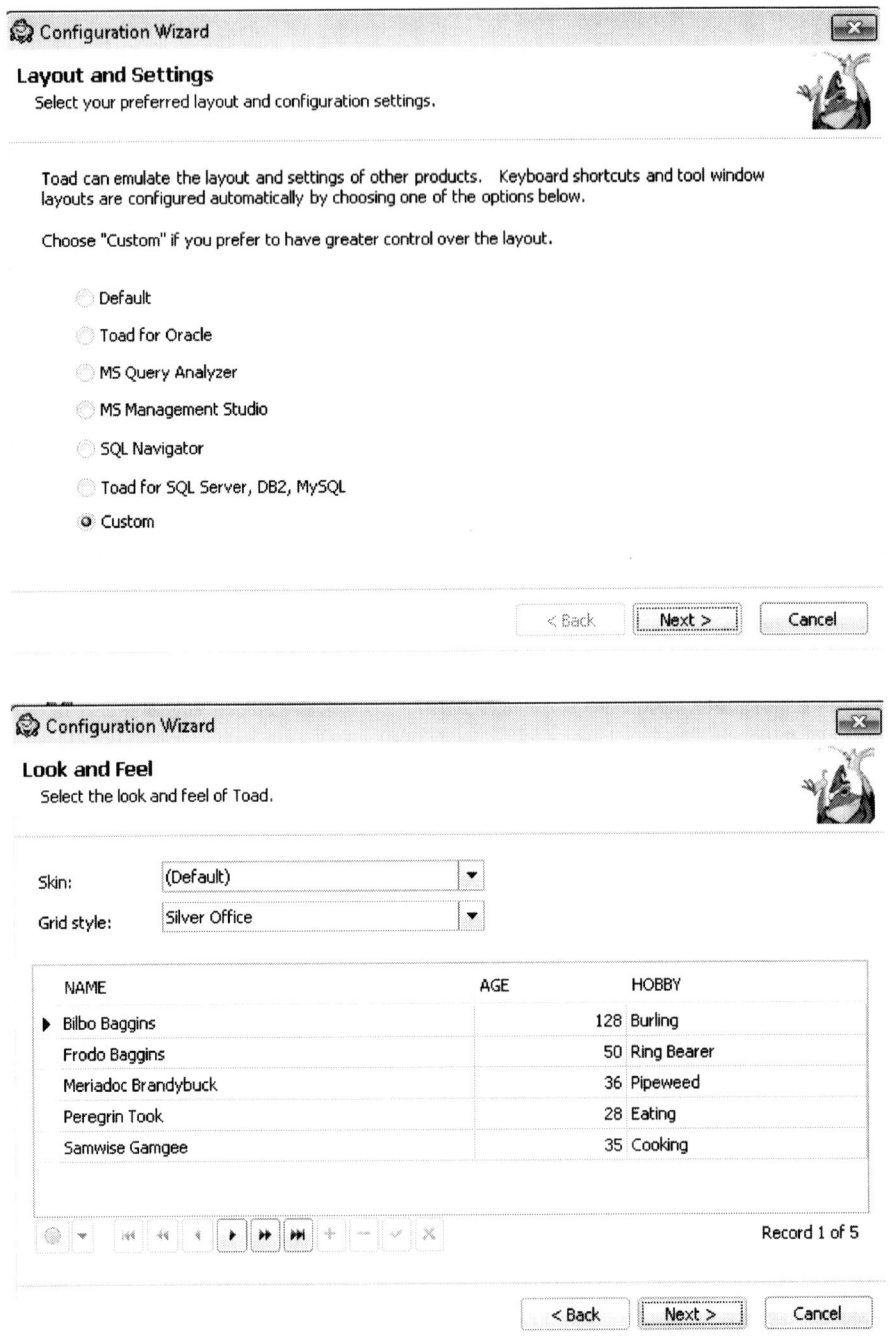

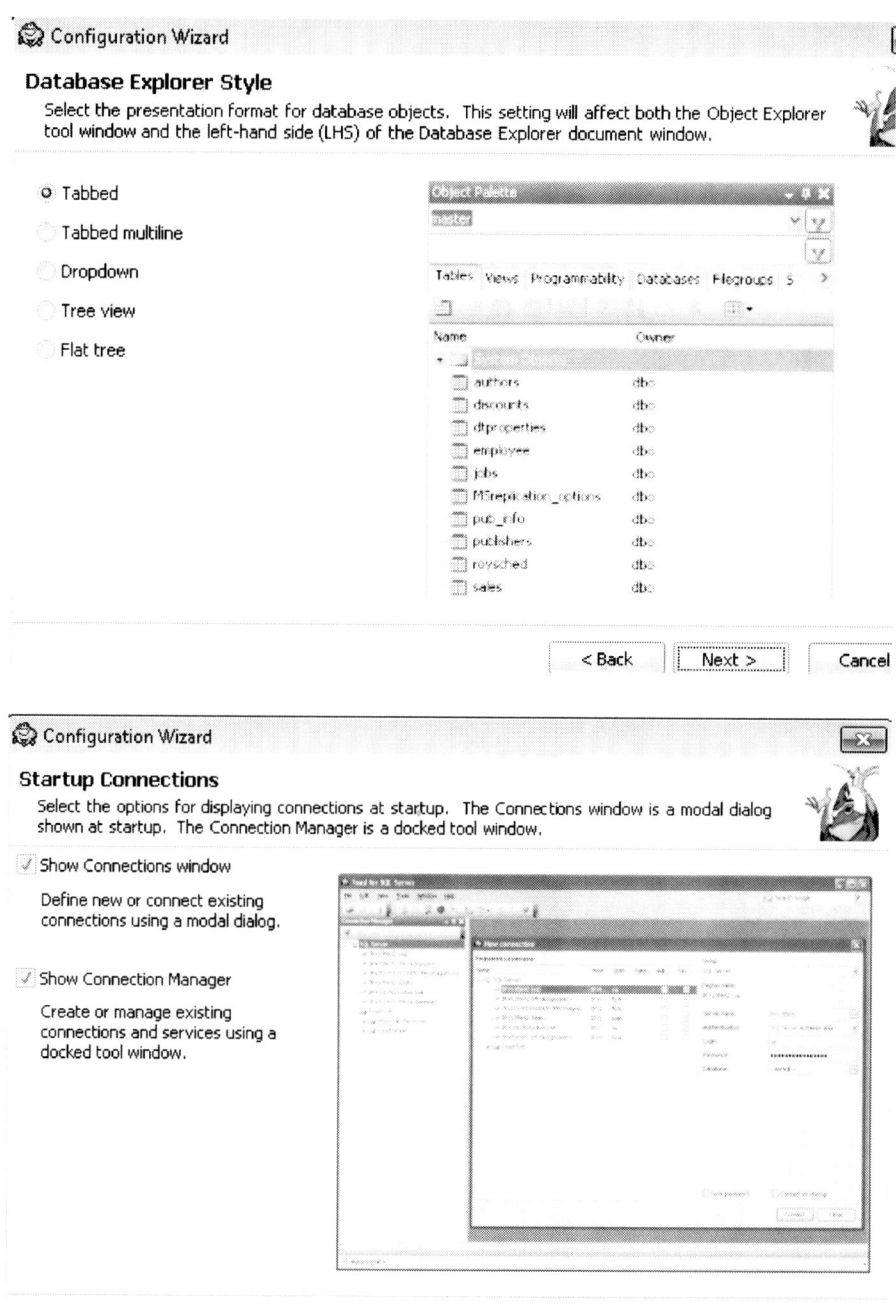

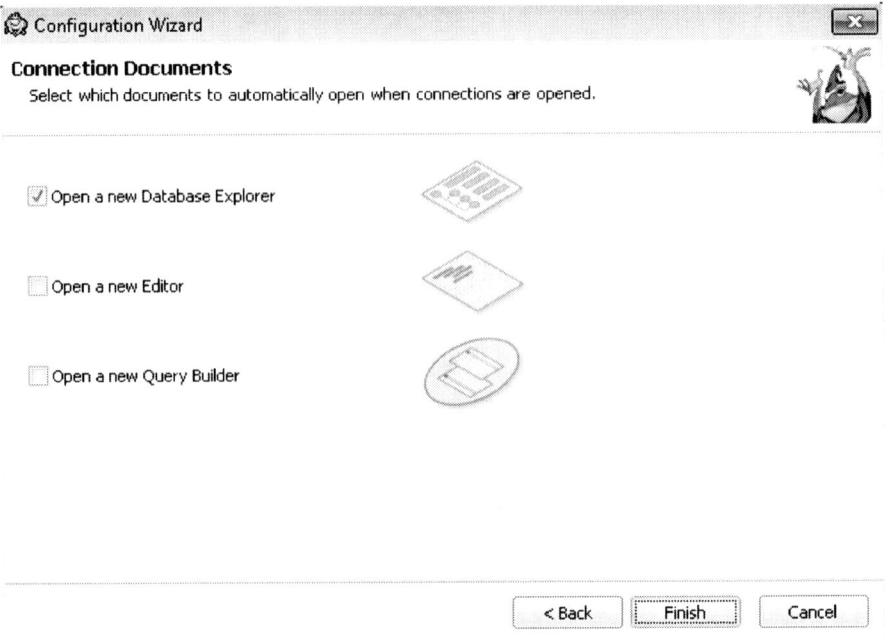

Under Tools > Options > Database > Diagramming select *Maximum objects to add* greater or equal to the number of tables (ie. in PShop 144 just put 200) :

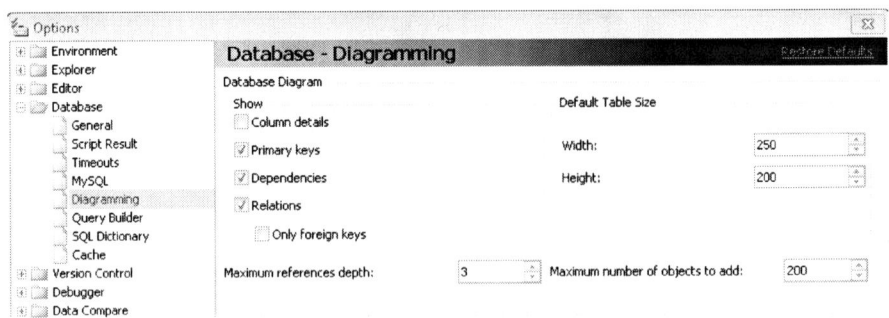

Now let's connect the PShop database :

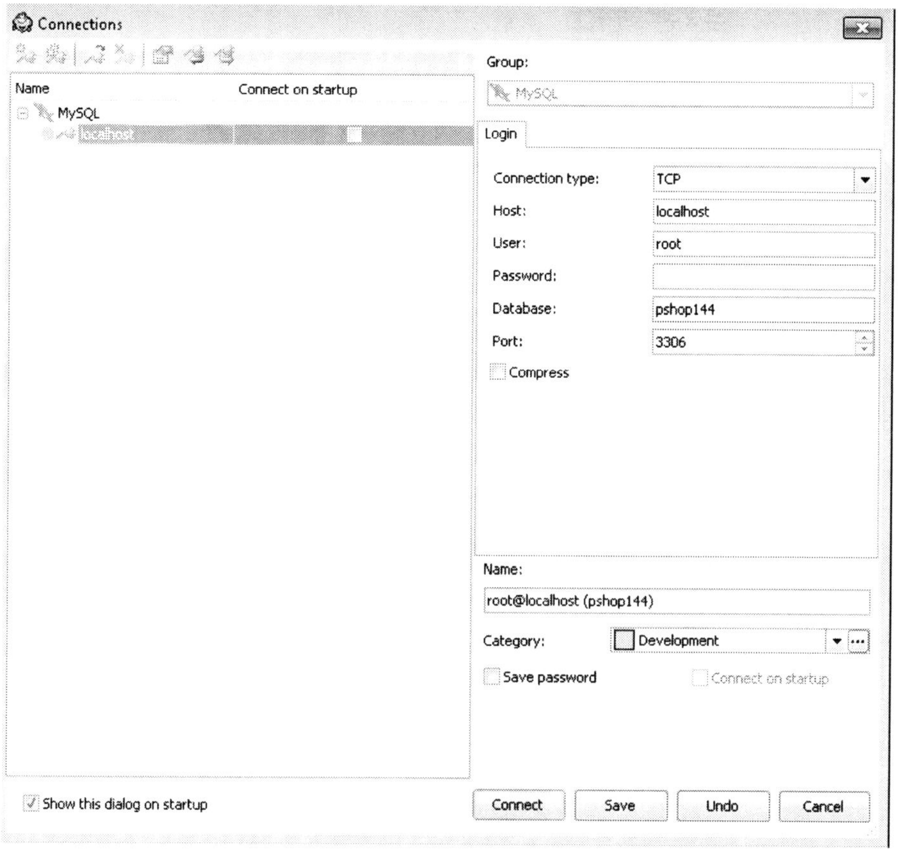

Then click on Create diagram of database and from Object Explorer (left side) select all the tables and drag & drop them over the central area :

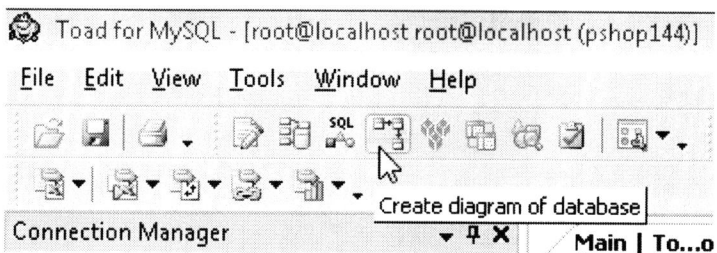

Finally you'll get the database diagram of PShop where (manually with left mouse) you can add relations between foreign keys:

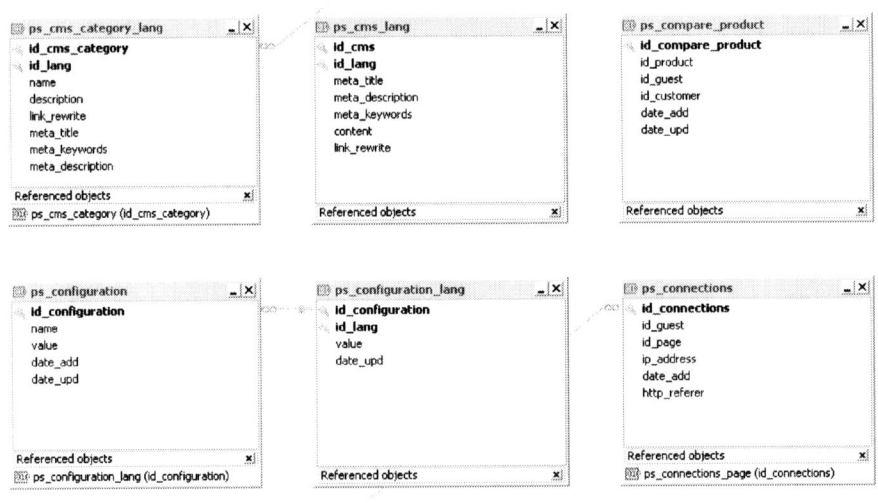

SQL queries

CRUD is the short for Create, Retrieve, Update and Delete and all these actions can be executed to process data stored in the database. SQL (structured Query Language) can be used in phpMyAdmin to process your data, here we'll see few examples of the basic keywords:

Select : this keyword is used to retrieve data from the tables. For instance in phpMyAdmin by selecting the table ps_customer (left pane) you'll get its data displayed in the central area. All customers which have been registered in our shop will be listed there, in this example we've six customers :

id_customer	id_gender	id_default_group	firstname	lastname
1	1	1	John	DOE
2	1	1	bob	collins
3	9	1	Alex	Manni
4	1	1	Andrea	Rizzo
5	9	1	romina	falcone
6	2	1	Giuliana	Turuani

If we want to retrieve only those with the firstname starting with A, we can click on the SQL tab and enter the following string :

```
SELECT * FROM `ps_customer`
WHERE left(`firstname` ,1) ='A'
```

id_customer	id_gender	id_default_group	firstname
3	9	1	Alex
4	1	1	Andrea

Update : with this keyword we can update the database in many ways:

Table store

store_location	Orders	Date
LA	$1500	Feb-05-2011

NYC		$250	Feb-06-2011
LA		$300	Feb-07-2011
Boston		$700	Feb-08-2011

```
UPDATE store
SET Sales = 500
WHERE store_location = "LA"
AND Date = "Feb-07-2011"
```

store_location	Orders	Date
LA	$1500	Feb-05-2011
NYC	$250	Feb-06-2011
LA	**$500**	Feb-07-2011
Boston	$700	Feb-08-2011

Other commonly used keywords are : INSERT INTO and DELETE

`INSERT INTO "table_name" ("column1", "column2", ...) VALUES ("value1", "value2", ...)`	`INSERT INTO store (store_name, orders, date) VALUES ('LA', 900, 'Feb-08-2011')`

`DELETE FROM "table_name" WHERE {condition}`	`DELETE FROM store WHERE store_location = "LA"`

A useful quick reference of SQL keywords can be found here [3.4].

Data Import

Data import into the database can be very convenient if you have a lot of data to handle.
For instance if you've to manage a Hardware shop with 5000 products ranging from the tiny screw to the lawnmower then automating the import could save weeks. This option is useful when you want to do a

bulk import and keep your products in a format easy to update (Excel). To access the option Import navigate to BO > Tools > Import , there are three main panes : Upload, Import and Fields Available. The last two are closely related; let's start creating a file to be imported :

- Open Excel and write in the first row the following fields : ID_Code, Title, Short_Descr, Price, Long_Descr, ID_Supplier, Picture_URL, Qty, Category then fillup them with some data like below. Make sure you create a folder in under \uploads and save there a sample picture (test.jpg) :

ID_Code	Title	Short_Descr
FO-26DC	Toner original Sharp FO-26DC	FO26DC black
SF-880ST1	Toner original Sharp SF-880ST1	SF880ST1 black
SF-880ST1	Toner original Sharp SF-880ST1	SF880ST1 black

Price	Long_Descr	ID_Supplier	Picture_URL	Qty	Category
33	2600 Fo Fax Laser	EU-T00371	C:\xampp\htdocs\pshop144\upload\pictures\test.jpg	10	Toner original
33	8800 Sf copier	EU-T00372	C:\xampp\htdocs\pshop144\upload\pictures\test.jpg	8	Toner original
33	8870 Sf copier	EU-T00373	C:\xampp\htdocs\pshop144\upload\pictures\test.jpg	4	Toner original

Save the file as sample_import.csv and import it using the dialog as below :

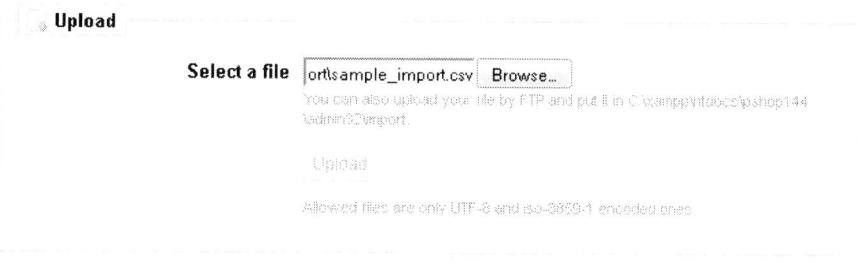

2. Click Upload then select the entity Products as below and click Next step :

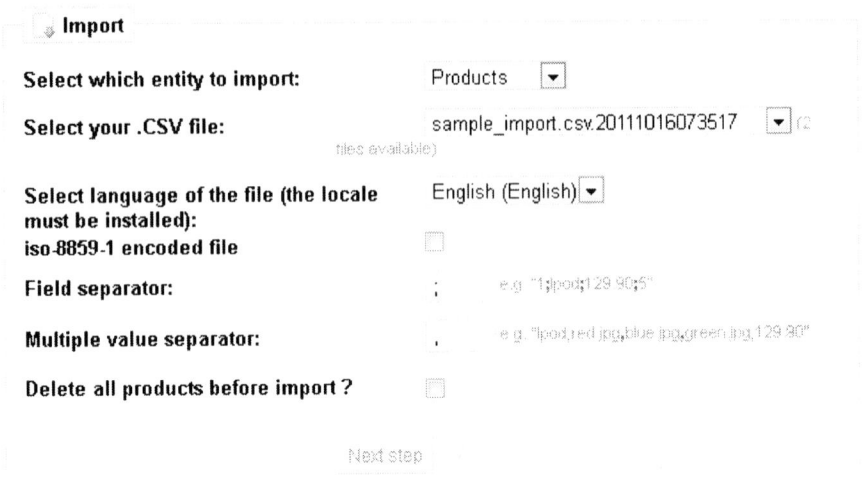

PShop automatically put a suffix code at the end of the imported filename.

3. In the next window you can Map each imported field into a selectable field of the database table, like below : (make sure to skip the first line containing the field names of the CSV file)

Do not forget to move to the next page by clicking   :

4. When completed just click Import CSV data , if there are no errors PShop will import your CSV file and return to the first page.

Web Service

With the Webservice we can access PrestaShop's database from JAVA, .NET, C++, Python, PHP... Data exchange is accomplished through XML files and it's more easy now than before to create applications interacting with the back end database. Webservice is a feature available from PShop 1.4 and in the following examples it's assumed that you've installed XAMPP and PShop in your PC (or anyway you can test the following code and access PHP system files wherever they are).

Webservice uses Representational state transfer (REST) [3.5] architecture to manage client & server applications. When related to data exchange this architecture can be represented by the four basic functions of a DBMS called create, read, update and delete (CRUD) [3.6] .

The material discussed here is based on the following article published on PrestaShop website http://www.prestashop.com/blog/article/the feature_of_the_week_the_webservice/

CRUD functions can be applied as in the table below (see Tutorials) :

Operation	SQL	HTTP/REST
Create	INSERT	POST
Read (Retrieve)	SELECT	GET
Update	UPDATE	PUT
Delete (Destroy)	DELETE	DELETE

In this chapter we'll use PHP code to implement CRUD on the installed PShop database (pshop144)

Enable the Webservice

- 1. BO > Tools > Generators and click on *Generate .htaccess*

file
- 2. BO > Tools > Webservice > Add New and generate a key
- 3. Scroll down to Permissions and select the full row *Products*
- 4. BO > Tools > Webservice and enable it

Check if the Webservice is running by typing the following URL in your browser (FireFox) :
http://localhost/pshop144/api
you should get 'true' for all the four methods related to *Products* as below :

```
products xlink:href=" http://localhost/pshop144/api/prod-
ucts" get=" true" put=" true" post=" true" delete=" true"
head=" true" >
...
```

If you type : *http://localhost/pshop144/api/products/1*

You should get a list of the product ID=1 similar to the one below (truncated) :

```
<prestashop><product><id>1</id><id_manufactur-
er xlink:href="http://localhost/ pshop144/api/
manufacturers/1">1</id_manufacturer><id_sup-
plier xlink:href="http://localhost/ pshop144/
api/suppliers/1">1</id_supplier><id_category_de-
```

```
fault xlink:href="http://localhost/ pshop144/
api/categories/2">2</id_category_default><out_
of_stock>2</out_of_stock><new/><cache_default_
attribute/><id_default_image xlink:href="http://
localhost/pshop144/api/images/products/1/37" not_
filterable="true">37</id_default_image>
...
```

Retrieve Data

To access data programmatically we need to define few more things.

3. search in your xampp/php/php.ini for 'Dynamic extensions' and add the line : extension=php_curl.dll then reboot the Apache server (from XAMPP tray icon)
4. download the following file from : http://doc.prestashop.com/download/attachments/720902/PSWebServiceLibrary.php
5. open it and increase the max supported version (line 47) as below :

```
[code    xampp/htdocs/webservice/ PSWebServiceLibrary.php]
const psCompatibleVersionsMax =  '1.4.4.1' ;  // we use PShop
1.4.4
```

- copy it to : *C:\xampp\htdocs\webservice*
- in the same folder copy the file below (remember to replace with your Auth Key)

```
[code   xampp/htdocs/webservice/ProductList.php]
<html><head><title>Product list</title></head><body>
<?php
define('PS_SHOP_PATH', 'http://localhost/pshop144/');
define('PS_WS_AUTH_KEY', 'K8OB97RZJ5YJ3AQRQ0GQZV2R-FM8HLS39');  // your Auth key ! require_once('./PSWebServiceLibrary.php');   // see edit above
```

```php
try
{
    $webService = new PrestaShopWebservice(PS_SHOP_PATH, PS_WS_AUTH_KEY, DEBUG);
    $opt['resource'] = 'products';
    $xml = $webService->get($opt);
    $resources = $xml->products->children();  // we get products ID
}
catch (PrestaShopWebserviceException $e)
{
    $trace = $e->getTrace();
    if ($trace[0]['args'][0] == 404) echo 'Bad ID';
    else if ($trace[0]['args'][0] == 401) echo 'Bad auth key';
    else print_r($e);  // print error
}

echo "<h1>Product List</h1>";  // page title
echo '<table border="5">';

if (isset($resources))
{
        echo '<tr><th>Id</th></tr>';
        foreach ($resources as $resource)
        {
            echo '<tr><td>'.$resource->attributes().'</td></tr>';
        }
}
echo '</table>';
?>
</body></html>
```

In FireFox run the following : *http://localhost/webservice/ProductList.php*

Product List

Id
7
8
10
11
13
14
15

Update Data

To update a table in the database programmatically try the following :

- Repeat the steps defined above in 'Enable the Webservice' but this time check the row 'Customers' instead of 'Products'
- Repeat the steps 1-4 defined above in 'Retrieve Data'
- In the folder 'webservice' download and copy the file below (remember to replace with your Auth Key) : doc.prestashop.com/download/attachments/720902/2-Update.php
- Replace the first lines of the file as below:

```
[code    xampp/htdocs/webservice/2-Update.php ]
define('PS_SHOP_PATH', 'http://localhost/pshop144/');
define('PS_WS_AUTH_KEY', '3REFFVW5MY0IIBSFBCMD2Y-QT5XOZ5EBW');   // copy here the AuthKey generated by your PShop for 'Customers'
```

By running the code above in your sever (XAMPP) you'll be able to :

- get first the list of customers stored in your database
- select one of them for editing2

change data and update the PShop database (through a call to the webservice)

Customers List

Id	More
1	Update
2	Update
3	Update
4	Update
5	Update

Successfully updated.

Customers Update

Return to the list

id	1
id_default_group	1
newsletter_date_add	2011-10-24 09:45:08
ip_registration_newsletter	
last_passwd_gen	2011-07-31 08:27:48
secure_key	47ce86627c1f3c792a807
deleted	0
passwd	c9c6a94b2b32aebfdf8c:

SQL Injection

Using SQL Injection hackers may try to access data saved in the database and possibly disrupt it or just stole sensitive informations.

For instance this can be done by executing unintended commands submitted in a user form. Therefore to fight external attacks we should first make sure that our software is protected by external SQL Injections.

Let's assume that your program is asking some details to the user, like while login :

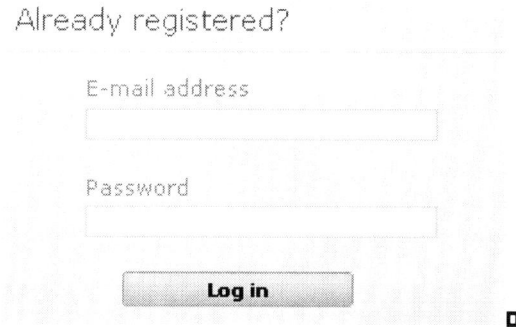

Let's assume that your software will do a query based on the data entered as below :

$query= "SELECT * FROM users WHERE email = '" .$userEmail. "';"

Now suppose the hacker enter the following in the field E-mail address : ' or '1'='1
This means that $userEmail=" ' or '1'='1 " and the resulting query will be :

$query= SELECT * FROM users WHERE email = '' OR '1'='1';

This way the hacker is able to get the full list of the table 'users' from the database.

Suppose now that the hacker enter the following string:
$userEmail=" a';DROP TABLE users; SELECT * FROM userinfo WHERE 't' = 't' "

This will result in the following (the table users will be deleted from the database) :

Database - Pag. 65

```
$query= SELECT * FROM users WHERE email = 'a';DROP
TABLE users; SELECT * FROM userinfo WHERE 't' =
't';
```

To stop SQL Injection there is a special function called pSQL and defined in /classes/DB.php :

```
function pSQL($string, $htmlOK = false)
{
      if (_PS_MAGIC_QUOTES_GPC_)
            $string = stripslashes($string);
      if (!is_numeric($string))
      {
            $link = Db::getInstance()-
>getRessource();
            $string = _PS_MYSQL_REAL_ESCAPE_STRING_
? mysql_real_escape_string($string, $link) :
addslashes($string);
            if (!$htmlOK)
                  $string = strip_
tags(nl2br2($string));
      }

      return $string;
}
```

Therefore when we make a call to the database it's a good practice to 'sanitize' data which will be used to query the database as in the following example :

[code /Controllers/PasswordController.php]
$email = Db::getInstance()->getValue('SELECT `email` FROM '._DB_PREFIX_.'customer c WHERE c.`secure_key` = "'.pSQL($token).'" AND c.id_customer='.(int)($id_customer));

Credits

[3.1] http://en.wikipedia.org/wiki/Foreign_key
[3.2] http://en.wikipedia.org/wiki/Database_schema
[3.3] http://en.wikipedia.org/wiki/SQL
[3.4] http://www.1keydata.com/sql
[3.5] http://en.wikipedia.org/wiki/REST
[3.6] http://en.wikipedia.org/wiki/Create,_read,_update_and_delete
[3.7] http://en.wikipedia.org/wiki/SQL_injection

Classes

DB class	69
Tools class	72
Validate class	77
Employee class	80
MySQL class	82
ObjectModel class	83
Module class	85
Namespaces	87
Cookies	89
Autoload	91
Override	92
Hooks	94
Credits	99

If you're not familiar with OOP I would suggest to have a look at it before moving forward. There are a lot of books on the web or you may have a look at the tutorials included in this book. In this chapter we'll see few important classes used in PShop and other tools. As for the previous chapter I would suggest to install XAMPP on your PC and install PShop in a sub-folder of the htdocs. For the purpose of this book we'll use the following PShop root: C:\xampp\htdocs\pshop144
If you do not want to install XAMPP you can test your scripts by uploading them on your remote server. (see Developer's Tools later in this book)

From PShop 1.4 base classes have the suffix 'core' and only few of them are discussed here. In PShop classes are saved in a filename having the same name, ie. the base class OrderCore is saved in the file Order.php.
In case you've customized your own classes and you want to upgrade your shop, you should rename them by adding the suffix 'core' as described in the upgrade procedure of the official site (the filename. php remain the same). More about the core classes can be found in Prestashop Wiki

DB class

This abstract class is defined in /classes/Db.php , its constructor connect to the database through the following variables: $server, $user, $password, $database

Public Member Functions
```
      getRessource ()
      __construct ($server, $user, $password, $data-
base)
      autoExecute ($table, $values, $type,
$where=false, $limit=false, $use_cache=1)
      autoExecuteWithNullValues ($table, $values,
$type, $where=false, $limit=false)
      connect ()
      Insert_ID ()
      Affected_Rows ()
      NumRows ()
      delete ($table, $where=false, $limit=false,
$use_cache=1)
```

```
Execute ($query, $use_cache=1)
ExecuteS ($query, $array=true, $use_cache=1)
nextRow ($result=false)
getServerVersion ()
getRow ($query, $use_cache=1)
getValue ($query, $use_cache=1)
getMsgError ()
```

Static Public Member Functions
```
static      getInstance ($master=1)
static      s ($query, $use_cache=1)
static      ps ($query, $use_cache=1)
static      ds ($query, $use_cache=1)
```

Protected Attributes
```
$_server
$_user
$_password
$_type
$_database
$_link
$_result
$_lastQuery
$_lastCached
```

Static Protected Attributes
```
static      $_db
static      $_instance = array()
static      $_servers
static      $_idServer
```

The function autoExecute is able to apply INSERT or UPDATE statements:

```
DbCore::autoExecute ( $ table, $ values, $ type,
$ where = false, $ limit = false, $ use_cache = 1 )
```

If use_cache=1 the result of the query will be cached. The constant _DB_PREFIX_ is a prefix to the name of the table (by default is 'PS_'). Below are described few examples using autoExecute :

```
Db::getInstance()->autoExecute('user_table', array(
     'id_user'   =>     (int)$ID,
     'user_name' =>     pSQL($name),
), 'INSERT');
```

which is equivalent to :

```
INSERT INTO `user_table` (`id_user`, `name`) VALUES
(9, 'Bob')
```

To update a row of a table we can call the function autoExecute or Execute respectively like in /classes/Product.php or /product.php :

```
Db::getInstance()->AutoExecute(_DB_
PREFIX_.'product_attribute', $data, 'UPDATE', '`id_
product_attribute` = '.(int)($id_product_attri-
bute))
```

```
Db::getInstance()->Execute('
          UPDATE `'._DB_PREFIX_.'category_
product`
          SET `position` = '.(int)($posi-
tion).'
          WHERE `id_product` = '.(int)
($movedProduct['id_product']).'
          AND `id_category`='.(int)
($movedProduct['id_category'])));
```

The method ExecuteS will save the results into a multidimensional array:

```
$sql = 'SELECT * FROM '._DB_PREFIX_.'user_table';
if ($result = Db::getInstance()->ExecuteS($sql))
     foreach ($result as $row)
          echo $row['id'].' ::
'.$row['lastname'].'<br />';
```

To delete data we can call the method 'delete ' of the class like below:

```
Db::getInstance()->delete('user_table', 'ID < 10', 5);
```

which is equivalent to the SQL string :

```
DELETE FROM target_table WHERE ID < 10 LIMIT 5
```

To get the first row from a table we can use the method getRow() :

```
$sql = 'SELECT * FROM '._DB_PREFIX_.'user_table'
       WHERE id = 100';
if ($row = Db::getInstance()->getRow($sql))
       echo $row['id'].' = '.$row['lastname'];
```

To get the first value of the row we can use the method getValue() :

```
$sql = 'SELECT COUNT(*) FROM '._DB_PREFIX_.' user_table';
       $totCount = Db::getInstance()->getValue($sql);
```

Tools class

This class is defined in /classes/Tools.php and is used everywhere in PShop having many useful functions :

```
Static Public Member Functions
       static      passwdGen ($length=8)
       static      redirect ($url, $baseUri=__PS_BASE_URI__)
       static      redirectLink ($url)
       static      redirectAdmin ($url)
       static      getProtocol ($use_ssl=null)
       static      getHttpHost ($http=false, $entities=false)
```

```
static      getShopDomain ($http=false,
$entities=false)
static      getShopDomainSsl ($http=false,
$entities=false)
static      getServerName ()
static      getRemoteAddr ()
static      usingSecureMode ()
static      getCurrentUrlProtocolPrefix ()
static      secureReferrer ($referrer)
static      getValue ($key,
$defaultValue=false)
static      getIsset ($key)
static      setCookieLanguage ()
static      switchLanguage ()
static      setCurrency ()
static      displayPrice ($price,
$currency=NULL, $no_utf8=false)
static      displayPriceSmarty ($params,
&$smarty)
static      convertPrice ($price,
$currency=NULL, $to_currency=true)
static      dateFormat ($params, &$smarty)
static      displayDate ($date, $id_lang,
$full=false, $separator= '-')
static      safeOutput ($string, $html=false)
static      htmlentitiesUTF8 ($string,
$type=ENT_QUOTES)
static      htmlentitiesDecodeUTF8 ($string)
static      safePostVars ()
static      deleteDirectory ($dirname, $delete_
self=true)
static      displayError ($string= 'Fatal er-
ror', $htmlentities=true)
static      dieObject ($object, $kill=true)
static      d ($object, $kill=true)
static      p ($object)
static      isSubmit ($submit)
static      getMetaTags ($id_lang, $page_name)
static      getHomeMetaTags ($id_lang, $page_
name)
static      completeMetaTags ($metaTags, $de-
faultValue)
```

Classes - Pag. 73

static	encrypt	($passwd)
static	getToken	($page=true)
static	getAdminToken	($string)
static	getAdminTokenLite	($tab)
static	getPath	($id_category, $path= '', $linkOntheLastItem=false, $categoryType= 'products')
static	getFullPath	($id_category, $end, $type_cat= 'products')
static	getCategoriesTotal	()
static	getProductsTotal	()
static	getCustomersTotal	()
static	getOrdersTotal	()
static	historyc_1	($key, $translations)
static	link_rewrite	($str, $utf8_decode=false)
static	str2url	($str)
static	truncate	($str, $maxLen, $suffix= '...')
static	dateYears	()
static	dateDays	()
static	dateMonths	()
static	hourGenerate	($hours, $minutes, $seconds)
static	dateFrom	($date)
static	dateTo	($date)
static	getExactTime	()
static	strtolower	($str)
static	strlen	($str, $encoding= 'UTF-8')
static	stripslashes	($string)
static	strtoupper	($str)
static	substr	($str, $start, $length=false, $encoding= 'utf-8')
static	ucfirst	($str)
static	orderbyPrice	(&$array, $orderWay)
static	iconv	($from, $to, $string)
static	isEmpty	($field)
static	getTimezones	($select=false)
static	ps_set_magic_quotes_runtime	($var)
static	ps_round	($value, $precision=0)
static	ceilf	($value, $precision=0)
static	floorf	($value, $precision=0)

Classes - Pag. 74

```
static      file_exists_cache ($filename)
static      file_get_contents ($url,
$useIncludePath=false, $streamContext=NULL)
static      simplexml_load_file ($url, $class_
name=null)
static      minifyHTML ($html_content)
static      toCamelCase ($str,
$capitaliseFirstChar=false)
static      getBrightness ($hex)
static      minifyHTMLpregCallback ($preg_
matches)
static      packJSinHTML ($html_content)
static      packJSinHTMLpregCallback ($preg_
matches)
static      packJS ($js_content)
static      minifyCSS ($css_content,
$fileuri=false)
static      replaceByAbsoluteURL ($matches)
static      addJS ($js_uri)
static      addCSS ($css_uri, $css_media_type=
'all')
static      cccCss ()
static      cccJS ()
static      getMediaServer ($filename)
static      generateHtaccess ($path, $re-
write_settings, $cache_control, $specific= '',
$disableMuliviews=false)
static      jsonDecode ($json, $assoc=false)
static      jsonEncode ($data)
static      displayAsDeprecated ()
static      displayParameterAsDeprecated ($pa-
rameter)
static      enableCache ($level=1)
static      restoreCacheSettings ()
static      isCallable ($function)
static      pRegexp ($s, $delim)
static      str_replace_once ($needle, $re-
place, $haystack)
static      property_exists ($class, $property)
static      checkPhpVersion ()
static      selectionVersionSmarty ()
static      ZipTest ($fromFile)
```

```
        static     ZipExtract ($fromFile, $toDir)
        static     getProductsOrder ($type,
$value=null)
        static     convertBytes ($value)
        static     display404Error ()
        static     dieOrLog ($msg, $die=true)
        static     clearCache ($smarty)

Static Protected Attributes
        static     $file_exists_cache = array()
        static     $_forceCompile
        static     $_caching
```

As listed above this class can be called without instantiation (no object required) , below are listed few examples using some of its member functions :

```
[Code   admin/login.php]
<a href="https://'.Tools::getServerName().$_
SERVER['REQUEST_URI'].'">https://'.
Tools::getServerName().$_SERVER['REQUEST_URI'].'</
a>
…

if (Tools::isSubmit('Submit'))
…

Tools::displayError('E-mail is empty');
…

[Code   classes/Customer.php]
  if (empty($password))
      $password = Tools::passwdGen();

…

$this->passwd = Tools::encrypt($password);
…
```

Classes - Pag. 76

One useful method used to attach the file.css is addCSS , below you'll find an example of how to use it for the module block currencies :

```
[Code    modules/blockcurrencies/blockcurrencies.php]
Tools::addCSS(($this->_path).'blockcurrencies.css',
'all');
...
```

Validate class

This class is defined in /classes/Validate.php and is also used everywhere in PShop having many useful functions to validate data :

```
static Public Member Functions
    static   isIp2Long ($ip)
    static   isAnything ($data)
    static   isEmail ($email)
    static   isModuleUrl ($url, &$errors)
    static   isMd5 ($md5)
    static   isSha1 ($sha1)
    static   isFloat ($float)
    static   isUnsignedFloat ($float)
    static   isOptFloat ($float)
    static   isCarrierName ($name)
    static   isImageSize ($size)
    static   isOptId ($id)
    static   isName ($name)
    static   isHookName ($hook)
    static   isMailName ($mailName)
    static   isMailSubject ($mailSubject)
    static   isModuleName ($moduleName)
    static   isTplName ($tplName)
    static   isTplFileName ($tplFileName)
    static   isIconFile ($icon)
    static   isIcoFile ($icon)
    static   isImageTypeName ($type)
    static   isPrice ($price)
    static   isLanguageIsoCode ($isoCode)
    static   isLanguageCode ($s)
    static   isStateIsoCode ($isoCode)
```

```
static    isNumericIsoCode ($isoCode)
static    isGenderIsoCode ($isoCode)
static    isGenderName ($genderName)
static    isDiscountName ($discountName)
static    isCatalogName ($name)
static    isMessage ($message)
static    isCountryName ($name)
static    isLinkRewrite ($link)
static    isZoneName ($name)
static    isAddress ($address)
static    isCityName ($city)
static    isValidSearch ($search)
static    isGenericName ($name)
static    isCleanHtml ($html)
static    isReference ($reference)
static    isPasswd ($passwd, $size=5)
static    isPasswdAdmin ($passwd)
static    isConfigName ($configName)
static    isDateFormat ($date)
static    isDate ($date)
static    isBirthDate ($date)
static    isBool ($bool)
static    isPhoneNumber ($phoneNumber)
static    isEan13 ($ean13)
static    isUpc ($upc)
static    isPostCode ($postcode)
static    isZipCodeFormat ($zip_code)
static    isOrderWay ($orderWay)
static    isOrderBy ($orderBy)
static    isTableOrIdentifier ($table)
static    isValuesList ($list)
static    isTagsList ($list)
static    isInt ($value)
static    isUnsignedInt ($value)
static    isUnsignedId ($id)
static    isNullOrUnsignedId ($id)
static    isLoadedObject ($object)
static    isColor ($color)
static    isUrl ($url)
static    isUrlOrEmpty ($url)
static    isAbsoluteUrl ($url)
static    isFileName ($name)
```

```
static   isTabName ($name)
static   isWeightUnit ($unit)
static   isDistanceUnit ($unit)
static   isProtocol ($protocol)
static   isSubDomainName ($subDomainName)
static   isVoucherDescription ($text)
static   isGranularityValue ($value)
static   IsSortDirection ($value)
static   isLabel ($label)
static   isPriceDisplayMethod ($data)
static   isDniLite ($dni)
static   isDni ($dni)
static   isDniBool ($dni)
static   isCookie ($data)
static   isString ($data)
static   isReductionType ($data)
static   isBool_Id ($ids)
static   isLocalizationPackSelection ($data)
static   isSerializedArray ($data)
static   isCoordinate ($data)
static   isLangIsoCode ($iso_code)
static   isLanguageFileName ($file_name)
static   isArrayWithIds ($ids)
static   isSceneZones ($zones)
```

below are listed few examples using some of its member functions :

```
[Code   admin/login.php]
if (empty($email))
         $errors[] = Tools::displayError('E-mail is empty');
     elseif (!Validate::isEmail($email))
...

if (!Validate::isCleanHtml($url))
...
```

```
[Code   classes/Order.php]
if ($pd AND Validate::isUnsignedInt($pd) AND
$product['download_hash'])
…

if (!Validate::isLoadedObject($orderState) OR !Vali
date::isLoadedObject($order))
…
```

Employee class

This class is defined in /classes/Employee.php and is used to manage employee details

```
Public Member Functions
      getFields ()
      add ($autodate=true, $nullValues=true)
      getByEmail ($email, $passwd=NULL)
      isLastAdmin ()
      setWsPasswd ($passwd)
Static Public Member Functions
      static     getEmployees ()
      static     employeeExists ($email)
      static     checkPassword ($id_employee, $pass-
wd)
      static     countProfile ($id_profile,
$activeOnly=false)
Public Attributes
      $id
      $id_profile
      $id_lang
      $lastname
      $firstname
      $email
      $passwd
      $last_passwd_gen
      $stats_date_from
      $stats_date_to
      $bo_color
```

```
    $bo_theme
    $bo_uimode
    $active = 1
Protected Attributes
    $fieldsRequired = array('lastname', 'firstname',
'email', 'passwd', 'id_profile', 'id_lang')
    $fieldsSize = array('lastname' => 32, 'first-
name' => 32, 'email' => 128, 'passwd' => 32, 'bo_
color' => 32, 'bo_theme' => 32)
    $fieldsValidate
    $table = 'employee'
    $identifier = 'id_employee'
    $webserviceParameters
```

Some examples of this class are listed below :

```
[Code  admin/login.php]
    /* Seeking for employee */
        $employee = new Employee();
        $employee = $employee->getByemail($email,
$passwd);
...
```

```
[Code  tabs/AdminEmployees.php]
 elseif (Employee::employeeExists($email) AND
!Tools::getValue('id_employee'))
...

$employee = new Employee((int)Tools::getValue('id_
employee'));
                if (!(int)$this->tabAccess['edit'])
                    $_POST['id_profile'] = $_
GET['id_profile'] = $employee->id_profile;
...
```

MySQL class

This is a child class of the DB class and is defined in /classes/MySQL.php :

```
Public Member Functions
      connect ()
      getServerVersion ()
      set_db ($db_name)
      disconnect ()
      getRow ($query, $use_cache=1)
      getValue ($query, $use_cache=1)
      Execute ($query, $use_cache=1)
      ExecuteS ($query, $array=true, $use_cache=1)
      nextRow ($result=false)
      delete ($table, $where=false, $limit=false, $use_cache=1)
      NumRows ()
      Insert_ID ()
      Affected_Rows ()
      getMsgError ($query=false)
      getNumberError ()
      displayMySQLError ($query=false)
Static Public Member Functions
      static    tryToConnect ($server, $user, $pwd, $db, $newDbLink=true)
      static    tryUTF8 ($server, $user, $pwd)
Protected Member Functions
      q ($query, $use_cache=1)
```

Few examples of its usage are given below:

[Code classes/Db.php]

```
self::$_instance[(int)($idServer)] = new MySQL(self::$_servers[(int)($idServer)]['server'], self::$_servers[(int)($idServer)]['user'], self::$_servers[(int)($idServer)]['password'], self::$_servers[(int)($idServer)]['database']);
...
```

```
[Code  classes/ToolsInstall.php]
switch(MySQL::tryToConnect(trim($srv),
trim($login), trim($password), trim($name)))
```

ObjectModel class

This class is defined in /classes/ObjectModel.php and is used to access the tables of the database as an object.

```
Public Member Functions
      getFields ()
      __construct ($id=NULL, $id_lang=NULL)
      save ($nullValues=false, $autodate=true)
      add ($autodate=true, $nullValues=false)
      update ($nullValues=false)
      delete ()
      deleteSelection ($selection)
      toggleStatus ()
      validateFields ($die=true, $errorReturn=false)
      validateFieldsLang ($die=true,
$errorReturn=false)
      validateControler ($htmlentities=true)
      validateController ($htmlentities=true)
      getWebserviceParameters
($wsParamsAttributeName=NULL)
      getWebserviceObjectList ($sql_join, $sql_fil-
ter, $sql_sort, $sql_limit)
      getFieldsRequiredDatabase ($all=false)
      addFieldsRequiredDatabase ($fields)
      clearCache ($all=false)
      deleteImage ()
Static Public Member Functions
      static    getValidationRules ($className=__
CLASS__)
      static    displayFieldName ($field, $class-
Name=__CLASS__, $htmlentities=true)
Public Attributes
      $id
```

```
Protected Member Functions
      getTranslationsFields ($fieldsArray)
      makeTranslationFields (&$fields, &$fieldsArray,
$id_language)
Protected Attributes
      $id_lang = NULL
      $table = NULL
      $identifier = NULL
      $fieldsRequired = array()
      $fieldsSize = array()
      $fieldsValidate = array()
      $fieldsRequiredLang = array()
      $fieldsSizeLang = array()
      $fieldsValidateLang = array()
      $tables = array()
      $webserviceParameters = array()
      $image_dir = NULL
      $image_format = 'jpg'
Static Protected Attributes
      static      $fieldsRequiredDatabase = NULL
      static      $_cache = array()
```

This class is extended by many child classes, for instance the method Update() update the object in the database and the method validateFields() check for fields validity before database interaction. Few examples of this class are given below :

```
[Code   classes/Customer.php]
      public function getFields()
      {
            parent::validateFields();   // parent
class is the ObjectModel
            if (isset($this->id))
                  $fields['id_customer'] = (int)
($this->id);
            $fields['secure_key'] = pSQL($this->secure_key);
```

Module class

This class is defined in /classes/Module.php , its constructor load from the database the list of installed modules :

```
$result = Db::getInstance()->ExecuteS('SELECT *
FROM `'.pSQL(_DB_PREFIX_.$this->table).'`');   //
table 0 'module'
```

```
Public Member Functions
      __construct ($name=NULL)
      install ()
      uninstall ()
      enable ()
      disable ()
      registerHook ($hook_name)
      displayFlags ($languages, $defaultLanguage,
$ids, $id, $return=false)
      unregisterHook ($hook_id)
      unregisterExceptions ($hook_id)
      registerExceptions ($id_hook, $excepts)
      editExceptions ($id_hook, $excepts)
      l ($string, $specific=false, $id_lang=null)
      updatePosition ($id_hook, $way,
$position=NULL)
      cleanPositions ($id_hook)
      getPosition ($id_hook)
      displayError ($error)
      displayConfirmation ($string)
      getExceptions ($id_hook)
      isRegisteredInHook ($hook)
      isCached ($template, $cacheId=NULL,
$compileId=NULL)
      isHookableOn ($hook_name)
Static Public Member Functions
      static     enableByName ($name)
      static     disableByName ($name)
      static     getModuleNameFromClass ($current-
Class)
      static     getInstanceByName ($moduleName)
```

```
static      preloadModuleNameFromId ($ids)
static      getInstanceById ($id_module)
static      configXmlStringFormat ($string)
static      getModulesOnDisk ($useConfig=false)
static      getModulesDirOnDisk ()
static      getNonNativeModuleList ()
static      getModulesInstalled ($position=0)
static      hookExec ($hook_name,
$hookArgs=array(), $id_module=NULL)
static      hookExecPayment ()
static      getPaymentModules ()
static      findTranslation ($name, $string,
$source)
static      isInstalled ($moduleName)
static      display ($file, $template,
$cacheId=NULL, $compileId=NULL)
```

Public Attributes
```
$id = NULL
$version
$name
$displayName
$description
$author
$need_instance = 1
$tab = NULL
$active = false
$warning
$beforeUninstall = NULL
$_errors = false
$limited_countries = array()
```

Static Public Attributes
```
static      $_db
static      $classInModule = array()
```

Protected Member Functions
```
_isTemplateOverloaded ($template)
_getApplicableTemplateDir ($template)
_clearCache ($template, $cacheId=NULL,
$compileId=NULL)
_generateConfigXml ()
```

Static Protected Member Functions
```
static      _isTemplateOverloadedStatic ($moduleName, $template)
```

```
Protected Attributes
      $_lang = array()
      $_path = NULL
      $table = 'module'
      $identifier = 'id_module'
Static Protected Attributes
      static      $modulesCache
      static      $_hookModulesCache
      static      $_INSTANCE = array()
      static      $_generateConfigXmlMode = false
      static      $l_cache = array()
      static      $exceptionsCache = NULL
```

The method registerHook() will register a new hook in the database, few examples of this class are given below :

```
[Code   classes/AdminTab.php]
      $currentClass = get_class($this);
      if (Module::getModuleNameFromClass($currentCla
ss))
...
```

```
[Code   blockmanufacturer/Blockmanufacturer.php]
      $output .= $this->displayConfirmation($this-
>l('Settings updated'));
      // this class extend the base class Module
```

Namespaces

Smarty is the template engine used in PShop and is responsible of rendering the HTML pages by inserting special tags in the template document [4.1] You can have a look at the Smarty's tutorial later in this book.

A Namespace is a container for encapsulating items or symbols [4.2]. For instance we may have two identical filenames saved in two different folders, when we access them outside the native folder we must prefix the filename with the full path. The folder in this case is a namespace.

In PHP we can use Namespaces to group classes, functions or constants with two main benefits : [4.3]

- Avoid name collisions between your code and internal PHP code or third-party code
- Ability to alias (or shorten) Extra_Long_Names improving readability of the source code.

A small example will clarify their use :

```
[Code]
<?php
namespace my\name;
class MyClass {}
function myfunction() {}
const MYCONST = 1;

$a = new MyClass;
$c = new \my\name\MyClass;
$a = strlen('hi');
$d = namespace\MYCONST;
$d = __NAMESPACE__ . '\MYCONST';
echo constant($d);
?>
```

If you run the code above your browser will print the value of $d=1
Note that the namespace must be the first statement in your script :

```
[Code]
<html>
<?php
namespace MyProject; // fatal error - namespace must be the first statement in the script
?>
```

In PShop there are the following Namespaces:

AddressStandardizationSolution
Archive
Artichow
EasySwift

FirePHPCore
JSMin
Minify
PEAR
Services_JSON
Smarty
Swift
Swift_Authenticator
Swift_Cache
Swift_Connection
Swift_Events
Swift_Log
Swift_Message
Swift_Plugin
XML_Feed_Parser

PEAR , Services_JSON, Smarty, FirePHPCore will be discussed in a separate chapter
Minify and JSmin are used to parses through php and javascript respectively and removes superfluous characters. [4.4]

Cookies

A cookie, also known as an HTTP cookie, web cookie, or browser cookie, is used for an origin website to send state information to a user's browser and for the browser to return the state information to the origin site.[4.5]
Basically they store text data on the user's PC to track user's browsing activities. Coockies cannot be programmed therefore they carry no viruses or malware but hackers can use them to spy the user's acitivities. In PShop the class Cookie take care of managing them, its constructor get data if the cookie exist or create a new one through the variables : $name, $path, $expire

```
Public Member Functions
      __construct ($name, $path= '', $expire=NULL)
      setExpire ($expire)
      __get ($key)
```

```
    __isset ($key)
    __set ($key, $value)
    __unset ($key)
    isLogged ($withGuest=false)
    isLoggedBack ()
    logout ()
    mylogout ()
    makeNewLog ()
    update ($nullValues=false)
    write ()
    getFamily ($origin)
    unsetFamily ($origin)
    getName ()
Protected Member Functions
    getDomain ()
    _setcookie ($cookie=NULL)
Protected Attributes
    $_content
    $_name
    $_expire
    $_domain
    $_path
    $_cipherTool
    $_key
    $_iv
    $_modified = false
```

The following code clarify the use of this class by looking at the authentication process of an employee in the BO :

```
[Code  admin/login.php]
// first we check if the employee exist

    if (!$employee)
        {
            $errors[] = Tools::displayError('Employee does not exist or password is incorrect.');
            $cookie->logout();
        }
```

```
            else
// we create a cookie
            {
                    /* Creating cookie */
                    $cookie->id_employee = $employee->id;
                    $cookie->email = $employee->email;
                    $cookie->profile = $employee->id_profile;
                    $cookie->passwd = $employee->passwd;
                    $cookie->remote_addr = ip2long(Tools::getRemoteAddr());
                    $cookie->write();
```

If we want to use the employee's email in our code it's enough to declare global cookie; in our function like below :

```
[Code classes/AdminTab.php]
public function display()
    {
    global $currentIndex, $cookie;
...
```

Autoload

There are basically two entry points in PShop

- /index.php   for the FO
- /admin/index.php for the BO

Both require the file /config/config.inc.php which in turn require the file /config/autoload.php .
In the file autoload.php there is a function called __autoload() which basically do the following :

Classes - Pag. 91

- get the current class name and path to load
- strip the suffix 'core' from the base class to load the class.php
- check the override folder to switch between overriden classes or default classes (see next paragraph)

Later we'll come back again on this function..

Override

Method overriding, in OOP, is a language feature that allows a subclass or child class to provide a specific implementation of a method that is already provided by one of its parent classes. The implementation in the subclass overrides (replaces) the implementation in the superclass by providing a method that has same name, same parameters or signature, and same return type as the method in the parent class.

The version of a method that is executed will be determined by the object that is used to invoke it. If an object of a parent class is used to invoke the method, then the version in the parent class will be executed, but if an object of the subclass is used to invoke the method, then the version in the child class will be executed. [4.6]

In PShop the Override concept is used to execute new releases of Module's templates, Class and Controllers by replacing the old ones.

Module's templates are usually saved under the folder /modules and can be represented with three files extensions : mymodule.tpl, mymodule.css, mymodule.js

Assuming we're using the default template, to override them it's enough to save their new versions under the folder /themes/prestashop/modules/mymodule/

Overriding classes is quite straightforward , for instance if we need to override the base class OrderCore we could do the following:

- the filename of the class remain the same but must save it under /override/classes
- the name of the overriding class become Order (without the

suffix 'Core')

The same applies to Controllers, below are few examples:

```
/override/classes/myclass.php
/override/controllers/mycontroller.php
```

Suppose you don't want your employee to add a new Category while editing a product.
Assuming the email of your employee is 'employeename@mydomain.com' , this could be done as below:

1. edit the file : tabs/AdminCategories.php by replacing the function public function display($token = NULL) with the one below
2. copy the file to /override/classes/AdminCategories.php

```
public function display($token = NULL)
    {
    global $currentIndex, $cookie;

    $this->getList((int)($cookie->id_lang), !$cookie->__get($this->table.'Orderby') ? 'position' : NULL, !$cookie->__get($this->table.'Orderway') ? 'ASC' : NULL);
    echo '<h3>'.(!$this->_listTotal ? ($this->l('There are no subcategories')) : ($this->_listTotal.' '.($this->_listTotal > 1 ? $this->l('subcategories') : $this->l('subcategory')))).' '.$this->l('in category').' "'.stripslashes($this->_category->getName()).'"</h3>';

    if ($cookie->email!='employeename@mydomain.com')
            {

    echo '<a href="'.__PS_BASE_URI__.substr($_
```

```
SERVER['PHP_SELF'], strlen(__PS_BASE_URI__)).'
?tab=AdminCatalog&add'.$this->table.'&id_par
ent='.Tools::getValue('id_category').'&token='.
($token!=NULL ? $token : $this->token).'"><img
src="../img/admin/add.gif" border="0" /> '.$this-
>l('Add a new subcategory').'</a>';
      echo ,<div style="margin:10px;">';
      $this->displayList($token);
            echo ,</div>';
      
      }
      else
      {
      echo ,<a href="'.__PS_BASE_URI__.sub-
str($_SERVER[,PHP_SELF'], strlen(__PS_BASE_URI__)
).'?tab=AdminCatalog&add'.$this->table.'&id_par
ent='.Tools::getValue(,id_category').'&token='.
($token!=NULL ? $token : $this->token).'"></a>';
            echo ,<div style="margin:10px;">';
            $this->displayList($token);
            echo ,</div>';
            }
      }
```

Hooks

The term hooking covers a range of techniques used to alter or augment the behaviour of an operating system, of applications, or of other software components by intercepting function calls or messages or events passed between software components. Code that handles such intercepted function calls, events or messages is called a "hook". [4.7] In PShop Hooks can be seen as shortcuts to the methods defined in the Module assigned to them. For instance hooks are used to help positioning modules over the page or to manage actions like updating the order's status (hookUpdateOrderStatus). In the left column of your homepage you may have the following modules : Information, Categories and Latest Products all of them located in the left hook. When a hook is found on a page, PShop will load the related module.

Therefore additional functionality is inserted or "hooked" into PShop by using "hook" in the controller code, which can be exploited by userinstallable modules (also called plugins). These modules have the ability to add new functionality (business logic) to PShop. Hooks can be managed directly in the BO > Modules but this feature will be described in the chapter related to Themes.

Hooks are especially used to manage templates. For instance the header.tpl contain three main hooks that indicate the positions where the associated modules will be displayed.
Suppose you want to hide the right column in the homepage but you want to display it in the other pages. To do this in the standard theme, open /themes/prestashop/header.tpl and change the div right_column as the following :

```
[code   /themes/prestashop/header.tpl]
{if $page_name != 'index'}
<div id="right_column" class="column">
{$HOOK_RIGHT_COLUMN}
</div>
{/if}
```

The class HookCore is defined as below :

Public Member Functions
      getFields ()
Static Public Member Functions
      static   get ($hookName)
      static   getHooks ($position=false)
      static   getModulesFromHook ($id_hook)
      static   preloadModulesFromHooks ($position=false)
      static   getModuleFromHook ($id_hook, $id_module)
      static   newOrder ($cart, $order, $customer, $currency, $orderStatus)
      static   updateOrderStatus ($newOrderStatusId, $id_order)
      static   postUpdateOrderStatus ($newOrderStatusId, $id_order)
      static   updateQuantity ($product, $order=null)

```
    static      productFooter ($product, $category)
    static      productOutOfStock ($product)
    static      addProduct ($product)
    static      updateProduct ($product)
    static      deleteProduct ($product)
    static      updateProductAttribute ($id_prod-
uct_attribute)
    static      orderConfirmation ($id_order)
    static      paymentReturn ($id_order, $id_mod-
ule)
    static      PDFInvoice ($pdf, $id_order)
    static      backBeforePayment ($module)
    static      updateCarrier ($id_carrier, $car-
rier)
Public Attributes
    $name
Static Public Attributes
    static      $preloadModulesFromHooks = array()
Protected Attributes
    $fieldsRequired = array('name')
    $fieldsSize = array('name' => 32)
    $fieldsValidate = array('name' => 'isHookName')
    $table = 'hook'
    $identifier = 'id_hook'
```

Use a new hook

- Insert in the database table 'ps_hook' a new row with your hook like :

```
INSERT INTO `ps_hook` (`name`, `title`, `descrip-
tion`)
    VALUES ('MyHook', 'Test Hook', 'just a test
hook');
```

- In your class add the new method :

```
public function NameOfMyHook($params)   { }
```

- In your module's Install function add (it's necessary to register the hook):

```
 return parent::install() && $this->registerHook('NameOfMyHook');
```

- open the page where you want the hook to appear, ie. for the homepage header : classes/FrontController.php . Locate the function displayHeader() and find the following code inside:

```
self::$smarty->assign(array(
    'HOOK_HEADER' => Module::hookExec('header'),
    'HOOK_TOP' => Module::hookExec('top'),
```

- below the above code add the line : 'HOOK_MyHook' :

```
self::$smarty->assign(array(
    'HOOK_HEADER' => Module::hookExec('header'),
    'HOOK_TOP' => Module::hookExec('top'),
    'HOOK_MyHook' => Module::hookExec('NameOfMyHook'),
    'HOOK_LEFT_COLUMN' => Module::hookExec('leftColumn')
    ));
```

- Finally put the following in the .tpl file where you want the hook to appear : {$HOOK_MyHook}

Use an existing hook

Just follow the steps above and replace 'HOOK_MyHook' with an existing hook :

```
'HOOK_FOOTER' => Module::hookExec('footer')
```

For instance the blockcurrencies.php register its hook in the install function as below :

```
[Code    modules/blockcurrencies/blockcurrencies.php]
class BlockCurrencies extends Module
...

public function install()
{
   return (parent::install() AND $this->registerHook('top') AND $this->registerHook('header'));
}
```

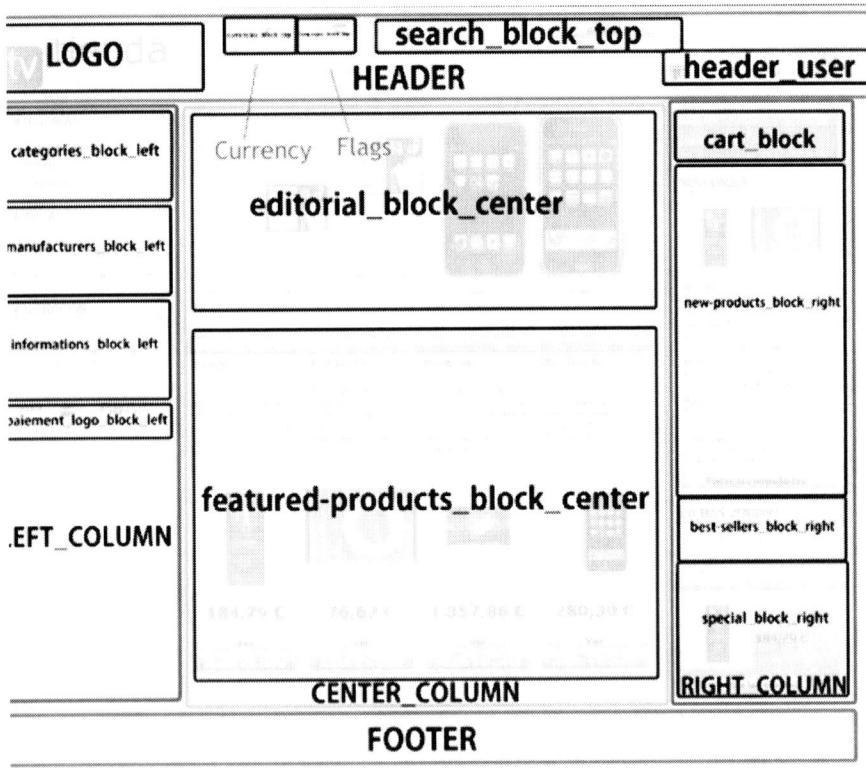

Hooks are defined in a Smarty array then the class Module through the method hookExec()execute them :

```
[Code    modules/blockmyaccount/blockmyaccount.php]
public function hookLeftColumn($params)
…
$smarty->assign(array(
      'voucherAllowed' => (int)
(Configuration::get('PS_VOUCHERS')),
      'returnAllowed' => (int)
(Configuration::get('PS_ORDER_RETURN')),
      'HOOK_BLOCK_MY_ACCOUNT' => Module::hookExec('myAccountBlock')
…
```

```
[Code    modules/blockmyaccount/blockmyaccount.php]
public static function hookExec($hook_name, $hookArgs = array(), $id_module = NULL)
```

Credits

[4.1] http://en.wikipedia.org/wiki/Smarty
[4.2] http://en.wikipedia.org/wiki/Namespace_(computer_science)
[4.3] http://www.php.net/manual/en/language.namespaces.rationale.php
[4.4] http://en.wikipedia.org/wiki/Minification_(programming)
[4.5] http://en.wikipedia.org/wiki/HTTP_cookie
[4.6] http://en.wikipedia.org/wiki/Method_overriding
[4.7] http://en.wikipedia.org/wiki/Hooking

PShop Programming Tools

SQL	101
CSS	104
HTML	112
Javascript	114
JQuery	120
JSON	126
PEAR	127
Swift Mailer	129
Credits	132

PShop run with many technologies and in this chapter we'll try to have a look at those most important.

SQL

SQL often referred to as Structured Query Language is a programming language designed for managing data in relational database management systems (RDBMS). [5.1]

In PShop the DB and other classes use it to access data in the database. SQL has various versions depending on the DBMS used. Common to all are four main statements : INSERT, DELETE, SELECT, and UPDATE. [5.2]

INSERT INTO

```
INSERT INTO "table1" ("column1", "column2", ...)
SELECT "column3", "column4", ...
FROM "table2"

INSERT INTO mytable1  (product, Sales, Date)
SELECT  product, Sales, Date
FROM mytable2
WHERE Year(Date) = 2011



INSERT INTO "table_name" ("column1", "column2",
...)
VALUES ("value1", "value2", ...)

INSERT INTO mytable  (product, Sales, Date)
VALUES ('iPAD', 90, 'Jan-10-2011')
```

DELETE

```
DELETE FROM "table_name"
```

```
WHERE {condition}

DELETE FROM mytable
WHERE product = "Los Angeles"
```

SELECT

```
SELECT "column_name" FROM "table_name"
SELECT product FROM mytable WHERE Year(Date) = 2011
```

UPDATE

```
UPDATE "table_name"
SET "column_1" = [new value]
WHERE {condition}

UPDATE mytable
SET Sales = 30
WHERE product = "iPAD"
AND Date = "Feb-08-2011"
```

With reference to MySQL, the partial list below include the syntax for the above statements [5.3]:

SELECT
    [ALL | DISTINCT | DISTINCTROW]
      [HIGH_PRIORITY]
      [STRAIGHT_JOIN]
      [SQL_SMALL_RESULT] [SQL_BIG_RESULT] [SQL_BUFFER_RESULT]
      [SQL_CACHE | SQL_NO_CACHE] [SQL_CALC_FOUND_ROWS]
    select_expr [, *select_expr* ...]
    [FROM *table_references*
    [WHERE *where_condition*]
    [GROUP BY {*col_name* | *expr* | *position*}

```
        [ASC | DESC], ... [WITH ROLLUP]]
    [HAVING where_condition]
    [ORDER BY {col_name | expr | position}
        [ASC | DESC], ...]
    [LIMIT {[offset,] row_count | row_count OFFSET
offset}]
    [PROCEDURE procedure_name(argument_list)]
    [INTO OUTFILE 'file_name'
        [CHARACTER SET charset_name]
        export_options
      | INTO DUMPFILE 'file_name'
      | INTO var_name [, var_name]]
    [FOR UPDATE | LOCK IN SHARE MODE]]


INSERT [LOW_PRIORITY | DELAYED | HIGH_PRIORITY]
[IGNORE]
    [INTO] tbl_name [(col_name,...)]
    {VALUES | VALUE} ({expr | DE-
FAULT},...),(...),...
    [ ON DUPLICATE KEY UPDATE
      col_name=expr
        [, col_name=expr] ... ]


DELETE [LOW_PRIORITY] [QUICK] [IGNORE] FROM tbl_name
    [WHERE where_condition]
    [ORDER BY ...]
    [LIMIT row_count]


UPDATE [LOW_PRIORITY] [IGNORE] table_reference
    SET col_name1={expr1|DEFAULT} [, col_
name2={expr2|DEFAULT}] ...
    [WHERE where_condition]
    [ORDER BY ...]
    [LIMIT row_count]
```

For instance in PShop SQL statements can be found in the class Db:

```
[Code admin/tabs/AdminEmployees.php]
    $query = 'INSERT INTO `'.$table.'` (';
        foreach ($values AS $key => $value)
            $query .= '`'.$key.'`,';
            $query = rtrim($query, ',').') VAL-
UES (';
            foreach ($values AS $key => $value)
                $query .= '\''.$value.'\',';
                $query = rtrim($query, ',').')';
...
```

CSS

Cascading Style Sheets (CSS) is a style sheet language used to describe the presentation semantics (the look and formatting) of a document written in a markup language. Its most common application is to style web pages written in HTML and XHTML, but the language can also be applied to any kind of XML document, including plain XML, SVG and XUL. [5.4]

The advantage of using external CSS files is to separate the text content (HTML) from its formatting (CSS). For instance to change the font used in a website it's possible to edit a single file.css. CSS internal to the HTML are usually deprecated

CSS syntax (rules) are made in two parts : selector and one or more declaration [5.5]

```
selector { declaration; declaration; }

/* comment*/
p
{
text-align:center;
color:white;
font-family:verdana;
}
```

Selectors

The table below describe the most used selectors [5.6]

Selector	Description	Example
ID	This selector uses the id attribute of the HTML element, and is defined with a "#" .	`#input1 { text-align:center; color:red; }`
C	The class selector uses the HTML class attribute, and is defined with a "." In the example all HTML elements with class="left" will be affected	`.left {text-align:left;}` /* this affect all elements in class="left" */ `p.left {text-align:left;}` /* this affect all p elements in class="left" */
S	the star selector affect all elements in the page	`* {margin: 0; padding: 0; }`
A B	descendant , for instance to target all anchors within an unordered list	`li a { text-decoration: none; }`
T	type selector, for instance to target all unordered list	`ul { margin-left: 0; }`
A:visited , B:link	Visited and not yet visited links	`a:link { color: red; }` /* target all anchors not yet visited */ `a:visted { color: purple; }` /* target all visited links */
A + B	this will affect only the first B element after A	`ul + p { color: red; }`

A[attribute]	will affect only those tags having the specific attribute	a[title] {
		    color: green; /* affect only anchors with 'title' attribute */
		}

A[href=]	will affect only those tags having the specific attribute	a[href="http://google.com"] { color: #1f6053;
A[href^=]	will affect only those tags having the specific attribute adding a small icon beside the link	
A: checked	will affect only those tags having the specific attribute (checked)	

A: hover	Apply the style when a user hover over the element	div:hover {
		    background: #e3e3e3;
		}

A: not	Useful if we want to affect all elements except the one indicated	

A: pseudo Element	Pseudo elements (::) affect portions of an element, such as the first line, or the first letter. They must be applied to block level elements	p::first-line {
		    font-weight: bold;
		    font-size: 1.2em;
		}

Units

in CSS we can usually find pixels (px), points (pt), percent (%) or ems (em). em is a unit of measurement in the field of typography, equal to the currently specified point size. The name of em is related to M. Originally the unit was derived from the width of the capital "M" [5.7]

The units px and pt do not scale if you change the font size of your page. The em and % does but while the em scales too much (smallest size too small and largest size too large) the % seems to offer a better readability to the user. [5.8] Notably with professional browsers

supporting zoom the unit px seems to regain in popularity.
Margins : This property define the space around elements.
Paddings : This property define the space between the element border and the element content.
Overflow : The overflow property specifies what happens if content overflows an element's box.
!Important : using this property we make sure that the declaration is always applied even if we change it through the CSS :

```
p { color: #ff0000 !important; } /* this will be applied */
p { color: #000000; }
```

CSS3 is split up into "modules". The old specification has been split into smaller pieces, and new ones are also added. Some of the most important CSS3 modules are:

- Selectors
- Box Model
- Backgrounds and Borders
- Text Effects
- 2D/3D Transformations
- Animations
- Multiple Column Layout
- User Interface

The table below include some of the most used declarations in CSS

CSS Backgrounds	Set the background color of a page	background-color:#ededed;
	position a background image	background-image:url('img_tree.png'); background-repeat:no-repeat; background-position:right top;

CSS Text	Set the text color of different elements	`body {color:red;}`
		`h1 {color:#00ff00;}`
		`p.ex {color:rgb(0,0,255);}`

	Align the text	`p.date {text-align:right;}` `p.main {text-align:justify;}`
	Remove the line under links	`a {text-decoration:none;}`

	Control the letters in a text	`p.uppercase {text-transform:uppercase;}`
		`p.lowercase {text-transform:lowercase;}`
		`p.capitalize {text-`

	Indent text	`p {text-indent:50px;}`
	Specify the space between characters	`h1 {letter-spacing:2px;}` `h2 {letter-spacing:-3px;}`
	Text wrapping	`white-space:wrap;`

	Text transform	`h1 {text-transform:uppercase}`
		`h2 {text-transform:capitalize}`
		`p {text-transform:lowercase}`

CSS Fonts	Set the font of a text	`p.serif{font-family:"Times New Roman",Times,serif;}` `p.sansserif{font-`
	Set the size of the font	`h1 {font-size:200%;}` `p {font-size:100%;}`

	Set the size of the font in percent and em	`body {font-size:100%;}`
		`h1 {font-size:2.5em;}`
		`h2 {font-size:1.875em;}`
		`p {font-size:0.875em;}`

	Font style	`p.normal {font-style:normal;}` `p.italic {font-style:italic;}`

CSS Links	Link colors	`a:link {color:#FF0000;}` /* unvisited link */ `a:visited {color:#00FF00;}` /* visited link */ `a:hover {color:#FF00FF;}` /* mouse over link */ `a:active {color:#0000FF;}` /* selected link */
	Backgroud color for links	`a:visited {background-color:#FFFF85;}` /* visited link */

CSS List	list item markers	`ul.a {list-style-type:circle;}`
		`ul.b {list-style-type:disc;}`
		`ul.c {list-style-type:square;}`

CSS Tables	Table border	`table,th,td {`
		`border:1px solid black;`
		`}`

	Border collapse	`table {`
		`border-collapse:collapse;`
		`}`

	Table size	`table,td,th {`
		`border:1px solid black;`
		`}`
		`table {`
		`width:100%;`
		`}`
		`th {`
		`height:40px;`
		`}`

	Table text align	`td {`
		`text-align:right;`
		`}`

	Padding	`td {`
		`padding:15px;`
		`}`

CSS Border	Border width	`border-style:solid;` `border-width:1px;`

	Border style	`p.dotted {border-style:dotted;}`
		`p.dashed {border-style:dashed;}`
		`p.solid {border-style:solid;}`

	Border color	`border-color:#ff0000 #0000ff;` `border-top-color:#ff0000;`
CSS Outline	Border Outline	`border:1px solid red;` `outline:green dotted thick;`

CSS Margin	Specify margins for an element	`margin-top:100px;`
		`margin-bottom:100px;`
		`margin-right:50px;`
		`margin-left:50px;`

CSS Padding	Set the left padding of an element	`p.padding {padding-left:2cm;}` `p.padding2 {padding-left:50%;}`

CSS Positioning	Position an element relative to the browser window	`p.pos_fixed {`
		`position:fixed;`
		`top:30px;`
		`right:5px;`
		`}`

	Position an element relative to its normal position	`h2.pos_left {`
		`position:relative;`
		`left:-20px;`
		`}`

	Overlapping elements	`img {`
		`position:absolute;`
		`left:0px;`
		`top:0px;`
		`z-index:-1;`
		`}`

	Shape clipping	`img {` `position:absolute;`

| | create a scroll bar when an element's content is too big to fit | ```
div.scroll {
background-
color:#00FFFF;
width:100px;
height:100px;
overflow:scroll;
}
``` |
|---|---|---|
| | set the browser to automatically handle overflow | ```
div {
background-
color:#00FFFF;
width:150px;
height:150px;
overflow:auto;
}
``` |
| CSS Floating | Float image | ```
img {
float:right;
}
``` |

Image Sprite

A collection of images inside a single image is called Sprite, by changing the x,y coordinates we can show the desired portion of the Sprite, as below :

```
[Code   testSprite.htm]
<html>
<head>
<style type="text/css">
img.sprite1
{
width:64px;
height:69px;
background:url(sprites.png) 0 0;
}
img.sprite2
{
width:43px;
height:56px;
```
```

```
background:url(sprites.png) -130px 0;
}
</style>
</head>

<body>
<img class="sprite1" src="transparent.gif"
width="1" height="1" />
<br /><br />
<img class="sprite2" src="transparent.gif"
width="1" height="1" />
</body>
</html>
```

In the above example transparent.gif is a transparent image and sprites.png (186 x 64) is attached below. When we move the left_pointer to the left by 91px we get
displayed the last image, when we move it to zero the first image is displayed.

HTML

HyperText Markup Language (HTML) is the predominant markup language for web pages [5.9]
Any HTML document include tags enclosed in angle brackets , a typical document could be in the following form:

```
<html>
  <head>
    <title>Hello HTML</title>
  </head>
  <body>
    <p>Hello World!</p>
  </body>
</html>
```

Where html define the whole html document , p means paragraph, head means header of the document and body contain the body of the html document. Html, body , p and head are called tag elements. The slash before a tag terminate its scope.

Some of the most used HTML tags are listed below

HTML Basic	`<h1>My First Heading</h1>` `<p>My first paragraph.</p>`
	`<a href="http://www.google.com">This is a link to Google</a>`
Comment	`<!--This comment will not be displayed-->` `<p>This is a regular paragraph</p>`
Line breaks	`<p>This is a para graph with line breaks</p>`

Image with link	`<a href="default.asp">`
	`<img src="smiley.gif" alt="HTML tutorial" width="32" height="32" />`
	`</a>`

Email	`<a href="mailto:someone@example.com?Subject=Hello%20again">Send Mail</a>`

Table	`<p> Each table starts with a table tag. Each table row starts with a tr tag.`
	`Each table data starts with a td tag. Th is a table header</p>`
	
	`<h4>One column:</h4>`
	`<table border="1">`
	`<tr>`
	`  <td>100</td>`
	`</tr>`
	`</table>`

Unordered list	`<ul>`
	`   <li>Coffee</li>`
	`   <li>Tea</li>`
	`   <li>Milk</li>`
	`</ul>`

Ordered list	```<ol>
<li>Coffee</li>
<li>Tea</li>
<li>Milk</li>
</ol>```
Input fields	```<form action="">
First name: <input type="text" name="firstname" />
Last name: <input type="text" name="lastname" />
</form>```
Checkbox	```<input type="checkbox" name="vehicle" value="Bike" /> I have a bike ```
Radio button	```<input type="radio" name="sex" value="male" /> Male ```
Drop down	```<select name="cars">
<option value="volvo">Volvo</option>
<option value="saab">Saab</option>
<option value="fiat">Fiat</option>
<option value="audi">Audi</option>
</select>```
Button	```<input type="button" value="Hello world!">```
Meta tags	```<meta name="author" content="Hege Refsnes" />
<meta name="description" content="Free Web tutorials ">
<meta name="keywords" content="HTML, CSS">```
Div	```<div style="color:#00FF00">
<h3>This is a header</h3>
<p>This is a paragraph.</p>
</div>```
Span	```<p>My mother has <span class="blue">light blue</span> eyes.</p>```

Javascript

JavaScript is designed to add interactivity to HTML pages, it's a client-side script. JavaScript is used in billions of Web pages to add functionality, validate forms, communicate with the server, etc . [5.10] Few examples are given as below :

Write to the Document with JavaScript	`<script type="text/javascript">`
	`// Write a paragraph`
	`document.write("<p>" + Date() + "</p>");`
	`</script>`

Change HTML elements with JavaScript	`<p id="demo">test</p>`
	`<script type="text/javascript">`
	`document.getElementById("demo").innerHTML=Date();`
	`</script>`

external JavaScript	`<script type="text/javascript" src="test.js">`
	`/* multiple line comment */`
	`</script>`

JavaScript statements.	`<script type="text/javascript">`
	`document.write("<h1>This is a heading</h1>");`
	`document.write("<p>This is a paragraph.</p>");`
	`</script>`

Variables	`<script type="text/javascript">` `var firstname;` `firstname="Bob";` `document.write(firstname);` `document.write(" ");` `firstname="Tom";` `document.write(firstname);` `</script>`

If statement	```
	<script type="text/javascript">
	var d = new Date();
	var time = d.getHours();
	
	if (time < 10)
	  {
	  document.write("<b>Good morning</b>");
	  }
	</script>
	``

If...else statement	```
	<script type="text/javascript">
	var d = new Date();
	var time = d.getHours();
	if (time < 10)
	{
	document.write("<b>Good morning</b>");
	}
	else
	{
	document.write("<b>Good day</b>");
	}
	</script>
	``

| Switch statement | ```
<script type="text/javascript">
var d=new Date();
var theDay=d.getDay();
switch (theDay)
{
case 5:
  document.write("Finally Friday");
  break;
case 6:
  document.write("Super Saturday");
  break;
case 0:
  document.write("Sleepy Sunday");
  break;
default:
  document.write("I'm really looking forward to this weekend!");
}
</script>
``` |
| Random number | `var r=Math.random();     // 0-1` |
| Alert box | ```
<script type="text/javascript">
function disp_alert()
{
alert("Hello ! This is how we" + '\n' + "add line breaks to an alert box!");
}
</script>
</head>
<body>

<input type="button" onclick="disp_alert()" value="Display alert box" />

</body>
``` |

| Confirm box | ```html
<script type="text/javascript">
function show_confirm()
{
var r=confirm("Press a button!");
if (r==true)
  {
  alert("You pressed OK!");
  }
else
  {
  alert("You pressed Cancel!");
  }
}
</script>
</head>
<body>

<input type="button" onclick="show_confirm()" value="Show a confirm box" />

</body>
``` |
| Prompt box | ```html
<script type="text/javascript">
function show_prompt()
{
var name=prompt("Please enter your name","Harry Potter");
if (name!=null && name!="")
  {
  document.write("Hello " + name + "! How are you today?");
  }
}
</script>
</head>
<body>

<input type="button" onclick="show_prompt()" value="Show prompt box" />

</body>
``` |

Function call	```
	<script type="text/javascript">
	function myfunction(txt)
	{
	alert(txt);
	}
	</script>
	</head>
	<body>
	
	<form>
	<input type="button"
	onclick="myfunction('Hello')"
	value="Call function">
	</form>
	
	<p>By pressing the button above, a function will be called with "Hello" as a parameter. The function will alert the parameter.</p>
	
	</body>
	``

Return function	```
	<script type="text/javascript">
	function myFunction()
	{
	return ("Hello world!");
	}
	</script>
	</head>
	<body>
	
	<script type="text/javascript">
	document.write(myFunction())
	</script>
	
	</body>
	``

JQuery

JQuery is a cross-browser JavaScript library designed to simplify the client-side scripting of HTML.[5.11]

JQuery library can be downloaded from the official website [5.13], below there is an example just save it as test.htm and run it in your browser. With jQuery you select (query) HTML elements and perform "actions" on them. jQuery uses the $ sign as a shortcut for jQuery. jQuery selectors allow you to select HTML elements (or groups of elements) by element name, attribute name or by content.

jQuery Syntax

The jQuery syntax is tailor made for **selecting** HTML elements and perform some **action** on the element(s).
The basic syntax is: **$(selector).action()**

jQuery Element Selectors

jQuery uses CSS selectors to select HTML elements.

```
$("p") selects all <p> elements.
$("p.intro") selects all <p> elements with class="intro".
$("p#demo") selects all <p> elements with id="demo".
```

jQuery Attribute Selectors

jQuery uses XPath expressions to select elements with given attributes.

```
$("[href]") select all elements with an href attribute.
$("[href='#']") select all elements with an href value equal to "#".
```

The following example changes the background-color of all p elements to yellow:$("p").css("background-color","yellow");

```
$(this)             Current HTML element
$("p")              All <p> elements
$("p.intro")        All <p> elements with class="intro"
$("p#intro")        All <p> elements with id="intro"
```

```
$("p#intro:first")      The first <p> element with
id="intro"
$(".intro")             All elements with class="intro"
$("#intro")             The first element with id="intro"
```

jQuery Event Functions

The jQuery event handling methods are core functions in jQuery.

```
$(document).ready(function(){
  $("button").click(function(){
    $("p").hide();
  });
});
```

In the example above, a function is called when the click event for the button is triggered:
`$("button").click(function() {..some code... } )`
The method hides all <p> elements:
`$("p").hide();`

Event Method	Description
$(document).ready(function)	Binds a function to the ready event of a document (when the document is finished loading)
$(selector).click(function)	Triggers, or binds a function to the click event of selected elements
$(selector).dblclick(function)	Triggers, or binds a function to the double click event of selected elements
$(selector).focus(function)	Triggers, or binds a function to the focus event of selected elements

| $(selector).mouseover(function) | Triggers, or binds a function to the mouseover event of selected elements |

Adding (or removing) a class can be done by using .addClass() or removeClass() which will apply the bold style to all elements, This example demonstrate the use of the click event :

```html
<!DOCTYPE html>
<html lang="en">
<head>
  <meta charset="utf-8">
  <title>jQuery demo</title>
  <style>
    a.test { font-weight: bold; }
  </style>
</head>
<body>
  <a href="http://jquery.com/">jQuery</a>
  <script src="http://ajax.googleapis.com/ajax/libs/jquery/1.5/jquery.min.js"></script>
  <script>
  $("a").addClass("test");
    $(document).ready(function(){
      $("a").click(function(event){
        alert("As you can see, the link no longer took you to jquery.com");
        event.preventDefault();
      });
    });
  </script>
</body>
</html>
```

JQuery Effects

Function	Description
$(selector).hide()	Hide selected elements
$(selector).show()	Show selected elements
$(selector).toggle()	Toggle (between hide and show) selected elements

| $(selector).slide-Down() | Slide-down (show) selected elements |
| $(selector).fadeIn() | Fade in selected elements |

Callback functions : A callback function is executed after the current animation (effect) is finished.

```
$("p").hide(1000,function(){
   alert("The paragraph is now hidden");
});
```

JQuery CSS methods

Method	Description
addClass()	Adds one or more classes to selected elements
css()	Sets or returns one or more style properties for selected elements
hasClass()	Checks if any of the selected elements have a specified class
height()	Sets or returns the height of selected elements
offset()	Sets or returns the position (relative to the document) for selected elements
offsetParent()	Returns the first parent element that is positioned
position()	Returns the position (relative to the parent element) of the first selected element
removeClass()	Removes one or more classes from selected elements
scrollLeft()	Sets or returns the horizontal position of the scrollbar for the selected elements

jQuery AJAX Methods

Ajax is an acronym for Asynchronous JavaScript and XML.
AJAX is the art of exchanging data with a server, and update parts of a web page - without reloading the whole page.

Method	Description
ajaxComplete()	Specifies a function to run when the AJAX request completes
ajaxError()	Specifies a function to run when the AJAX request completes with an error
ajaxSend()	Specifies a function to run before the AJAX request is sent
$.ajaxSetup()	Sets the default values for future AJAX requests
ajaxStart()	Specifies a function to run when the first AJAX request begins
ajaxStop()	Specifies a function to run when all AJAX requests have completed
ajaxSuccess()	Specifies a function to run an AJAX request completes successfully
$.get()	Loads data from a server using an AJAX HTTP GET request
$.getJSON()	Loads JSON-encoded data from a server using a HTTP GET request
$.getScript()	Loads (and executes) a JavaScript from the a server using an AJAX HTTP GET request
load()	Loads data from a server and puts the returned HTML into the selected element

Hide and Show	```$("#hide").click(function(){
$("p").hide();
});
$("#show").click(function(){
$("p").show();
});```
$.ajax() : Performs an AJAX request (low level)	```$("button").click(function(){
$.ajax({url:"demo_ajax_load.txt",
success:function(result){
$("div").html(result);
}});
});```

For instance in PShop JQuery is used in BO > Employees to setup the color for the back office or to upload the product file through Ajax :

```
[Code   admin/tabs/AdminProducts.php]
      function uploadFile()
      {
         $.ajaxFileUpload (
            {
            url:'./uploadProductFile.php',
...
```

```
[Code   admin/tabs/AdminEmployees.php]
echo '<script type="text/javascript" src="'._PS_JS_
DIR_.'/jquery/jquery-colorpicker.js"></script>
...
```

The feature Live Edit available in BO > Modules > (choose one) then 'Manage Hooks' gives to the admin the option to change the theme by dragging & dropping the modules on the FO. For instance it's possible to move the block 'My Account' on the bottom-right side of the home page or to remove the block 'Categories'..
The Live Edit feature can be implemented with different libraries like Google API [5.21] or with JQuery [5.22]. In PShop Live Edit is made using JQuery libraries and is mainly controlled by three files : /classes/FrontController.php , admin/tabs(AdminModulesPositions.php , /js/hookLiveEdit.js

FrontController will load the Smarty template and the Javascript with a call to methods of the class Tools which will add the Javascript and the CSS as below :

```
[Code   /classes/FrontController.php]
      self::$smarty->assign(array('ad' => $ad,
'live_edit' => true));
      self::$smarty->display(_PS_ALL_THEMES_
DIR_.'live_edit.tpl');
...
```

```
    Tools::addJS(array(
    _PS_JS_DIR_.'jquery/jquery-ui-1.8.10.custom.
min.js',
    _PS_JS_DIR_.'jquery/jquery.fancybox-1.3.4.js',
    _PS_JS_DIR_.'hookLiveEdit.js')
    );
    Tools::addCSS(_PS_CSS_DIR_.'jquery.fancybox-
1.3.4.css');
...
```

JSON

JSON: **J**ava**S**cript **O**bject **N**otation. JSON is a syntax for storing and exchanging text information. The JSON text format is syntactically identical to the code for creating JavaScript objects.Much like XML but For AJAX applications, JSON is faster and easier than XML[5.15]

JSON Object creation :

```
<p>
Name: <span id="jname"></span><br />
Age: <span id="jage"></span><br />
Address: <span id="jstreet"></span><br />
Phone: <span id="jphone"></span><br />
</p>

<script type="text/javascript">
var JSONObject = {
  "name":"John Johnson",
  "street":"Oslo West 16",
  "age":33,
  "phone":"555 1234567"};
document.getElementById("jname").
innerHTML=JSONObject.name
document.getElementById("jage").
innerHTML=JSONObject.age
document.getElementById("jstreet").
innerHTML=JSONObject.street
document.getElementById("jphone").
innerHTML=JSONObject.phone
</script>
```

For instance PShop uses JSon in the product page to get manufacturers and suppliers or customers with Ajax :

```
[Code   admin/ajax.php]
     $json = '{"customers" : ';
     foreach ($customers AS $customer)
          $jsonArray[] = '{"value":"0_'.(int)
($customer['id_customer']).'", "text":"'.
addslashes($customer['name']).' ('.addslashes($cust
omer['email']).')"}';
...
```

```
[Code   admin/tabs/AdminProducts.php]
     <script type="text/javascript">
          $(document).ready(function() {
          updateCurrentText();
          updateFriendlyURL();
          $.ajax({
          url: "'.dirname($currentIndex).'/ajax.php",
                  cache: false,
                  dataType: "json",
                  data: "ajaxProductManufacturers=1",
...
```

PEAR

The PHP Extension and Application Repository, or PEAR, is a repository of PHP software code. [5.16] PEAR is a framework and distribution system for reusable PHP components.[5.17]

PEAR is structured in packages, The smallest unit that can be managed by Pyrus or the PEAR Installer is a package. A package is a collection of files that are organized and defined by a meta-information file called package.xml . The following is a partial list of PEAR packages :

PEAR Packages [5.18]

Authentication
Benchmarking
Caching
Configuration
Console
Database
Date and Time
Encryption
Event
File Formats
File System
Gtk
Gtk2
HTML
HTTP
Images
....

For instance the Database class PEAR MDB2 is a merge of the PEAR DB and Metabase php database abstraction layers. It provides a common API for all supported RDBMS. The main difference to most other DB abstraction packages is that MDB2 goes much further to ensure portability.
The following is the static function connect() of the MDB2 package:

```
static function connect($dsn, $options = false)
{

    $db = MDB2::factory($dsn, $options);
    if (PEAR::isError($db)) {
        return $db;
    }

    $err = $db->connect();
    if (PEAR::isError($err)) {
        $dsn = $db->getDSN('string', 'xxx');
        $db->disconnect();
        $err->addUserInfo($dsn);
        return $err;
    }
    return $db;
}
```

Swift Mailer

Swift Mailer is a component-based library for sending e-mails from PHP applications [5.19]

Swift Mailer is made up of many classes. Each of these classes can be grouped into a general "component" group which describes the task it is designed to perform.

- The mailer class, Swift_Mailer is the central class in the library
- Transports are the classes in Swift Mailer that are responsible for communicating with a service in order to deliver a Message
- MIME Entities : everything that forms part of a Message is called a MIME Entity
- Encoders are used to transform the content of Messages generated in Swift Mailer into a format that is safe to send across the internet and that conforms to RFC specifications
- Plugins exist to extend, or modify the behaviour of Swift Mailer

Below you'll find a table of Transports classes:

Class	Features
Swift_SmtpTransport	Sends messages over SMTP; Supports Authentication; Supports Encryption
Swift_SendmailTransport	Communicates with a locally installed sendmail executable (Linux/UNIX)
Swift_MailTransport	Uses PHP's built-in mail() function
Swift_LoadBalancedTransport	Cycles through a collection of the other Transports to manage load-reduction
Swift_FailoverTransport	Works in conjunction with a collection of the other Transports to provide high-availability

Below you'll find an example of how to send an email with Swift Mailer [5.19]:

```php
require_once 'lib/swift_required.php';

//Create the Transport
$transport = Swift_SmtpTransport::newInstance('smtp.example.org', 25)
  ->setUsername('your username')
  ->setPassword('your password')
  ;

/*
You could alternatively use a different transport such as Sendmail or Mail:

//Sendmail
$transport = Swift_SendmailTransport::newInstance('/usr/sbin/sendmail -bs');

//Mail
$transport = Swift_MailTransport::newInstance();
*/

//Create the Mailer using your created Transport
$mailer = Swift_Mailer::newInstance($transport);

//Create a message
$message = Swift_Message::newInstance('Wonderful Subject')
  ->setFrom(array('john@doe.com' => 'John Doe'))
  ->setTo(array('receiver@domain.org', 'other@domain.org' => 'A name'))
  ->setBody('Here is the message itself')
  ;

//Send the message
$result = $mailer->send($message);
```

In PShop the class MailCore take care of sending emails by including the Swift class:

```php
include_once(_PS_SWIFT_DIR_.'Swift.php');
include_once(_PS_SWIFT_DIR_.'Swift/Connection/SMTP.php');
include_once(_PS_SWIFT_DIR_.'Swift/Connection/NativeMail.php');
include_once(_PS_SWIFT_DIR_.'Swift/Plugin/Decorator.php');

class MailCore
{
    public static function Send($id_lang, $template, $subject, $templateVars, $to, $toName = NULL, $from = NULL, $fromName = NULL, $fileAttachment = NULL, $modeSMTP = NULL, $templatePath = _PS_MAIL_DIR_, $die = false)
...
```

```
Static Public Member Functions    // class MailCore
    static      Send ($id_lang, $template, $subject, $templateVars, $to, $toName=NULL,
            $from=NULL, $fromName=NULL, $fileAttachment=NULL, $modeSMTP=NULL,
            $templatePath=_PS_MAIL_DIR_, $die=false)
    static      sendMailTest ($smtpChecked, $smtpServer, $content, $subject, $type, $to, $from,
            $smtpLogin, $smtpPassword, $smtpPort=25, $smtpEncryption)
    static      l ($string, $id_lang=null)
```

For instance PShop send an email to the customer when the order has been shipped as below (for the meaning of the symbol @ prefixed before the class see the PHP Tutorial later in this book):

```
[Code   tabs/AdminOrders.php]
@Mail::Send((int)($order->id_lang), 'in_transit',
Mail::l('Package in transit'), $templateVars,
                        $customer->email,
$customer->firstname.' '.$customer->lastname, NULL,
NULL, NULL, NULL,
                        _PS_MAIL_DIR_,
true);
```

Credits

[5.1] http://en.wikipedia.org/wiki/SQL
[5.2] http://www.1keydata.com/sql
[5.3] http://dev.mysql.com/doc/refman/5.1/en/sql-syntax-data-manipulation.html
[5.4] http://en.wikipedia.org/wiki/CSS
[5.5] http://w3schools.com/css/default.asp
[5.6] http://net.tutsplus.com/tutorials/html-css-techniques/the-30-css-selectors-you-must-memorize/
[5.7] http://en.wikipedia.org/wiki/Em_(typography)
[5.8] http://kyleschaeffer.com/best-practices/css-font-size-em-vs-px-vs-pt-vs/
[5.9] http://en.wikipedia.org/wiki/Html
[5.10] http://en.wikipedia.org/wiki/JavaScript
[5.11] http://en.wikipedia.org/wiki/Jquery
[5.12] http://www.w3schools.com/css3/css3_intro.asp
[5.13] http://jquery.com/
[5.14] http://en.wikipedia.org/wiki/Ajax_(programming)
[5.15] http://www.w3schools.com/json/default.asp
[5.16] http://en.wikipedia.org/wiki/PEAR
[5.17] http://pear.php.net/
[5.18] http://pear.php.net/packages.php
[5.19] http://swiftmailer.org
[5.20] http://www.firephp.org/Wiki/Libraries/FirePHPCore
[5.21] http://www.michelhiemstra.nl/scripts/jsportal/index.php
[5.22] http://demo.webdeveloperplus.com/drag-drop-panels/

Modules

Structure	134
Installation	135
Positions	137
Theme	138
Language	140
Create a new Module	140
Credits	154

In this chapter we'll first examine an existing module as it's distributed in the standard package of PShop and then we'll create a new module from scratch to turn concepts in practical.

Structure

A module is a software design technique that increases the extent of the application [6.1] In PShop a module is a collection of template and core files which usually include the following file extensions : .tpl, .css, .js and .php
The folder structure may vary for each module but all modules must be saved in a folder under /modules. In this chapter we'll examine the standard module Follow-up saved under modules/followup

First we can see that this module include language files to manage different translations : english (en.php), spanish (es.php), french (fr. php), italian (it.php), german (de.php)
Then we have logo images (logo-2.gif, logo.gif) , the file index.php (used to setup few settings) and the main file followup.php. The folder mails contain the text of the emails generated by the module for the customers in all languages. The default language is the one you select in PShop.
In PShop there is an override mechanism which can be used to 'replace' a default class with one from your module (see Override) but

this module do not modify core PShop files since it uses the standard PShop classes.

Installation

To install the module (files are already present in the folder under /modules) just goto BO > Modules > Customer follow-up and install it :

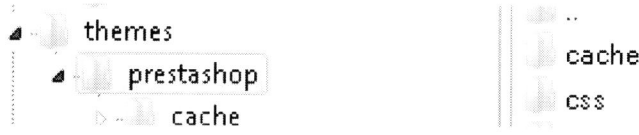

Next click on Configure and you'll get the configuration panel :

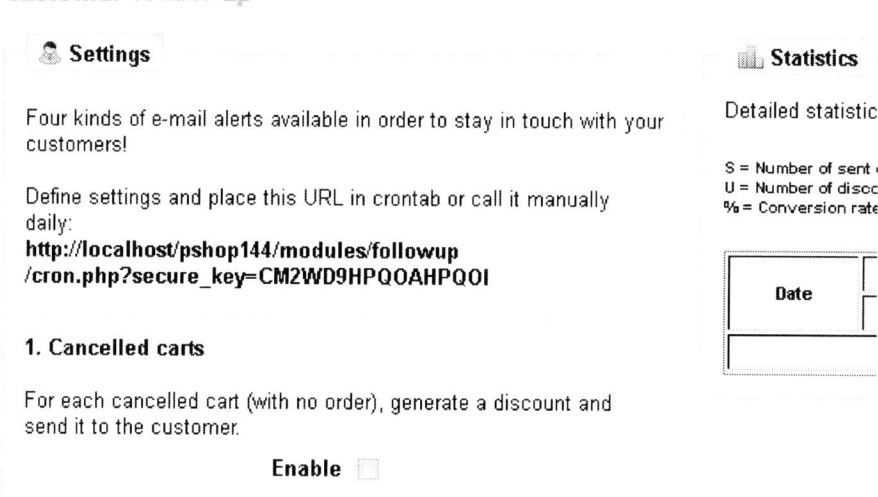

From here you can change the settings for this module. All these settings are defined in the main file followup.php

Open followup.php and look at the first line of code:

```
[code /modules/followup.php]
if (!defined('_CAN_LOAD_FILES_'))
```

```
    exit;
```

That will prevent users to run this file directly from the browser. The next statement define the class followup as a child class of the class module :

```
[code /modules/followup.php]
class Followup extends Module
```

Then the constructor (see PHP tutorial) which define some important variables :

```
[code /modules/followup.php]
    function __construct()
    {
        $this->name = 'followup';
        $this->tab = 'advertising_marketing';
        $this->version = '1.0';
        $this->author = 'PrestaShop';
        $this->need_instance = 0;

        $this->confKeys = array(
            'PS_FOLLOW_UP_ENABLE_1', 'PS_FOLLOW_UP_ENABLE_2', 'PS_FOLLOW_UP_ENABLE_3', 'PS_FOLLOW_UP_ENABLE_4',
            'PS_FOLLOW_UP_AMOUNT_1', 'PS_FOLLOW_UP_AMOUNT_2', 'PS_FOLLOW_UP_AMOUNT_3', 'PS_FOLLOW_UP_AMOUNT_4',
            'PS_FOLLOW_UP_DAYS_1', 'PS_FOLLOW_UP_DAYS_2', 'PS_FOLLOW_UP_DAYS_3', 'PS_FOLLOW_UP_DAYS_4',
            'PS_FOLLOW_UP_THRESHOLD_3',
            'PS_FOLLOW_UP_DAYS_THRESHOLD_4',
            'PS_FOLLOW_UP_CLEAN_DB');
...
```

In the code above is defined the Name of the module (followup) and the Tab in the BO where it's displayed (Advertising and Marketing), then the version and its author.
If we want PShop to load the class Followup when loading the modules in the BO > Modules then we should have need_instance=1
In the line starting with $this , the code load the associative array

confKeys with all its default keys.

After calling the parent constructor we have the following lines :

```
[code /modules/followup.php]
          $this->displayName = $this->l('Customer follow-up');
          $this->description = $this->l('Follow-up with your customers with daily customized e-mails.');
          $this->confirmUninstall = $this->l('Are you sure you want to delete all settings and your logs?');
...
```

The public attribute displayName display the name of the module in the Module list of the BO and the description attribute does the same for the description.
The message to uninstall the module is saved in the attribute confirmUninstall .
When we click Install in the BO we actually run the function Install() which does the following : create the table ps_log_email and save the array confKeys in the database.
Conversely the function uninstall() will drop the newly created table.
The function getContent() display the configuration page in the BO and process the data entry.

Positions

In order to display the module in the desired position we can 'hook' it in one of the existing positions (ie. leftColumn) and use a file .tpl to render it on the page.
In this module the template is made with the statement 'echo' inside the file followup.php therefore hooks are not used here.

```
[code /modules/followup.php]
          echo '
          <h2>'.$this->l('Customer follow-up').'</h2>
          <form action="'.$_SERVER['REQUEST_URI'].'" method="post">
```

```
                    <fieldset style="width: 400px; float: 
left;">
                        <legend><img src="'.$this->_
path.'logo.gif" alt="" title="" />'.$this-
>l('Settings').'</legend>
                        <p>'.$this->l('Four kinds of 
e-mail alerts available in order to stay in touch 
with your customers!').'<br /><br />
                        '.$this->l('Define settings 
and place this URL in crontab or call it manually 
daily:').'<br />
...
```

The member function l [$this->l('Customer follow-up')] stand for language and translate the text from english to the default language implemented in the shop.

The hooks available in PShop have been shown previously in this book.

Theme

This module do not make use of templates (.tpl) therefore the template engine Smarty is not implemented. Nevertheless we'll see how to hook a module and how to access it with Smarty. For this purpose let's take a look at the module \modules\blockmyaccount

The function install call the function MyAccountBlockHook() which will add our module name, description, position and title to the table PS_hook in the database :

```
[Code modules/blockmyaccount/blockmyaccount.php]
public function install()
{
if (!$this->addMyAccountBlockHook()
OR !parent::install() OR !$this-
>registerHook('leftColumn') OR !$this-
>registerHook('header'))
            return false;
        return true;
}
```

Conversely the function uninstall will remove that entry :

```
[Code modules/blockmyaccount/blockmyaccount.php]
public function uninstall()
{
  return (parent::uninstall() AND $this-
>removeMyAccountBlockHook());
}
```

The function hookLeftColumn() or hookRightColumn() , will take care to load the Smarty array so that it will be available in the template (blockmyaccount.tpl)

```
[Code modules/blockmyaccount/blockmyaccount.php]
public function hookLeftColumn($params)
{
            global $smarty;

            if (!$params['cookie']->isLogged())
                return false;
            $smarty->assign(array(
                'voucherAllowed' => (int)
(Configuration::get('PS_VOUCHERS')),
                'returnAllowed' => (int)
(Configuration::get('PS_ORDER_RETURN')),
                'HOOK_BLOCK_MY_ACCOUNT' => Module::
hookExec('myAccountBlock')
));
return $this->display(__FILE__, $this-
>name.'.tpl');
}


public function hookRightColumn($params)
{
      return $this->hookLeftColumn($params);
}
```

The function hookHeader() load the file CSS saved under themes\prestashop\css\modules\blockmyaccount\blockmyaccount.css :

```
[Code modules/blockmyaccount/blockmyaccount.php]
function hookHeader($params)
{
    Tools::addCSS(($this->_path).'blockmyaccount.
css', 'all');
}
```

In the blockmyaccount.tpl we can see the references to the module and a number of conditional statement related to the variables we've defined in the module (ie. {if $returnAllowed}which are used to display some part of the template programmatically.

```
<h4><a href="{$link->getPageLink('my-account.php',
true)}">{l s='My account' mod='blockmyaccount'}</
a></h4>
```

Language

The member function l() (lower case of L) is used in this module to translate the text displayed into the default language selected in BO. If we're using existing sentences in english then the language pack loaded into PShop will take care to translate them properly. If we are using sentences which are not present in the english standard language pack then we can update that language pack and ask the user to load it into the BO before installing our module. This can be done in BO > Tools > Languages

Create a new Module

Starting from the module Followup described above we'll now modify it to create our own new module.

Mission : we want a module giving our employee the privileges to work on all products but , for safety reasons, the employee will not be allowed to add or delete any Categories. This means the employee can only manage products associated with the existing Categories. We'll call our module ePlus.

Assuming the employee is male, we basically need to :

- identify him
- modify some class
- override the existing class with our one
- make the main file eplus.php
- pack and deploy

Identify the employee : the easiest way is to use his email . We'll get it from the array created when he login to the BO. For flexibility purposes in the configuration panel of ePlus we will :

- enter the email of the employee
- enable/disable the categories for him to manage

we'll use the associative array confKeys to store the above info having two keys : PS_EMAIL_1 and PS_ENABLED_1 (we keep the suffix _1 in case of future extensions)

There are basically two classes which we need to modify : /classes/AdminTab.php and /tabs/AdminCategories.php

- /classes/AdminTab.php : in this class we'll remove the line icons to edit a category and the button 'Delete Selection'
- /tabs/AdminCategories.php : in this class we'll remove the icon 'Add new Category'

In the **AdminTab.php** find the first occurrence of line below :

```
[code /classes/AdminTab.php]
if (isset($params['active']) AND isset($tr[$key])
```

and replace it with :
```
if (isset($params['active']) AND isset($tr[$key])
AND ($cookie->email==$conf['PS_EMAIL_1']   AND
```

```
$conf['PS_ENABLED_1']=='1' ))
```

next, one line below, replace the following:
```
elseif (isset($params['activeVisu']) AND
isset($tr[$key])
```

with :
```
elseif (isset($params['activeVisu']) AND
isset($tr[$key]) AND ($cookie->email==$conf['PS_
EMAIL_1']  AND  $conf['PS_ENABLED_1']=='1' ))
```

Remove 'Core' from the class name at the top of this file :
```
abstract class AdminTab
```

we need now to define the public array in the class, copy the following definition before the class constructor public function __construct() :

```
[code /classes/AdminTab.php]
    public $confKeys = array(
    'PS_ENABLED_1',
    'PS_EMAIL_1');
```

Add the following in the first lines of the function `displayListContent()`. This code retrieve in the array $conf() which has been saved when we click the Save button in the BO > Module configuration.

```
$conf = Configuration::getMultiple($this->confKeys);
    foreach ($this->confKeys AS $k)
        if (!isset($conf[$k])) $conf[$k] = '';
```

Then replace the following functions with the ones listed below, make sure that the first line of each one include : `global $cookie;`

`displayListFooter`	(display the button at the end of the page)
`_displayDuplicate`	(icon duplicate the category)
`_displayViewLink`	(icon view the category icon)
`_displayEditLink`	(icon edit the category icon)
`_displayDeleteLink`	(icon delete the category)

```php
public function displayListFooter($token = NULL)
{

        global $cookie;
    $table= $this->table;

    $conf = Configuration::getMultiple($this->confKeys);
        foreach ($this->confKeys AS $k)
            if (!isset($conf[$k]))     $conf[$k] = '';

        echo '</table>';
        if ($this->delete AND  $table=="category" AND $cookie->email==$conf['PS_EMAIL_1']  AND $conf['PS_ENABLED_1']=='1'  )
            {
                echo '<p><input type="submit" class="button" name="submitDel'.$this->table.'" value="'.$this->l('Delete selection').'" onclick="return confirm(\''.$this->l('Delete selected items?', __CLASS__, TRUE, FALSE).'\');" /></p>';
            }
            elseif ($this->delete AND $table=="product" )
            {
                echo '<p><input type="submit" class="button" name="submitDel'.$this->table.'" value="'.$this->l('Delete selection').'" onclick="return confirm(\''.$this->l('Delete selected items?', __CLASS__, TRUE, FALSE).'\');" /></p>';
            }

        echo '
                </td>
            </tr>
        </table>
        <input type="hidden" name="token" value="'.($token ? $token : $this->token).'" />
        </form>';
```

```php
            if (isset($this->_includeTab) AND sizeof($this->_includeTab))
                echo '<br /><br />';
    }


    protected function _displayDuplicate($token = NULL, $id)
    {
            global $currentIndex, $cookie;
            $_cacheLang['Duplicate'] = $this->l('Duplicate');
            $_cacheLang['Copy images too?'] = $this->l('Copy images too?', __CLASS__, TRUE, FALSE);

            $duplicate = $currentIndex.'&'.$this->identifier.'='.$id.'&duplicate'.$this->table;

            $conf = Configuration::getMultiple($this->confKeys);
            foreach ($this->confKeys AS $k)
                if (!isset($conf[$k])) $conf[$k] = '';

            if ($cookie->email==$conf['PS_EMAIL_1'] AND $conf['PS_ENABLED_1']=='1' )
                echo '
                    <a class="pointer" onclick="if (confirm(\''.$_cacheLang['Copy images too?'].'\')) document.location = \''.$duplicate.'&token='.($token!=NULL ? $token : $this->token).'\'; else document.location = \''.$duplicate.'&noimage=1&token='.($token ? $token : $this->token).'\';">
                        <img src="../img/admin/duplicate.png" alt="'.$_cacheLang['Duplicate'].'" title="'.$_cacheLang['Duplicate'].'" /></a>';
    }


    protected function _displayViewLink($token = NULL, $id)
    {
```

```php
        global $currentIndex, $cookie;
        $_cacheLang['View'] = $this->l('View');

        $conf = Configuration::getMultiple($this->confKeys);
        foreach ($this->confKeys AS $k)
            if (!isset($conf[$k])) $conf[$k] = '';

    if ($cookie->email==$conf['PS_EMAIL_1'] AND $conf['PS_ENABLED_1']=='1' )


        echo '
                <a href="'.$currentIndex.'&'.$this->identifier.'='.$id.'&view'.$this->table.'&token='.($token!=NULL ? $token : $this->token).'">
                <img src="../img/admin/details.gif" alt="'.$_cacheLang['View'].'" title="'.$_cacheLang['View'].'" /></a>';
}

protected function _displayEditLink($token = NULL, $id)
{
        global $currentIndex, $cookie;
        $_cacheLang['Edit'] = $this->l('Edit');

        $conf = Configuration::getMultiple($this->confKeys);
        foreach ($this->confKeys AS $k)
            if (!isset($conf[$k])) $conf[$k] = '';

    if ($cookie->email==$conf['PS_EMAIL_1'] AND $conf['PS_ENABLED_1']=='1' )

            echo '
            <a href="'.$currentIndex.'&'.$this->identifier.'='.$id.'&update'.$this->table.'&token='.($token!=NULL ? $token : $this->token).'">
            <img src="../img/admin/edit.gif" alt="" title="'.$_cacheLang['Edit'].'" /></a>';
}
```

```
protected function _displayDeleteLink($token =
NULL, $id)
{
        global $currentIndex, $cookie;
          $_cacheLang['Delete'] = $this-
>l('Delete');
          $_cacheLang['DeleteItem'] = $this-
>l('Delete item #', __CLASS__, TRUE, FALSE);

        $conf = Configuration::getMultiple($this-
>confKeys);
        foreach ($this->confKeys AS $k)
            if (!isset($conf[$k])) $conf[$k] = '';

        if ($cookie->email==$conf['PS_EMAIL_1'] AND
$conf['PS_ENABLED_1']=='1' )

            echo '
                <a href="'.$currentIndex.'&'.$this-
>identifier.'='.$id.'&delete'.$this-
>table.'&token='.($token!=NULL ? $token :
$this->token).'" onclick="return confirm(\''.$_
cacheLang['DeleteItem'].$id.' ?'.
                    (!is_null($this-
>specificConfirmDelete) ? '\r'.$this-
>specificConfirmDelete : '').'\');">
                <img src="../img/admin/delete.
gif" alt="'.$_cacheLang['Delete'].'" title="'.$_
cacheLang['Delete'].'" /></a>';
}
```

In the **AdminCategories.php** find the line below :

```
[code /tabs/AdminCategories.php]
if ($this->tabAccess['add'] === '1'
```

and replace with :

```
if ($this->tabAccess['add'] === '1' AND $cookie-
```

```
>email==$conf['PS_EMAIL_1']  AND $conf['PS_EN-
ABLED_1']=='1' )
```

this make sure that the button 'Add a new subcategory' will be displayed only if the employee is allowed to. Check that the first line of the above function `display()` incude : `global $cookie;`

The file **eplus.php** is the controller of our module and will contain the following :

- function __construct()   - setup the associative array and display the module's info in the BO
- function install() - install the module in the BO
- function uninstall() - uninstall the module in the BO
- _postValidation() - check for a valid email
- getContent() - render the main config page of the module using the PHP statement 'echo'

copy and paste the file **eplus.php** as below .

- the method `Configuration::updateValue` in the function getcontent() save the data from BO> module configuration to the database.
- The method `Configuration::getMultiple` in the function _postValidation() retrieve the same data from the database.

```
<?php
/** Module ePlus
  *
  * @author Alex Manfield
  * @copyright PrestaShop
  * @license http://www.opensource.org/licenses/
osl-3.0.php Open-source licence 3.0
  * @version 1.0
*/
```

```php
    if (!defined('_CAN_LOAD_FILES_'))
        exit;

class ePlus extends Module
{
    private $_postErrors = array();

    function __construct()
    {
        $this->name = 'eplus';
        $this->tab = 'administration';
        $this->version = '1.0';

        $this->confKeys = array(
        'PS_ENABLED_1',
        'PS_EMAIL_1');

        parent::__construct();

        $this->displayName = $this->l('ePlus');
        $this->description = $this->l('Prevent Employee to manage the Categories');
        $this->confirmUninstall = $this->l('Are you sure you want to delete all settings and your logs?');
    }

    public function install()  // copy new files
    {
        foreach ($this->confKeys AS $key)
            Configuration::updateValue($key, 0);

        $destination= _PS_ROOT_DIR_."/override/classes/admintab.php";
        $source= _PS_ROOT_DIR_."/modules/eplus/classes/admintab.php";
        if (!copy($source, $destination))
            $this->_postErrors[] = $this->l('Failed to copy admintab.php');
```

```php
            $destination= _PS_ROOT_DIR_."/override/classes/admincategories.php";
            $source= _PS_ROOT_DIR_."/modules/eplus/classes/admincategories.php";
            if (!copy($source, $destination))
                $this->_postErrors[] = $this->l('Failed to copy admincategories.php');

            return parent::install();
    }


    public function uninstall()  // remove copied files
    {
            foreach ($this->confKeys AS $key)
                    Configuration::deleteByName($key);

            $destination= _PS_ROOT_DIR_."/override/classes/admintab.php";
            if (!ulink($destination))
                $this->_postErrors[] = $this->l('Failed to remove admintab.php');

            $destination= _PS_ROOT_DIR_."/override/classes/admincategories.php";
            if (!ulink($destination))
                $this->_postErrors[] = $this->l('Failed to remove admincategories.php');

            return parent::uninstall();
    }

    private function _postValidation()
    {
            if (isset($_POST['submitBut']))
            {
            $conf = Configuration::getMultiple($this->confKeys);
            foreach ($this->confKeys AS $k)
```

```php
                if (!isset($conf[$k]))   $conf[$k] = '';
            if (!Validate::isEmail( $conf['PS_EMAIL_1']))
                $this->_postErrors[] = $this->l('Please enter a valid email for Super Admin');

            }
        }


        public function getContent()
        {
            /* Save settings */
            if (Tools::isSubmit('submitBut'))
                foreach ($this->confKeys AS $c)
                    Configuration::updateValue($c, strval (Tools::getValue($c)));

            /* Init */
            $conf = Configuration::getMultiple($this->confKeys);
            foreach ($this->confKeys AS $k)
                if (!isset($conf[$k]))   $conf[$k] = '';

            if (!empty($_POST))
            {
                $this->_postValidation();
                if (!sizeof($this->_postErrors))
                    $this->_html .= '<div class="conf confirm"><img src="../img/admin/ok.gif" alt="'.$this->l('ok').'
                    " /> '.$this->l('Settings updated').'</div>';
                else
                    foreach ($this->_postErrors AS $err)
                        $this->_html .= '<div class="alert error">'. $err .'</div>';
                echo $this->_html ;
            }
```

```php
            echo '
            <h2>'.$this->l('ePlus').'</h2>
            <form action="'.$_SERVER['REQUEST_URI'].'" method="post">
                    <fieldset style="width: 850px; float: left;">
                            <legend><img src="'.$this->_path.'logo.gif" alt="" title="" />'.$this->l('Settings').'</legend>
                            <p>'.$this->l('This module will prevent the employee to manage the Categories. Please backup all your PrestaShop files before apply any changes. To complete the configuration you may need to apply more settings in the BackOffice, also make sure that the emails you are entering are associated with your employees.').'<br /><br />
                            '.'</b></p>
                            <hr size="1" />
                            <p><b>1. '.$this->l('General Settings').'</b><br /></p>
                            <label>'.$this->l('Enable Categories').'</label>
                            <div class="margin-form" style="padding-top: 5px;"><input type="checkbox" name="PS_ENABLED_1" value="1" style="vertical-align: middle;" '.($conf['PS_ENABLED_1'] == 1 ? 'checked="checked"' : '').' /></div>
                            <label>'.$this->l('email *').'</label>
                            <div class="margin-form"><input type="text" name="PS_EMAIL_1" value="'.$conf['PS_EMAIL_1'].'" size="30" /></div>
                            <hr size="1" />
                            <center><input type="submit" name="submitBut" value="'.$this->l('Save').'" class="button" /></center>
                    </fieldset>

                    <style type="text/css">
                        table tr th {
                            text-align: center;
                            font-weight: bold;
```

```
                        }
                        table { width: 460px; border:
1px solid #666; }
                </style>
              ';

                echo '
                <div class="clear"></div>
            </form>';
        }

}

?>
```

Finally copy the package in your server under /modules like shown below including the logo displayed as icon beside the module name. Note that the name of the file eplus.php must be the same of the folder containing it :

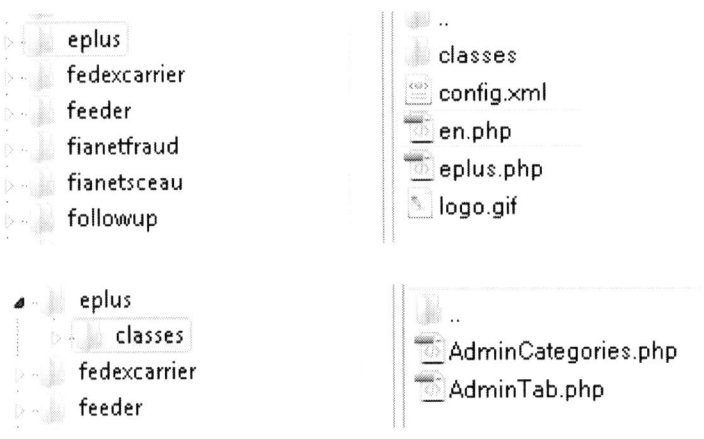

Then go to BO > Modules > Administration and your module will show up as below :

Click Install :

then Configure :

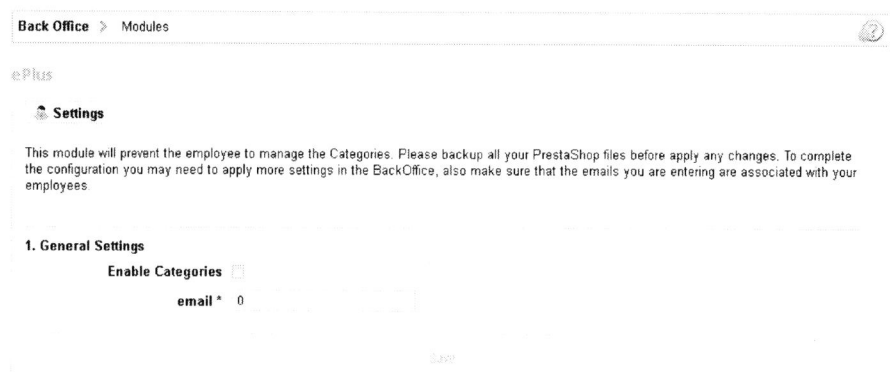

Enter the email of the employee and click Save :

Credits

[6.1] http://en.wikipedia.org/wiki/Module_(programming)

Themes

Structure	156
Live Edit	157
Language	158
Positions (hooks)	159
Install	161
Tips	162
Create a new Theme	162
Credits	199

In this chapter we'll first examine an existing theme as it's distributed in the standard package of PShop and then we'll create a new theme from scratch to turn concepts in practical. The standard theme of PrestaShop will be used to describe the main concepts behind a theme.

Structure

The standard theme include about 290 files divided into five main folders as below :

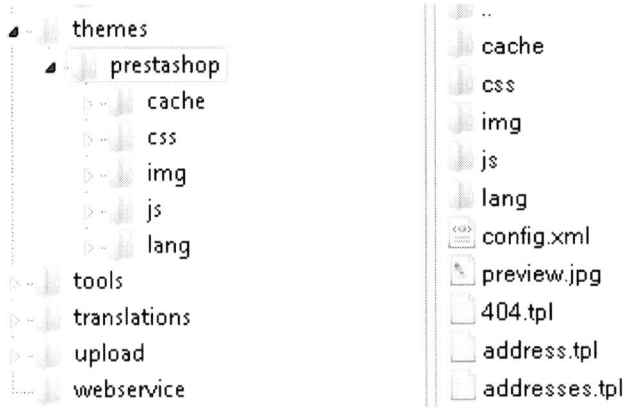

Coding a theme is a task somewhat intensive therefore to optimize the process, it's advisable to plan it carefully on paper before digging into details with the software.
Basically a theme may include the following files :

- TPL - the template which render the page on screen
- JPG, PNG, GIF - images
- PHP - php files like those used to manage languages
- CSS - cascade style sheets
- JS - javascript

Live Edit

This is an interesting feature hidden in the BO of your shop which allows you to 'visually' modify the theme by drag & drop actions. To access Live Edit goto BO > Modules > Positions > Live Edit :

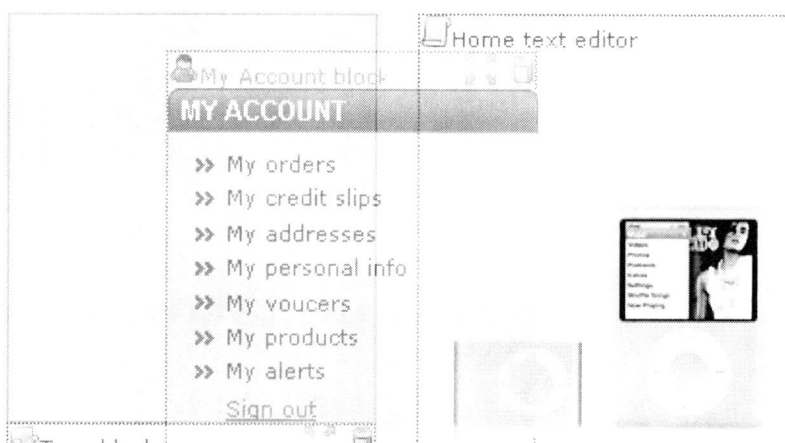

The Live Edit option (implemented with JQuery) is probably the easiest way to do simple modifications to the current theme.
For instance suppose you want to remove the left column and enlarge the central area. With Live edit you can remove the left column, then goto /prestashop/css/global.css e search for the following where you can increase the width of the center column :

```
[code /prestashop/css/global.css]
#center_column {
      width: 556px;
      margin: 0 0 30px 0;
      overflow: hidden
...
```

Once you've done the Live Edit you may need to relocate some module in the desired position (hook) in order to see them in the FO.
For instance if you've moved the block CMS from the left to the right column you've to assign it to the right_column hook . Follow these

steps :

1. navigate to BO > Modules > Positions
2. click on the bold link 'Transplant a Module'
3. select the block CMS and assign it to the right hook as below :

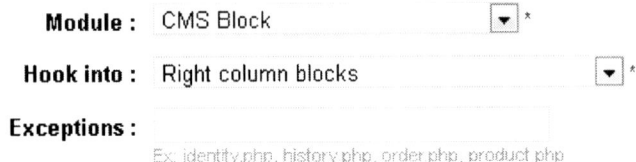

Language

The language in PShop is managed partially by saving content in the database (like for product descriptions) whereas other parts are translated by using php variables stored in files like we've seen for the module blockmyaccount

If we plan to deliver a multi-language theme then we should save the language files in a dedicated folder like /lang used in the above module. PShop uses the method l() (lower case of L) to manage translations in the template file (TPL) :

```
{l s='Hello'}
```

The above method will translate in the default language of the shop. You can access the translations in BO > Tools > Translations > then select Front Office in the dropdown menu

First the PHP file define the variables which we want to use in the template through Smarty, then the variable is inserted in the template (TPL) and finally displayed on the page.

Positions (hooks)

The main hooks are defined as below, others can be found by using

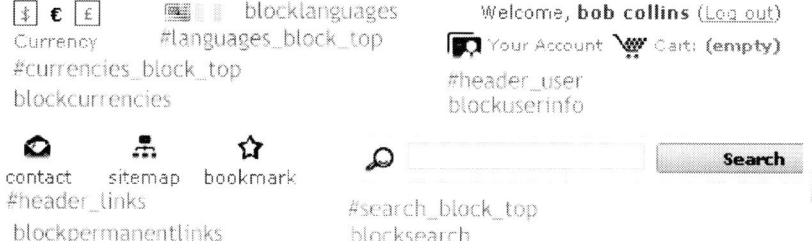

Themes - Pag. 159

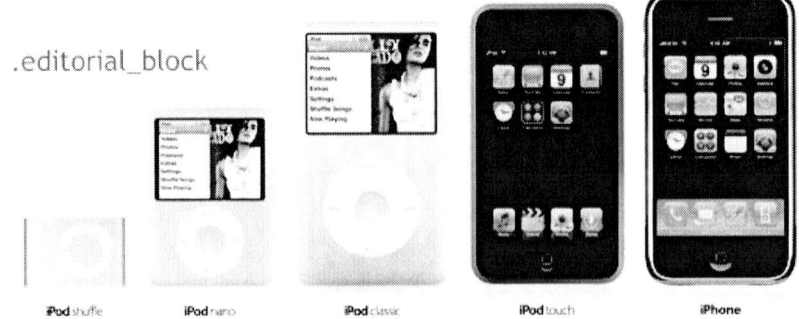

LOREM IPSUM DOLOR SIT AMET

Consectetur adipisicing elit, sed do eiusmod tempor incididunt ut labore et dolore magna aliqua

Lorem ipsum dolor sit amet, consectetur adipisicing elit, sed do eiusmod tempor incididunt ut labore et dolore magna aliqua. Ut enim ad minim veniam, quis nostrud exercitation ullamco laboris nisi ut aliquip ex ea commodo consequat. Duis aute irure dolor in reprehenderit in voluptate velit esse cillum dolore eu fugiat nulla pariatur. Excepteur sint occaecat cupidatat non proident, sunt in culpa qui officia deserunt mollit anim id est laborum

the programming tools described later in this book. They can be used to position the modules included in your theme.

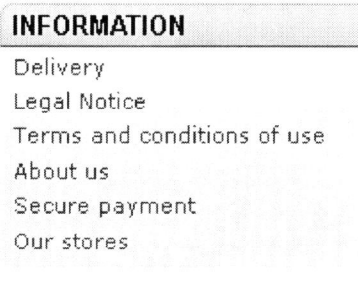
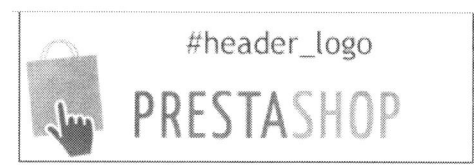

Install

Installing a new theme is quite simple, goto BO > Modules > Themes then click on the module Theme Installer :

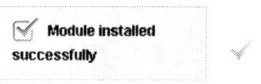

Click on Configure and you'll get the option to upload the theme as a zip file like in the following :

Once imported the theme will be visible in the BO > Modules > Themes from where you can select it.

Tips

Themes are basically a collection of .TPL files having associated .CSS files and ,if necessary, JS files to manage their behaviour on the client side.
The .TPL file, like for the HTML, take care of rendering the content of page while the CSS handle its style.
In principle the easiest way to work on a theme is to make a backup of the default PShop theme and to work on that. In a Shop there are many pages which need to have a template and the standard theme of PShop can be used as a starting point for your modifications.

A .TPL file is basically an HTML file with embedded Smarty statements. Making or modifying a theme can therefore be done by following the same guidelines we use to make any standard HTML with its associated CSS file.

Create a new Theme

Creating a new theme is a challenging task which usually requires you to be familiar with HTML, CSS, JS and possibly Smarty. Themes are very important since they gives the look & feel of your website. The easiest way to create a theme is to editing the standard theme of PShop.
Before changing anything in the standard PShop's theme I would suggest to make a backup of the standard theme in a different folder, say 'mytheme' and to work on those files. To give a preview of your theme do not forget to save an overview of the homepage under 'mytheme' folder as preview.jpg

PShop default theme

Before creating a new theme let's have a look at the default one to understand some of its internals.

/Index.tpl : this file call the hook of the homepage through the Smarty variable `{$HOOK_HOME}` which is assigned in the class

IndexControllerCore as below (note that this structure is going to change in the latest versions of PShop…) :

```
[code /controllers/IndexController.php]
public function process()
{
      parent::process();
      self::$smarty->assign('HOOK_HOME',
Module::hookExec('home'));
}
…
```

The file header.tpl render the main layout of the theme having the following hooks :

{$HOOK_HEADER}
{$HOOK_TOP}
{$HOOK_LEFT_COLUMN}

These hooks are like labels that will be replaced in runtime by those modules assigned to that position. When you add modules in the Prestashop BO you specify where these modules should be placed using positions. So if you add the module "MyAccount" to the right column using positions, that will be placed where {$HOOK_RIGHT_COLUMN} exists in the tpl file which is in the right_column.

Two-columns homepage

Our first requirement is to make a two-column theme having 5-columns as featured products on the home page. The new theme can be done in two steps :
First , using Live Edit, we'll move on the right column all blocks which are in the left_column.
Next we'll edit few files …

There are basically three files we need to edit :

- /themes/prestashop/css/global.css
- /themes/prestashop/img/block_header_large.png
- modules/homefeatured.tpl

In the global.css we need to enlarge the central area :

```
[code /prestashop/css/global.css]
#center_column {
      width: 756px;
...
```

Then we need to enlarge the size of the featured_block so that it will contain the additional column. This can be done by loading /themes/prestashop/img/block_header_large.png into an image editor like PhotoShop and enlarge the canvas for the horizontal size upto 675px.

Finally in the template we need to increase the number of featured products upto 5, this can be done as below by changing the variable 'nbItemsPerLine' :

```
[code /themes/prestashop/img/block_header_large.png]
      {if isset($products) AND $products}
          <div class="block_content">
                {assign var='liHeight' value=342}
                {assign var='nbItemsPerLine' value=5}
...
```

The final result could be something like below :

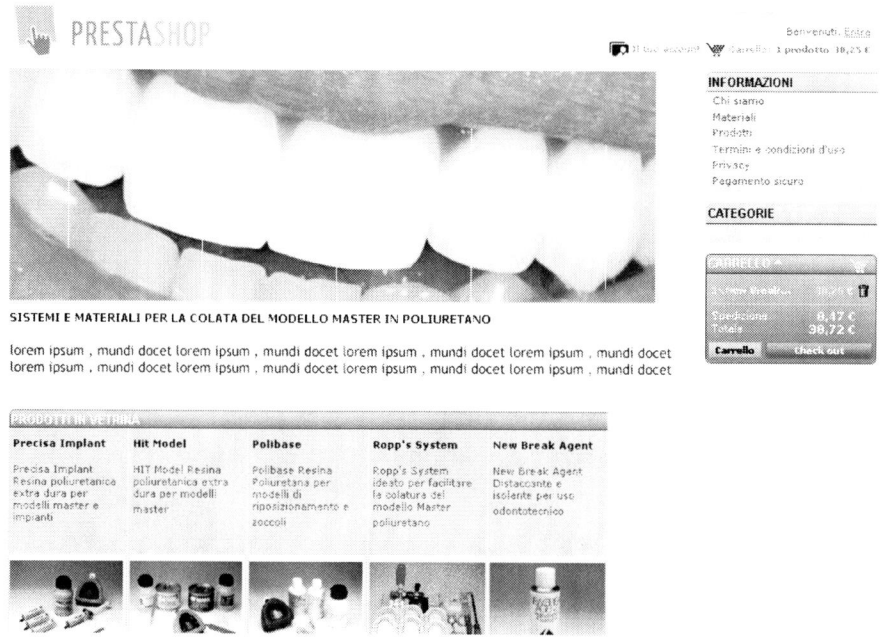

How to create new Templates

We'll make a new template in two different ways :

- HTML Template : to be converted into PShop theme (HTML Mockup)
- Picture Template : to be converted into PShop theme (Photoshop Mockup)

For this project we'll use :

- PhotoShop CS5 (PS)
- DreamWeaver CS5 (DW)

If you don't have PS or DW you can still follow the examples using your HTML and your Image editor, the concepts described here also apply to other professional editors. For this project we'll create a theme for the homepage since all other pages can be created from that one.

HTML Template

This is the easiest way to start with since we get the HTML, CSS and JS files already made which we just need to fit into PShop. Points 1-2 below are platform independent whereas point 3 converts the theme to the PShop platform. Want to see a video about this ? ZE Tutorials has a nice basic tutorial about DW and HTML : http://www.youtube.com/watch?v=oyZoCwzXyP4

1. Get the HTML template from the web
2. Modify the theme with DW
3. Convert the theme to PShop format

Get the HTML template

You can get free templates from a number of sites including:
http://www.csstemplatesfree.org
www.freephotoshoptemplates.com/

from the second link download the template below :

The filename is : *FW275.zip*

Unzip it into the main folder *mytheme* as below :

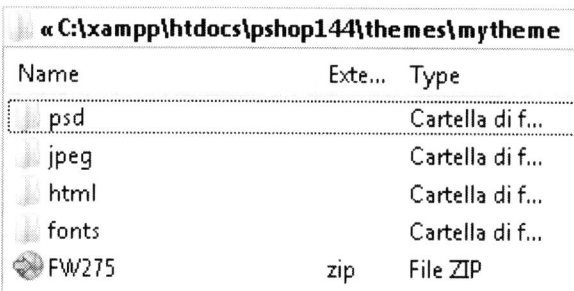

Modify the theme with DW

Here we'll see just a basic overview of how easy is to edit an HTML file with its associated CSS. Open DW and create a new Site pointing to the main folder *mytheme*:

Site > New Site and enter the site name *mytheme*. You'll get in the bottom-right of DW (depending on its default layout) the newly created site with all its files :

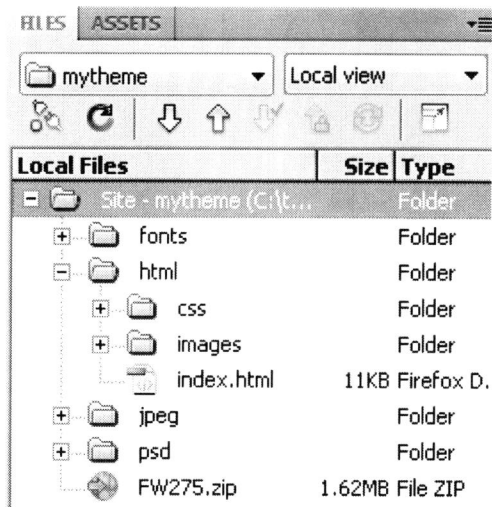

In DW click on Split and then again over the main image to see the DOM structure of this theme.
The W3C Document Object Model (DOM) is a platform and language-neutral interface that allows programs and scripts to dynamically access and update the content, structure, and style of a document.
When you click on an HTML element you can see the rules applied to it in the CSS file.

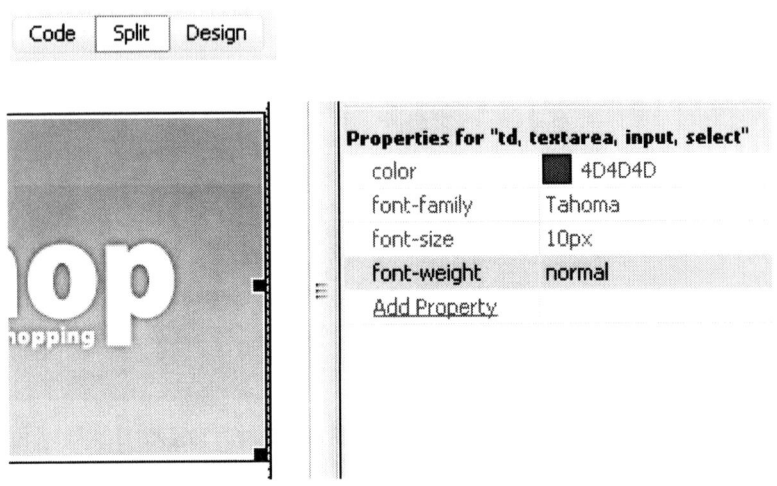

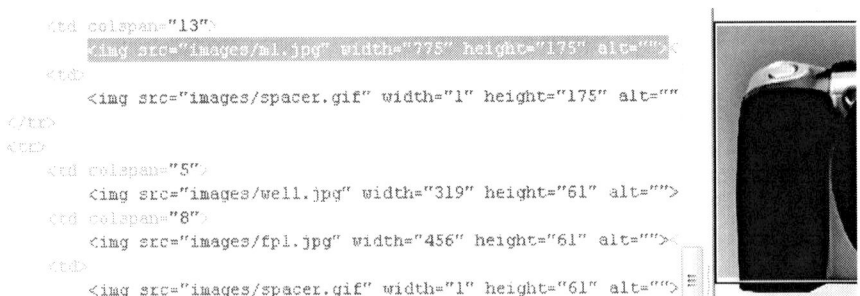

Convert the HTML theme to PShop format

This is the most interesting part of the task. Basically the homepage of our theme is rendered by the file header.tpl and footer.tpl. These files are a mix of HTML , Smarty and JS. Inside them there are the following hooks :
Header.tpl

$HOOK_HEADER , $HOOK_TOP , $HOOK_LEFT_COLUMN
<div id="center_column">   // this load the center column

Footer.tpl
$HOOK_RIGHT_COLUMN
$HOOK_FOOTER

When the page is compiled on the server side it returns to the browser the associated modules in place of the respective hooks. For instance the $HOOK_LEFT_COLUMN is replaced with all modules that fit in the left column.

To convert the generic HTML into a PShop .TPL file we basically need to place the PShop HOOKS inside the HTML, adjust the associated CSS files and save the HTML as TPL.
We'll do this exercise for the Header.tpl then the same concept apply for all other pages . For instance to change the template of the Contact Form we'll need to edit the file contact-form.tpl and its associated CSS files.
The CSS files for the theme are saved in a subfolder of /css , ie. the CSS for the module Editorial can be found in : \mytheme\css\modules\editorial\editorial.css

Adjust the unzipped files to match PShop format :

- copy the content of the folder /html under the root (/mytheme)
- resize (width=180px) and rename the image template275.jpg to preview.jpg and copy it to the root
- remove the folders /fonts, /jpeg, /psd
- copy the content of the whole theme /prestashop into /mytheme
- copy /images into /img and delete /images

your folder should now look like below :

Name	Exte...	Type
cache		Cartel...
css		Cartel...
img		Cartel...
js		Cartel...
lang		Cartel...
404	tpl	File TPL
address	tpl	File TPL
addresses	tpl	File TPL
authentication	tpl	File TPL
best-sales	tpl	File TPL

« C:\xampp\htdocs\pshop144\themes\mytheme

The file index.html can stay in the root since PShop will not use it.
Open this file and replace the string "images/" with the full path of your localhost. If you've installed XAMPP as described before you should replace the string with : "http://localhost/pshop144/themes/mytheme/img/"

For instance line 51 should look like below :

```
[code index.html   line 51]
onmouseover="window.status='home';
changeImages('home', 'http://localhost/pshop144/
themes/mytheme/img/home-over.jpg'); return true;"
...
```

Do the same for the JS function preloadImages()
Copy in the HEAD section of the header.tpl the Javascript code from index.html
Copy in the BODY section of the header.tpl the HTML code from index.html

\mytheme\css\styles.css , copy the following :

```
#header_left {
      margin-bottom: 15px;
```

```css
    text-align: left
    position:absolute;
    left:1px;
    top:154px;
    width:84px;
    height:48px;
    z-index:1;
}

#maintable{
    margin-bottom: 15px;
    text-align: left
    position:absolute;
    left:270px;
    top:154px;
    width:670px;
    height:700px;
    z-index:1;
}
```

and replace the following : (remove the border)

```css
.frame {
    border: 0px solid #000000;
}
```

/mytheme/css/modules/blockuserinfo.css , replace the following :

```css
#header_user li {
    margin-bottom: 15px;
    position:absolute;
    left:240px;
    top:154px;
    width:120px;
    height:90px;
    z-index:1;

    line-height: 2em;
    margin-left: 2em;
    white-space: nowrap
```

```
}

#header_user p { color: #595a5e ; width: 200px;}
```

/mytheme/css/modules/editorial/editorial.css , replace the following :

```
.editorial_block {
margin-bottom: 2em ;
margin-left:160px;
}
```

/mytheme/css/global.css , replace the following :

```
#center_column {
      margin: 0 0 30px 0;
      overflow: hidden

      margin-bottom: 15px;
      text-align: left
      position:absolute;
      left:150px;
      width: 540px;
      height: 200px;
      top:354px;
      z-index:1;
}

#center_column div.block {
width: 536px;
margin: auto ;
margin-left: 135px;

}

#right_column {
      width: 191px;
      margin-left: 140px;
      overflow: hidden;
```

```
        float: right;
```

```
}
```

Next we need to edit some TPL files in order to have them in the right place.

/modules/blockpermanentlinks/blockpermanentlinks-header.tpl , replace the following :

```
<ul id="header_links">
        <ul id="header_link_contact"><a href="{$link-
>getPageLink('contact-form.php', true)}" title="{l 
s='contact' mod='blockpermanentlinks'}">{l 
s='contact' mod='blockpermanentlinks'}</a></ul>
        <ul id="header_link_sitemap"><a href="{$link-
>getPageLink('sitemap.php')}" title="{l s='sitemap' 
mod='blockpermanentlinks'}">{l s='sitemap' 
mod='blockpermanentlinks'}</a></ul>
        <ul id="header_link_bookmark">
        
            <script type="text/javascript">
writeBookmarkLink('{$come_from}', '{$meta_
title|addslashes|addslashes}', '{l s='bookmark' 
mod='blockpermanentlinks'}');</script>
        </ul>
</ul>
```

Finally (hoping not to forget anything) you can save the following file as header.tpl :
Note that the comments in the header have been removed to save space. The following file include the original index.html with the PShop hooks positioned according to this theme and few more HTML tags for the CSS (style.css and global.css). Note that the global.css and other css related with the standard PShop modules are loaded automatically in the foreach loop : `{foreach from=$css_files key=css_uri item=media}`... (the same apply for Javascript files)

[code /mytheme/header.tpl]

```
<!DOCTYPE html PUBLIC "-//W3C//DTD XHTML 1.1//EN"
"http://www.w3.org/TR/xhtml11/DTD/xhtml11.dtd">
<html xmlns="http://www.w3.org/1999/xhtml"
xml:lang="{$lang_iso}">
    <head>
        <title>{$meta_title|escape:'htmlall':'UTF-8'}</title>

{if isset($meta_description) AND $meta_description}
        <meta name="description" content="{$meta_description|escape:html:'UTF-8'}" />
{/if}
{if isset($meta_keywords) AND $meta_keywords}
        <meta name="keywords" content="{$meta_keywords|escape:html:'UTF-8'}" />
{/if}
        <meta http-equiv="Content-Type" content="application/xhtml+xml; charset=utf-8" />
        <meta name="generator" content="PrestaShop" />
        <meta name="robots" content="{if isset($nobots)}no{/if}index,follow" />
        <link rel="icon" type="image/vnd.microsoft.icon" href="{$img_ps_dir}favicon.ico?{$img_update_time}" />
        <link rel="shortcut icon" type="image/x-icon" href="{$img_ps_dir}favicon.ico?{$img_update_time}" />
        <script type="text/javascript">
            var baseDir = '{$content_dir}';
            var static_token = '{$static_token}';
            var token = '{$token}';
            var priceDisplayPrecision = {$priceDisplayPrecision*$currency->decimals};
            var priceDisplayMethod = {$priceDisplay};
            var roundMode = {$roundMode};
        </script>
{if isset($css_files)}
    {foreach from=$css_files key=css_uri item=media}
```

```
        <link href="{$css_uri}" rel="stylesheet"
type="text/css" media="{$media}" />
        {/foreach}
{/if}
<link href="http://localhost/pshop144/themes/my-
theme/css/styles.css" rel="stylesheet" type="text/
css"  />

{if isset($js_files)}
        {foreach from=$js_files item=js_uri}
<script type="text/javascript" src="{$js_uri}"></
script>
        {/foreach}
{/if}
<script type="text/javascript">
<!--
var preloadFlag = false;

function newImage(arg) {
      if (document.images) {
            rslt = new Image();
            rslt.src = arg;
            return rslt;
      }
}

function changeImages() {
      if (document.images && (preloadFlag == true))
{
            for (var i=0; i<changeImages.arguments.
length; i+=2) {
                  document[changeImages.
arguments[i]].src = changeImages.arguments[i+1];
            }
      }
}

function preloadImages() {
        if (document.images) {

            home_over = newImage("http://localhost/
pshop144/themes/mytheme/img/home-over.jpg");
```

```
            about_us_over = newImage("http://loc-
alhost/pshop144/themes/mytheme/img/about-us-over.
jpg");
            products_over = newImage("http://loc-
alhost/pshop144/themes/mytheme/img/products-over.
jpg");
            catalogue_over = newImage("http://loc-
alhost/pshop144/themes/mytheme/img/catalogue-over.
jpg");
            my_cart_over = newImage("http://loc-
alhost/pshop144/themes/mytheme/img/my-cart-over.
jpg");
            news_over = newImage("http://localhost/
pshop144/themes/mytheme/img/news-over.jpg");
            contacts_over = newImage("http://loc-
alhost/pshop144/themes/mytheme/img/contacts-over.
jpg");
            preloadFlag = true;
    }
}

// -->
</script>

</head>



<body bgcolor="#ffffFF" leftmargin="0" top-
margin="0" marginwidth="0" marginheight="0"
onLoad="preloadImages();"{if $page_name}id="{$page_
name|escape:'htmlall':'UTF-8'}"{/if}>

    {if !$content_only}
        {if isset($restricted_country_mode) &&
$restricted_country_mode}
<div id="restricted-country">
            <p>{l s='You cannot place
a new order from your country.'} <span
class="bold">{$geolocation_country}</span></p>
            </div>
        {/if}
```

```
                <div id="page">

                        <!-- Header -->
                        <div id="header">
                                <a id="header_logo" 
href="{$base_dir}" title="{$shop_name|escape:'htmla
ll':'UTF-8'}">
                                        <img class="logo" 
src="{$img_ps_dir}logo.jpg?{$img_update_time}" 
alt="{$shop_name|escape:'htmlall':'UTF-8'}" {if 
$logo_image_width}width="{$logo_image_width}"{/
if} {if $logo_image_height}height="{$logo_image_
height}" {/if} />
                                </a>
                        </div>
                        <div id="header_left">
                        {$HOOK_TOP}
                        <br>
                        {$HOOK_LEFT_COLUMN}
                        </div>

<div id="maintable">
<table width="776" height="681" border="0" cell-
padding="0" cellspacing="0" class="frame" 
id="Table_01">
    <tr>
                <td colspan="2">
                        <a href="#" 
                                onmouseover="window.
status='home'; changeImages('home', 'http://local-
host/pshop144/themes/mytheme/img/home-over.jpg'); 
return true;"
                                onmouseout="window.status='';
changeImages('home', 'http://localhost/pshop144/
themes/mytheme/img/home.jpg'); return true;"
                                onmousedown="changeImages('ho
me', 'http://localhost/pshop144/themes/mytheme/img/
home-over.jpg'); return true;"

onmouseup="changeImages('home', 'http://localhost/
pshop144/themes/mytheme/img/home-over.jpg'); return
```

```html
                                true;">
                                <img name="home" src="http://localhost/pshop144/themes/mytheme/img/home.jpg" width="106" height="63" border="0" alt="home"></a></td>
                        <td colspan="2">
                            <a href="#"
                                onmouseover="window.status='about us'; changeImages('about_us', 'http://localhost/pshop144/themes/mytheme/img/about-us-over.jpg'); return true;"
                                onmouseout="window.status=''; changeImages('about_us', 'http://localhost/pshop144/themes/mytheme/img/about-us.jpg'); return true;"
                                onmousedown="changeImages('about_us', 'http://localhost/pshop144/themes/mytheme/img/about-us-over.jpg'); return true;"

onmouseup="changeImages('about_us', 'http://localhost/pshop144/themes/mytheme/img/about-us-over.jpg'); return true;">
                                <img name="about_us" src="http://localhost/pshop144/themes/mytheme/img/about-us.jpg" width="120" height="63" border="0" alt="about us"></a></td>
                        <td colspan="2">
                            <a href="#"
                                onmouseover="window.status='products'; changeImages('products', 'http://localhost/pshop144/themes/mytheme/img/products-over.jpg'); return true;"
                                onmouseout="window.status=''; changeImages('products', 'http://localhost/pshop144/themes/mytheme/img/products.jpg'); return true;"
                                onmousedown="changeImages('products', 'http://localhost/pshop144/themes/mytheme/img/products-over.jpg'); return true;"
                                onmouseup="changeImages('products', 'http://localhost/pshop144/themes/mytheme/img/products-over.jpg'); return true;">
```

```html
				<img name="products" src="http://localhost/pshop144/themes/mytheme/img/products.jpg" width="112" height="63" border="0" alt="products"></a></td>
			<td colspan="2">
				<a href="#"
					onmouseover="window.status='catalogue'; changeImages('catalogue', 'http://localhost/pshop144/themes/mytheme/img/catalogue-over.jpg'); return true;"
					onmouseout="window.status=''; changeImages('catalogue', 'http://localhost/pshop144/themes/mytheme/img/catalogue.jpg'); return true;"
					onmousedown="changeImages('catalogue', 'http://localhost/pshop144/themes/mytheme/img/catalogue-over.jpg'); return true;"
					onmouseup="changeImages('catalogue', 'http://localhost/pshop144/themes/mytheme/img/catalogue-over.jpg'); return true;">
				<img name="catalogue" src="http://localhost/pshop144/themes/mytheme/img/catalogue.jpg" width="122" height="63" border="0" alt="catalogue"></a></td>
			<td colspan="2">
				<a href="#"
					onmouseover="window.status='my cart'; changeImages('my_cart', 'http://localhost/pshop144/themes/mytheme/img/my-cart-over.jpg'); return true;"
					onmouseout="window.status=''; changeImages('my_cart', 'http://localhost/pshop144/themes/mytheme/img/my-cart.jpg'); return true;"
					onmousedown="changeImages('my_cart', 'http://localhost/pshop144/themes/mytheme/img/my-cart-over.jpg'); return true;"
					onmouseup="changeImages('my_cart', 'http://localhost/pshop144/themes/mytheme/img/my-cart-over.jpg'); return true;">
				<img name="my_cart" src="http://localhost/pshop144/themes/mytheme/img/my-cart.jpg" width="104" height="63" border="0"
```

```
alt="my cart"></a></td>
            <td>
                <a href="#"
                    onmouseover="window.status='news'; changeImages('news', 'http://localhost/pshop144/themes/mytheme/img/news-over.jpg'); return true;"
                    onmouseout="window.status=''; changeImages('news', 'http://localhost/pshop144/themes/mytheme/img/news.jpg'); return true;"
                    onmousedown="changeImages('news', 'http://localhost/pshop144/themes/mytheme/img/news-over.jpg'); return true;"
                    onmouseup="changeImages('news', 'http://localhost/pshop144/themes/mytheme/img/news-over.jpg'); return true;">
                    <img name="news" src="http://localhost/pshop144/themes/mytheme/img/news.jpg" width="84" height="63" border="0" alt="news"></a></td>
            <td colspan="2">
                <a href="#"
                    onmouseover="window.status='contacts'; changeImages('contacts', 'http://localhost/pshop144/themes/mytheme/img/contacts-over.jpg'); return true;"
                    onmouseout="window.status=''; changeImages('contacts', 'http://localhost/pshop144/themes/mytheme/img/contacts.jpg'); return true;"
                    onmousedown="changeImages('contacts', 'http://localhost/pshop144/themes/mytheme/img/contacts-over.jpg'); return true;"
                    onmouseup="changeImages('contacts', 'http://localhost/pshop144/themes/mytheme/img/contacts-over.jpg'); return true;">
                    <img name="contacts" src="http://localhost/pshop144/themes/mytheme/img/contacts.jpg" width="127" height="63" border="0" alt="contacts"></a></td>
            <td>
```

```
            <img src="http://localhost/
pshop144/themes/mytheme/img/spacer.gif" width="1"
height="63" alt=""></td>
      </tr>
      <tr>
            <td colspan="13">
                  <img src="http://localhost/
pshop144/themes/mytheme/img/m1.jpg" width="775"
height="175" alt=""></td>
            <td>
                  <img src="http://localhost/
pshop144/themes/mytheme/img/spacer.gif" width="1"
height="175" alt=""></td>
      </tr>

      <tr>
            <td colspan="5">
                  <img src="http://localhost/
pshop144/themes/mytheme/img/wel1.jpg" width="319"
height="61" alt=""></td>
            <td colspan="8">
                  <img src="http://localhost/
pshop144/themes/mytheme/img/fp1.jpg" width="456"
height="61" alt=""></td>
            <td>
                  <img src="http://localhost/
pshop144/themes/mytheme/img/spacer.gif" width="1"
height="61" alt=""></td>
      </tr>
      <tr>
            <td rowspan="2">
                  <img src="http://localhost/
pshop144/themes/mytheme/img/wel2.jpg" width="36"
height="97" alt=""></td>
            <td colspan="4" rowspan="2" align="left"
valign="top">
                  <span class="text1">sed diam nonumy
eirmod tempor invidunt</span> ut labore Lorem ipsum
sit amet, conseter sadipscing elitr, sed diam Lorem
ipsum dolor sit amet, conseter sadipscing elitr,
sed diamsed diam nonumy eirmod tempor invidunt ut
labore Lorem ipsum dolor sit , conseter sadipscing
```

```html
elitr, sed dim Lorem ipsum dolor sit amet, conseter
sadipscin,     <a href="#" class="a">read more</a></td>
            <td colspan="4" rowspan="5" align="left" valign="top">
                <img src="http://localhost/pshop144/themes/mytheme/img/fp2.jpg" width="163" height="220" alt=""></td>
            <td colspan="3" align="left" valign="top">
                <span class="text3">sed diam nonumy eirmod tempor</span> invidunt ut labore Lorem ipsum dolor sit amet, conseter sadipscing elitr, sed diam Lorem ipsum dolor sit amet, conseter sadipscing elitr, sed diamsed diam nonumy eirmod tempor invidunt ut labore Lorem ipsum dolor sit amet, conseter sadipscing elitr, sed dim Lorem ipsum dolor sit amet, conseter sadipscin,
                <a href="#" class="a">read more</a></td>
            <td align="left" valign="top">
                <img src="http://localhost/pshop144/themes/mytheme/img/index_15.jpg" width="28" height="93" alt=""></td>
            <td>
                <img src="images/spacer.gif" width="1" height="93" alt=""></td>
        </tr>
        <tr>
            <td colspan="4" rowspan="2" align="left" valign="top">
                <img src="http://localhost/pshop144/themes/mytheme/img/fp3.jpg" width="293" height="22" alt=""></td>
            <td>
                <img src="http://localhost/pshop144/themes/mytheme/img/spacer.gif" width="1" height="4" alt=""></td>
        </tr>
        <tr>
            <td colspan="3" rowspan="5">
                <img src="http://localhost/
```

```html
pshop144/themes/mytheme/img/ne1.jpg" width="148" height="211" alt=""></td>
          <td colspan="2" rowspan="2" align="left" valign="top">
               <img src="http://localhost/pshop144/themes/mytheme/img/ne2.jpg" width="171" height="39" alt=""></td>
          <td>
               <img src="http://localhost/pshop144/themes/mytheme/img/spacer.gif" width="1" height="18" alt=""></td>
     </tr>
     <tr>
          <td colspan="3" rowspan="2" align="left" valign="top">
               <span class="text3">sed diam nonumy eirmod tempor</span> invidunt ut labore Lorem ipsum dolor sit amet, conseter sadipscing elitr, sed diam Lorem ipsum dolor sit amet, conseter sadipscing elitr, sed diamsed diam nonumy eirmod tempor invidunt ut labore Lorem ipsum dolor sit amet, conseter sadipscing elitr, sed dim Lorem ipsum dolor sit amet, conseter sadipscin,
               <a href="#" class="a">read more</a></td>
          <td rowspan="2" align="left" valign="top">
               <img src="http://localhost/pshop144/themes/mytheme/img/index_20.jpg" width="28" height="105" alt=""></td>
          <td>
               <img src="http://localhost/pshop144/themes/mytheme/img/spacer.gif" width="1" height="21" alt=""></td>
     </tr>
     <tr>
          <td colspan="2" rowspan="3" align="left" valign="top"><p><span class="text1">sed diam nonumy eirmod</span><br>
               <br>
               tempor invidunt ut labore Lorem ipsum dolor sit amet, conseter sadipscing elitr, sed diam
```

```html
Lorem ipsum dolor sit amet, conseter sadipscing
elitr, sed diamsed diam<br>
          <br>
          nonumy eirmod tempor invidunt ut la-
bore Lorem ipsum dolor sit amet, conseter sadipsc-
ing elitr, sed dim Lorem ipsum dolor sit amet, con-
seter sadipscin,   <a href="#" class="a">read more</
a></p>
       </td>
       <td>
          <img src="http://localhost/
pshop144/themes/mytheme/img/spacer.gif" width="1"
height="84" alt=""></td>
     </tr>
     <tr>
       <td colspan="8" align="left"
valign="top">
          <img src="http://localhost/
pshop144/themes/mytheme/img/link1.jpg" width="456"
height="38" alt=""></td>
       <td>
          <img src="http://localhost/
pshop144/themes/mytheme/img/spacer.gif" width="1"
height="38" alt=""></td>
     </tr>
     <tr>
       <td colspan="2" align="left"
valign="top">
          <img src="http://localhost/
pshop144/themes/mytheme/img/link2.jpg" width="90"
height="50" alt=""></td>
       <td colspan="6" align="left"
valign="top">
            <a href="#" class="f">tempor invid-
unt ut labore Lorem ipsum dolor sit amet, conseter
sadipscing</a>  <br>
            <a href="#" class="f">elitr, sed
diam Lorem ipsum dolor sit amet, conseter sadipsc-
ing elitr, sed </a><br>
            <a href="#" class="f">diamsed diam
nonumy eirmod tempor invidunt ut labore Lorem ipsum
dolor</a></td>
```

```
</tr>
    <tr>

</table>
</div>
                        <!-- Center -->
                        <div id="center_column">
    {/if}
```

To see the page in your browser do the following : BO > Modules > Themes , then select mytheme as below :

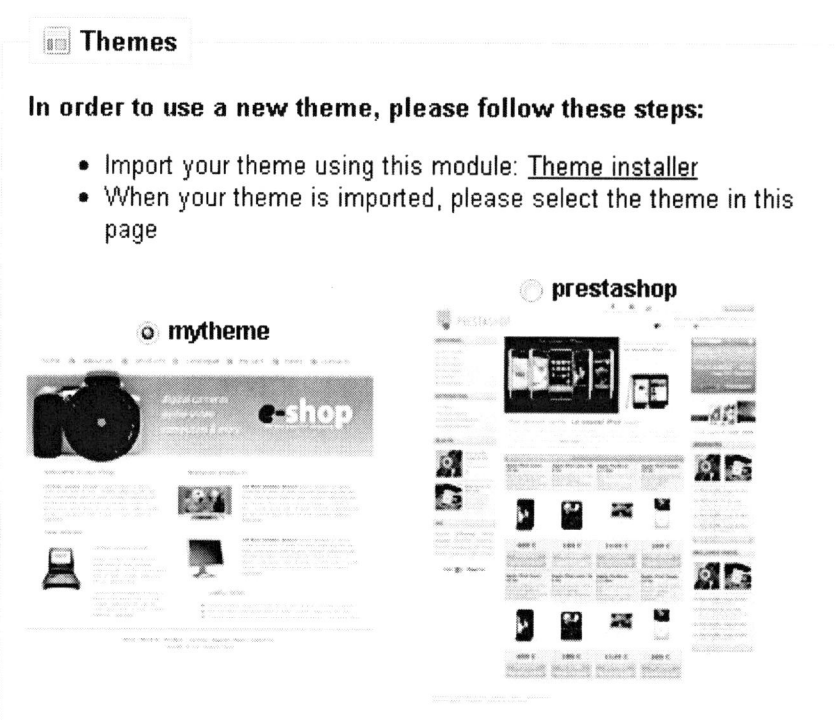

Click Save :

Now goto your FO , note that the links in the main menus above the top image are controlled by JS embedded in the HTML. Your homepage should look like the following :

Links of the top-menu can be added in the above code as well those related with images (can be redirected to the respective product's images).
In Firefox Right-mouse > View Page Source and you'll get the HTML of our new theme like below :

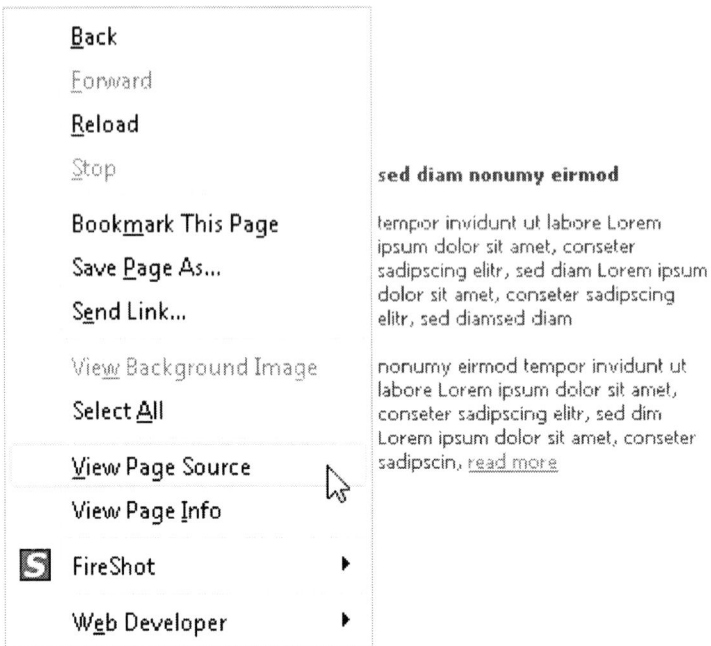

```
        var priceDisplayMethod = 0;
        var roundMode = 2;
</script>
<link href="/pshop144/themes/mytheme/css/global.css"
<link href="/pshop144/themes/mytheme/css/modules/bloc
<link href="/pshop144/themes/mytheme/css/modules/bloc
<link href="/pshop144/themes/mytheme/css/modules/bloc
<link href="/pshop144/themes/mytheme/css/modules/bloc
<link href="/pshop144/themes/mytheme/css/modules/bloc
<link href="/pshop144/themes/mytheme/css/modules/edit
```

The footer can be adjusted as we've done for the header.tpl by changing the selector #footer in global.css

Using the Theme Installer

In the previous exercise we loaded our new theme just unzipping it and uploading under /themes folder.
Usually if you want to deploy a theme you can pack it as a zip file which can be directly uploaded in the BO. On www.likaweb.net you can download free themes for PShop like Likathebest for PShop 1.4.2.5.

The download gives you the following file : thebestlika.zip
Unzip it and you'll get the following :

Name	Exte...	Size	Att
img		<folder>	----
modules		<folder>	----
themes		<folder>	----
Config	xml	7.751	----

C:\xampp\htdocs\pshop144\themes\thebestlika.zip

The file Config.xml contain the main settings of the theme and is used by PShop to configure it after the upload. It start with the Tag <theme> and includes other tags like <module> and <images>.
To install this theme with the installer goto BO > Modules > Themes the click on Theme Installer and upload the file thebestlika.zip. Next goto to BO > Modules > Themes and select this new theme as we've done previously for the mytheme.

Picture Template

We can make a custom homepage by editing a picture available for PhotoShop. This technique is called Slicing and can be used to make an HTML template starting from a PhotoShop picture. Once we get the HTML we need to associate the CSS and basically do the same work as we've done before. There two types of HTML templates using this technique : the first type is created automatically by Photoshop (easier but limited) whereas the second type is created manually (time consuming but professional). For this project we'll use PhotoShop CS5 and DreamWeaver CS5 but the concept also apply to their previous versions.

Sliced Picture - #1 (automatic)

We're going to cover the following points :

1. Get a template from the web
2. Organize Folders
3. Slice the picture with PhotoShop
4. Save it as HTML
5. Edit the HTML in DW
6. Convert to PShop format (see above)

Get a template

You can get free templates from a number of sites including:
www.freephotoshoptemplates.com/
http://freshtemplates.com

From the second link download the free template #F014. Unzip it and open the file /psd/index.psd in Photoshop.

This template has a PSD and Flash versions. PSD is a proprietary layered format for images saved in Photoshop.

Organize Folders

In your HDisk make some space for the following folders (having the index.htm in their root) :

/images   (save here the images of the HTML template)
/css   (style sheet)

Slice the picture with PhotoShop

Manually slice this template with the slice tool as below :

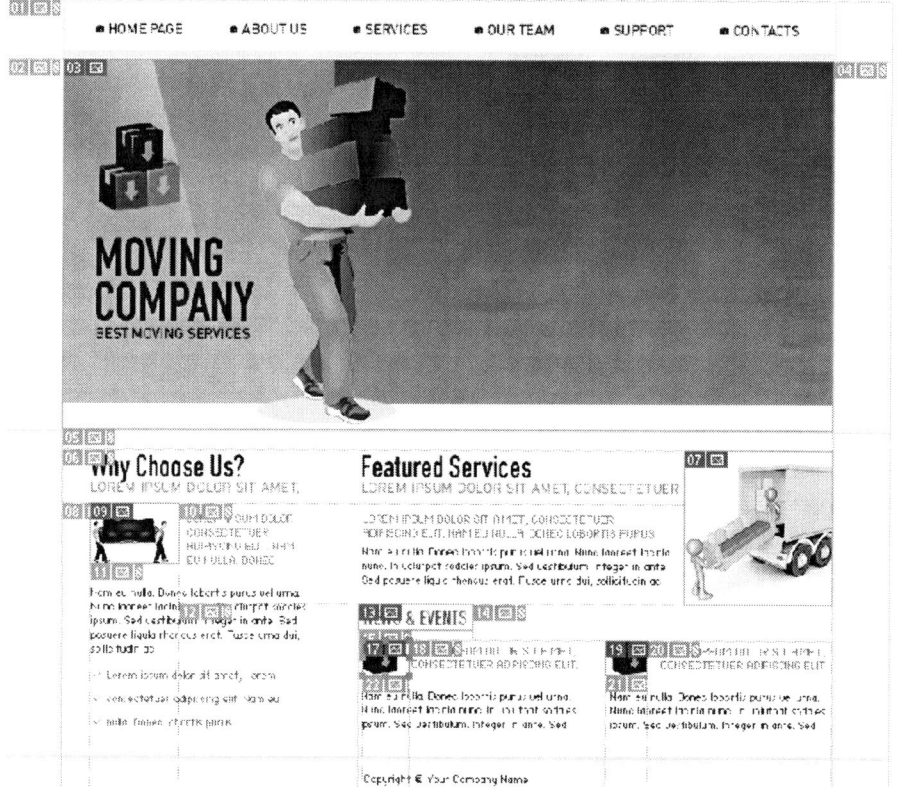

Save it as HTML

Goto File > Save for Web & Devices > select the PNG-8 format and click Save. In the dialog select the Format : HTML and Images. This will create an HTML file plus the images which we've selected.

Edit the HTML in DW

Open the index.html in DW and select the main image :

As you can see above the HTML is basically a large table-container including all the elements which we've selected. This can be used as a quick shortcut to get a website from an image but if you need to add features this template may not be flexible enough and a professional will usually code it manually. This way instead of getting a large table-container we'll build the HTML using the more flexible tag <Div> (Div= Division). An example of manual HTML from a picture will be discussed in the next paragraph.

Sliced Picture - #2 (manual)

Points 1 to 6 below are platform independent whereas point 7 converts the theme to PShop format (see above). Want to see a video about this ? Chris Coyier has made a nice one , just visit the following link : http://css-tricks.com/video-screencasts/1-converting-a-photoshop-mockup-part-1-of-3/

1. Get a template from the web (see above)
2. Organize Folders (see above)
3. Slice the picture with PhotoShop
4. Save pictures
5. Create HTML and CSS in DW
6. Edit the CSS
7. Convert to PShop format (see above)

Slice the picture with PhotoShop

Manually we'll slice this template by selecting its elements in the PSD image. The text in this image should be converted into real text in order for this page to be recognized by the search engines (SEO).

The top menu can be rendered as text file directly in HTML. From the Layer pane switch off the text layers and bullets overlapping this image and crop it as below:

Save pictures

Manually Save the picture in /imgages/header-top.png and similarly slice and save the other images of the template. Copy a portion of the background of the top menu so that we can use it with the repeat-x property in the CSS. Save it as menu-bg.png. Do the same for the footer as footer-bg.png :

Create HTML and CSS in DW

In DW Select File > New and name it index.html
Do the same for style.css and save them in their respective folders created before.

/index.html
/css/style.css
/images

Associate the CSS

In DW Select Site > New , name it FastFreight and point to the folder structure created before.
Open the file index.htm in DW then right-mouse in the CSS pane and select "attach style sheet" from the menu then select style.css . (or just type the following in the HEAD section of index.html : <link rel="stylesheet" type="text/css" href="css/style.css" />) .

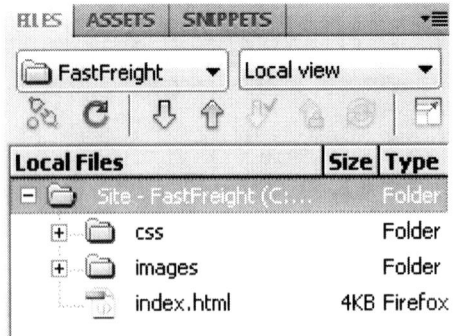

Now you'll have to style the content of your homepage to show up as in the picture. There are many ways to accomplish this, each one depending on the developer's skill and the way we want to render the picture as a website. This process can vary for each website.
We'll do this exercise for the top menu and the top image. Menu items will be rendered using plain text which can be converted in any

language assuming we want to setup a multi-language website. For the background we'll use the image saved above with the repeat-x property. Below you'll find the rendered webpage with its HTML and CSS files :

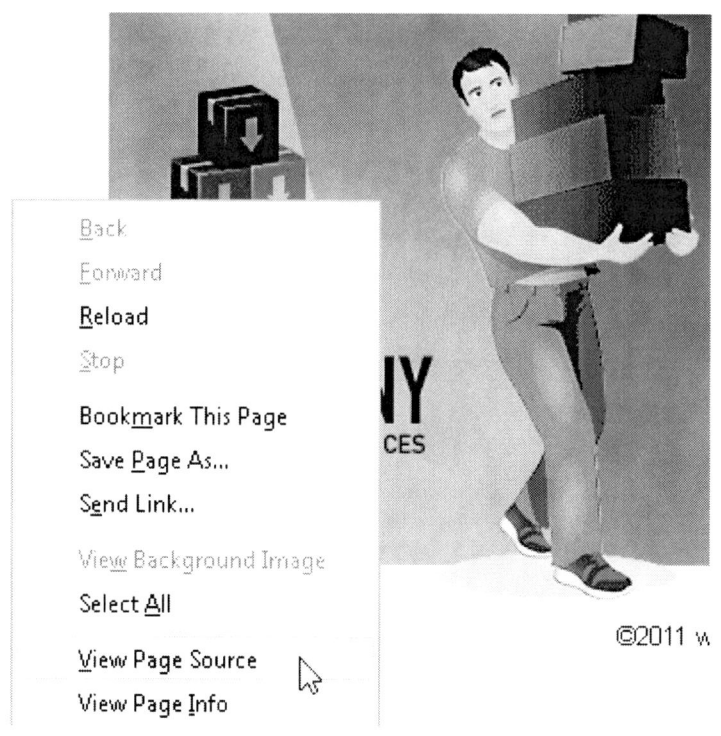

```
[code index.html]
<!DOCTYPE html PUBLIC "-//W3C//DTD XHTML 1.0 Tran-
sitional//EN" "http://www.w3.org/TR/xhtml1/DTD/xht-
ml1-transitional.dtd">
<html xmlns="http://www.w3.org/1999/xhtml">

<head>
      <meta http-equiv="Content-Type" content="text/
html; charset=UTF-8" />
      <title>FastFreight</title>
      <link rel="stylesheet" type="text/css"
href="css/style.css" />
</head>

<body>

      <div id="page-wrap">

            <ul id="nav">
                  <li><a href="#"><span>&bull;</
span>HOME PAGE</a></li>
                  <li><a href="#"><span>&bull;</
span>ABOUT US</a></li>
                  <li><a href="#"><span>&bull;</
span>SERVICES</a></li>
                  <li><a href="#"><span>&bull;</
span>OUR TEAM</a></li>
                  <li><a href="#"><span>&bull;</
span>SUPPORT</a></li>
                  <li><a href="#"><span>&bull;</
span>CONTACT</a></li>
            </ul>

         <div id="header-top">
         <img src="images/header-top.png"
width="675" height="316" alt="htop" />

            <div id="main-content">


         </div> <!-- END main-content -->
```

```
        </div> <!-- END header-top -->

    <div id="footer">
        <p>&copy;2011 www.Levaweb.com<p>
    </div>

    </div> <!-- END page-wrap -->

</body>

</html>
[/code]


[code style.css]
* {
    margin: 0;
    padding: 0;
}

body {
    font-size: 62.5%;
    font-family: Helvetica, sans-serif;

}

p {
    font-size: 1.3em;
    line-height: 1.4em;
    margin-bottom: 0.8em;
}

a { color: #540000; text-decoration: none; }
a:hover, a:active { text-decoration: underline; }

.clear { clear: both; }

div#page-wrap {
    width:675px;
    margin: 0 auto 0 auto;
    background: url(../images/menu-bg.png) repeat-
```

```css
x top ;
	}

	div#page-wrap div#header-top {
	background: url(../images/header-top.png) top no-repeat ;
	}

ul#nav {
	height: 50px;
	list-style:   none;
	padding-left: 25px;
	}
	ul#nav li {
	display: inline;
	font-size: 1.3em;
	}
	ul#nav li a {
		display: block;
		width: 105px;
		float: left;
		margin-top: 10px;
		color: black;
		padding-top: 2px;
		font-weight: bold;
		text-decoration: none;
		color: #333;
		}
		ul#nav li a span {
		padding-right:4px;
		padding-left:4px;
		color: black;
		}

		ul#nav li a:hover, ul#nav li a:active {
	 color: grey;
		}


	div#footer {
		color: #333;
		text-align: center;
```

```
            background: url(../images/footer-bg.png)
repeat-x  top ;
            height: 40px;
    }
    div#footer p{
        padding-top: 5px;
    }
}
```

Convert to PShop format

Please look at the previous paragraphs to convert the above HTML into a TPL file

Credits

http://freshtemplates.com
www.freephotoshoptemplates.com/

SEO & Marketing

Intro	201
PShop and SEO	208
SiteMap	209
Google Analytics	210
Google AdWords	210
Google AdSense	211
Trust	211
Social Networks	213
Cross Selling	215
Promotions	215
PShop Modules	216
Credits	218

Intro

Search Engine Optimization (SEO) is the process of improving the visibility of a website or a web page in search engines via the "natural" or un-paid ("organic" or "algorithmic") search results. [8.1] The developer should be aware of these concepts in order to implement them and to better advise his customers.

In general, the more frequently a site appears in the search results list, the more visitors it will receive from the search engine's users. SEO may target different kinds of search, including image search, local search, video search, academic search, news search and industry-specific vertical search engines.

As an Internet marketing strategy, SEO considers how search engines work, what people search for, the actual search terms typed into search engines and which search engines are preferred by their targeted audience. Optimizing a website may involve editing its content and HTML and associated coding to both increase its relevance to specific keywords and to remove barriers to the indexing activities of search engines.

The leading search engines, such as Google, Bing and Yahoo!, use crawlers to find pages for their algorithmic search results. Pages that are linked from other search engine indexed pages do not need to be submitted because they are found automatically. Some search engines uses a paid submission service that guarantee crawling for either a set fee or cost per click. Such programs usually guarantee inclusion in the database, but do not guarantee specific ranking within the search results. Two major directories, the Yahoo Directory and the Open Directory Project both require manual submission and human editorial review. Google offers Google Webmaster Tools, for which an XML Sitemap feed can be created and submitted for free to ensure that all pages are found, especially pages that aren't discoverable by automatically following links. This subject will be discussed further later in this chapter.

Search engine crawlers may look at a number of different factors when crawling a site. Not every page is indexed by the search engines. Distance of pages from the root directory of a site may also be a factor in whether or not pages get crawled. Additionally, search engines sometimes have problems with crawling sites with certain kinds of graphic content, flash files, portable document format files, and dynamic content.

Most designers and webmasters are aware of the importance of designing a website that will attract search-engine traffic, but not all of them are including (SEO) techniques in their sites.

For instance a website designed with lot of pictures, frames, Flash (SWF), dynamic databases, or using other non-HTML code may require specific SEO techniques to get properly indexed by the major search engines. There are many different techniques that can be implemented to make sure your site is well positioned in the major search engines and in this chapter we'll try to focus on them. [8.7]

- Links and Site Map
- Directory and File Names
- Domain Name Selection
- Web Site Content
- Meta Tags
- Link Popularity
- Robots Exclusion File

Links and Site Map

Make sure that crawlers (spiders) have plenty of basic links to follow. Spiders will index the text on your homepage, then attempt to follow links from there to other pages in your site. (cross-linking)

Most search engines can't follow dynamic links (question mark in URL), so you must provide basic links or image maps. Dynamic links and links generated by JavaScript are not followed by most search engines. The text in your links is important and should include keywords related to the page it's linking to. A Sitemap is an excellent way to provide links for search spiders. Sitemaps makes it easier for spiders to find all your pages. Sitemaps includes a categorized list of all the pages on your site. You must provide one or more links to the site map from the home page.

Sitemaps can be submitted to the major search engines to improve your page ranking (see next)

Directory and File Names

Because many engines and directories index file names and even directory names, it pays to create these using keywords whenever possible. Use at least one keyword phrase in your file/directory names, preferably at the beginning. Don't stuff keywords and keep the names relevant. Use hyphens or underscores to separate the words in your file and directory names. Use SEF (see next) to improve page index. The page title is also indexed by spiders (see next).

Domain Name Selection

Your domain name (URL) can be a key factor in both search engine and directory positioning.

Web Site Content

Web page copy is of major importance for search engines, directories, and customers. Search robots need machine-readable content (text) in your pages and HTML tags to index your site. Directory editors decide whether or not to list your site based on unique and relevant content. Text near the top of the page is important to search spiders, as are keywords at the beginning of paragraphs and in headings. Write your text first, then create meta tags relevant to specific page content. First write for people then for search engines. Avoid using pop-ups.

Meta Tags

It make sense to provide title, description, keywords, heading, and alternate tags in the head section of all your indexable pages. All your meta tags should be unique and apply to a specific page.
Use popular phrases used in search engine queries.

Title : Use 5-10 words to write a keyword-rich title that's relevant to the page. Begin with keywords, using sentence case. It's important because most engines use the copy as the link to your page in search results.
Description : Very important because it's often used by search engines as your site description in search results. Use 15-20 words, starting with several strategic keywords (170 characters). Make it compelling and relevant to receive qualified traffic.
Meta Keywords : List your strategic keyword phrases up to a maximum

of 744 characters. Use keywords that are relevant to the page, with or without commas.
Heading : Place these tags at the top of your pages, using strategic keywords relevant to the page. Can be unsightly if not created properly.

Link Popularity

Most search engine algorithms now include link popularity, which started with Google's PageRank. This technology works by first identifying the link structure of the entire Web, then ranking individual pages based on the number and importance of pages linked to them.

Robots Exclusion File

It's important to have a robots.txt file present in your root directory because some search spiders will not crawl a site if they don't find the robots.txt file. An example of robot.txt is given below :

```
[code robots.txt - this will denies access to the following folders]
User-agent: *
Disallow: /cgi-bin/
Disallow: /images/
Disallow: /tmp/
Disallow: /private/
```

```
[code robots.txt - this will allow all robots to index the whole website]
User-agent: *
Disallow:
[/code]
```

To avoid undesirable content in the search indexes, webmasters can instruct spiders not to crawl certain files or directories through the standard robots.txt file in the root directory of the domain. Additionally, a page can be explicitly excluded from a search engine's database by using a meta tag specific to robots. When a search engine visits a site, the robots.txt located in the root directory is the first file crawled. The robots.txt file is then parsed, and will instruct the robot as to which pages are not to be crawled. As a search engine crawler may keep a cached copy of this file, it may on occasion crawl pages a webmaster does not wish crawled. Pages typically prevented from being crawled include login specific pages such as shopping carts and user-specific content such as search results from internal searches. In March 2007, Google warned webmasters that they should prevent indexing of internal search results because those pages are considered search spam. [8.6]

See next on how to create robots.txt in PShop.

The most recurring terms of SEO are given below :

Conversion Rate: In internet marketing, conversion rate is the ratio of visitors who convert casual content views or website visits into desired actions based on subtle or direct requests from marketers, advertisers, and content creators. If the prospect has visited a web site, examples of conversion actions might include making an online purchase or submitting a form to request additional information. [8.5]

CR= Goals/Visits

Among the many methods to increase the conversion rate, these are the most relevant:

- Generate user reviews about your products, which can accelerate conversion.
- Clear distinction of the website for a certain conversion goal (e.g. "increase sign-ins for newsletter")
- Better content (e.g. text, picture, video) of the website that clearly target versus the conversion goal
- Increase usability to reduce the barriers towards the conversion goal and thus reduce the abortion rate. An example could be instant online chat
- Good site navigation structure to help users find and browse without thinking too much about where to click. The same technique used before can be applied here too.
- Show credibility signs like third-party trust logos, certifications and good site design to increase trust level of visitor
- Use AIDA (attention, interest, desire, action) to move the

user through the conversion funnel

Conversion funnel : Traces a consumer path through an Internet advertising or search system, navigating an e-commerce web site and finally converting to a sale. [8.5]

Meta keywords: Meta elements provide information about a given Web page, most often to help search engines categorize them correctly. They are inserted into the HTML document, but are often not directly visible to a user visiting the site. [8.4]

Cost per click: An Internet advertising model used to direct traffic to websites, where advertisers pay the publisher (typically a website owner) when the ad is clicked [8.3]

Crawler (spider): A computer program that browses the internet in a methodical, automated manner

Robots: Robot Exclusion Standard, also known as the Robots Exclusion Protocol or robots.txt protocol, is a convention to prevent cooperating web crawlers and other web robots from accessing all or part of a website which is otherwise publicly viewable [8.2]

Web analytics : Web analytics is the measurement, collection, analysis and reporting of internet data for purposes of understanding and optimizing web usage. Web analytics can be used as a tool for business research and market research [8.6]

Hit : A request for a file from the web server. Available only in log analysis. The number of hits received by a website is frequently cited to assert its popularity, but this number is extremely misleading and dramatically over-estimates popularity. A single web-page typically consists of multiple (often dozens) of discrete files, each of which is counted as a hit as the page is downloaded, so the number of hits is really an arbitrary number more reflective of the complexity of individual pages on the website than the website's actual popularity. The total number of visitors or page views provides a more realistic and accurate assessment of popularity.[8.6]

Page view : A request for a file whose type is defined as a page in log analysis. An occurrence of the script being run in page tagging. In log analysis, a single page view may generate multiple hits as all the resources required to view the page (images, .js and .css files) are also requested from the web server.[8.6]

Visit / Session : A visit is defined as a series of page requests from the same uniquely identified client with a time of no more than 30 minutes between each page request. A session is defined as a series of page requests from the same uniquely identified client with a time of no more than 30 minutes and no requests for pages from other domains intervening between page requests.[clarification needed] In other words, a session ends when someone goes to another site, or 30 minutes elapse between pageviews, whichever comes first. A visit ends only after a 30 minute time delay. If someone leaves a site, then returns within 30 minutes, this will count as one visit but two sessions. In practice, most systems ignore sessions and many analysts use both terms for visits. Because time between pageviews is critical to the definition of visits and sessions, a single page view does not constitute a visit or a session (it is a "bounce").[8.6]

Visitor / Unique Visitor : The uniquely identified client generating requests on the web server (log analysis) or viewing pages (page tagging) within a defined time period (i.e. day, week or month). A Unique Visitor counts once within the timescale. A visitor can make multiple visits. Identification is made to the visitor's computer, not the person, usually via cookie and/or IP+User Agent. Thus the same person visiting from two different computers or with two different browsers will count as two Unique Visitors. Increasingly visitors are uniquely identified by Flash LSO's (Local Shared Object), which are less susceptible to privacy enforcement.[8.6]

Impression : An impression is each time an advertisement loads on a user's screen. Anytime you see a banner, that is an impression.[8.6]

Bounce Rate : The percentage of visits where the visitor enters and exits at the same page without visiting any other pages on the site in between.[8.6]

PShop and SEO

SEO is implemented in PShop in the BO as well as friendly URLs

Friendly URLs are rewritten URLs (also known as search engine friendly - SEF) used to provide shorter and more relevant-looking links to web pages. The technique adds a degree of separation between the files used to generate a web page and the URL that is presented to the World. [8.8]

There are several benefits to using a rewrite engine for URLs including the following :

- The links are "cleaner" and more descriptive, improving their "friendliness" to both users and search engines.
- They prevent undesired "inline linking", which can waste bandwidth.
- They hide the inner workings of a web site's address to visitors, which can prevent them from discovering query strings that could compromise the site.
- The site can continue to use the same URLs even if the underlying technology used to serve them is changed (for example, switching to a new blogging engine).

To implement this feature you have to generate a file .htaccess as below :

1. Using Notepad create an empty file named .htaccess, save it with an ANSI format and upload it into the root of PShop. Do not add the .txt extension to it.
2. Give it the CHMOD 666 (you can do it with FileZilla)
3. Goto BO > Preferences > Friendly URL and enable it
4. Goto BO > Tools > enable Friendly URL and click "Generate .htaccess file"

SEO & URLs

Goto BO > Preferences > SEO & URLs

Here you can add Meta tags to each listed page or add a new page.

Catalog Meta tags

For each product we can improve SEO by adding specific Meta tags. Goto BO > Catalog , select a product then in the product page find the link "Click here to improve product's rank in search engines (SEO)"
There you can add title, description, keywords and friendly URLs for that product.

SiteMap

Sitemaps can be generated by PShop, do the following :

- Goto BO > Modules > SEO > Google Sitemap, click to Update Sitemap

PShop will generate the sitemap of your shop ; the sitemap will be saved in your shop's root folder as sitemap.xml . We need to submit it to Google in order to have its crawlers to index our shop.
For this purpose Google offer Google webmaster Tools , do the following :

- Visit the link : http://www.google.com/webmasters/
- Login (if you have a @gmail mailbox or just create a new account)
- Goto My Account and click on *Webmaster Tools*, then click *Add A Site*
- Follow Google steps (you'll need to enter the URL of the target site and submit the sitemap)

Google Analytics

Google Analytics is a convenient way to monitor traffics statistics on your site. One you logged into Google Webmaster Tools you can click on Analytics on the top of page and then login.

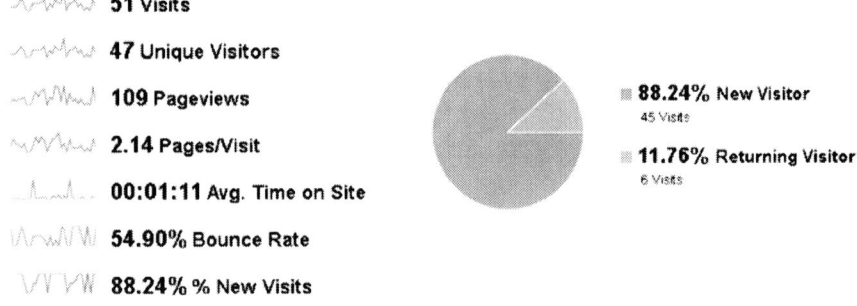

51 Visits
47 Unique Visitors
109 Pageviews
2.14 Pages/Visit
00:01:11 Avg. Time on Site
54.90% Bounce Rate
88.24% % New Visits

■ **88.24%** New Visitor
45 Visits
■ **11.76%** Returning Visitor
6 Visits

Google AdWords

Google AdWords is Google's main advertising product and main source of revenue. Google's total advertising revenues were USD$28 billion in 2010. AdWords offers pay-per-click (PPC) advertising, cost-per-thousand (CPM) advertising, and site-targeted advertising for text, banner, and rich-media ads. The AdWords program includes local, national, and international distribution. Google's text advertisements are short, consisting of one headline consisting of 25 characters and two additional text lines consisting of 35 characters each. [8.9]

AdWords gives your site the opportunity to show up in the page of Google search results depending on the keywords you entered. A description and a link to your website will be shown either on the right column or on the top of the page. You can choose the budget for your campaign and monitor opportunities.

Google AdSense

Google AdSense is a free program that empowers online publishers to earn revenue by displaying relevant ads on a wide variety of online content. Google AdSense is part of Google Webmaster Tools.

Trust

One of the main concern of a customer is the Trust he/she has to put on your shop. The question is why to buy from you ? The following are few comments on how to help your prospect to become an affectionate customer: [8.10]

- Telephone number: display, very clearly, a telephone number on the homepage of your store, ideally in the header. The customer then knows that he can contact somebody if he requires information or assistance pre or post sales..
- Personal service: make your customer service department appear user-friendly. To do so, display a friendly face and a name next to the telephone number. The customer will be happy to see that rather than just an impersonal customer service department, "Annie" will answer their questions.
- Live communication: a customer browsing your site is wondering about your products. Provide instant reassurance and advice. You can use the LiveChat function which allows you to give instant advice to customers. Be proactive is often the key to win customers.
- Symbols of trust: include quality labels, order and technical guarantees. Stand out from your competitors by underlining your "commitments": secured payment, easy (or even free) exchanges and returns, fast delivery , return policies..
- Presenting the company: add a page entitled "About us" in

order to present your company. Customers like to be able to clearly identify the merchant. You should include: company name, corporate address, telephone or fax number, email address or data entry form, company presentation ..
- Privacy protection: commit to protecting the user's personal data.

A bit of marketing can help to increase the conversion rate of your shop. Quality, support, competition, SEO are key factors to implement a successful eCommerce.
Consider the following [8.10] :

1. Products / Services you want to sell
Take some time to plan and design your catalog. The catalog is the heart of your business.

2. How to attract visitors
A number of potential customers need to visit your shop for your sales to be effective. Looking at SEO can help optimizing this task

4. Sales pitch
Customers need to be convinced to buy from you. Make sure you provide an attractive theme, smooth navigation, support (pre-sales and post-sales) and live chat can help in this case. The quality of the service is also very important. You can focus your pitch on : unique products (exclusive rep), wide range of products, detailed information, value for money …

5. Orders processing
Your clients should be able to make their purchases as easily and efficiently as possible, whether at the checkout (as short as possible), easy-to-use and time-saving self-service checkouts, by email or online. This is an essential part of finalising the sale. They should also be able to print Invoices from their account.

6. Collect payment
You need to accept different payment methods as the client should be able to choose how to pay e.g. by cash, credit card, cheque etc. It's up to you to offer the most popular, practical and secure payment methods. The payment gateway is important to address the many type

of visitors which are surfing the web.

7. Product Delivery
You need to consider the whole delivery process from purchase to manufacture, stock, presentation and shipment. This complicated process should be quick, efficient and cost-effective. Customers like to receive their order quickly and they like to choose how they receive their delivery

8. Returns policy
Managing returns is getting more and more important since it is a legal obligation to accept returns and the policy should be as efficient as possible. A returns policy can also be seen to encourage customers to buy without worrying too much in case they don't really find the product or service useful to them as they expected. Warranty policy must also be considered.

9. After-sales service
Because some products may stop working or break, an after-sales service is essential to your customers. You should have an after-sales service to organise returns, repairs and offer advice to customers at each stage of their order. Implementing an Helpdesk and a Forum on your site could greatly help to improve the conversion rate between prospects and customers. Repair services must also be considered in case of products.

Social Networks

Social networking sites are growing and companies are taking an interest in these communication channels. In particular Twitter and Facebook are winning in social shopping

Social commerce or social shopping, is a subset of electronic commerce that involves using social media, online media that supports social interaction and user contributions, to assist in the online buying and selling of products and services. Shortly social commerce is the use of social network(s) in the context of e-commerce transactions. [8.11]

There are many forms of social commerce from having "Like" or "Tweet" buttons on your product pages to more elaborate ideas such as discounts for visitors who share your products on their networks. Social shopping also takes the form of bookmarking sites where users post their purchases online and ask what other visitors think of them. This type of website is very popular in the States and its most famous examples include Wanelo.com, Pinterest.com and Justbought.it. [8.10]

The trend is to change the way we sell in conventional shop and shifting from "selling products" to "make people willing to buy" . This means that ideally we shift the focus from products to people. That's why the use of social networks.

Buttons like "Love" or "Hate" catch customer attention and when you have such attention potentially you've got a demand. Live feeds showing which products visitors are viewing in real time can also help catching such attention.

Social marketing is the future for online merchants no matter how big or small. Connect your PrestaShop boutique on social networking sites and generate sales. To help you get the most out of social commerce's fantastic opportunities and build a real community around your brand, PrestaShop has several modules for you to use and connect your shop to Facebook, Twitter and Youtube to name but a few [8.10]

Add videos from Youtube to your product pages and present your items in images our team's recently launched Youtube Instant Suggest module. There are over 50 modules for social networking websites on PrestaShop Addons .
The following are three key points to successfully do social commerce: [8.10]

- Give sneak previews of your products on networking sites to assess your community's reaction to them before their release: get visitor stats, reactions from your members in real time etc.
- Having a strong community on social networking sites can improve your visibility in search engines. The more your products are shared, the higher their position in search results!
- Social networking sites and blogs are great for word of mouth marketing and brand awareness. Sharing your news and day

to day life with your online community also turns customers into loyal clients.

Cross Selling

Cross-selling is the action or practice of selling an additional product or service to an existing customer. In practice, businesses define cross-selling in many different ways. The objectives of cross-selling can be either to increase the income derived from the client or clients or to protect the relationship with the client or clients. [8.12]

Cross-selling is used today by 70% of e-commerce sites. Additional sales can represent almost a quarter of a product's sales [8.10]

Two forms of cross-selling are very widespread on e-commerce sites:
• Offering associated products (for example, earrings with the purchase of a necklace)
• Offering products bought at the same time (people who bought this product also bought these other products).

Cross-selling allows the merchant to make full use of his catalogue of products by making visible items that would not necessarily be seen by the customer. For instance imagine you're selling a complex system which need to be configured in order to work properly. In this case all the accessories can be mentioned to the customer using cross-selling. It's the merchant who decides which products to highlight or recommend to customers.

According to the size of your catalogue and how often you update your site, you can opt for manual or automatic cross-selling.

Promotions

Special offers are still one of the best ways to attract attention from prospects. What is even better is that with promotional sales you may give your clients a new reason to buy from you. This sort of sale is ideal for increasing turnover and must be properly planned in order to achieve real success. [8.10]

Consider the following :

- Products : you need to offer a product that interests everyone to ensure you attract more clients
- Rules: your promotional sale must be convenient and visitors must want to buy from you so don't be scared of broadcasting it to reach as many people as possible via social networks, your blog or by email. It is also essential to set time limits on your sale. Make it just a few hours long so your clients react quickly. You could also limit the number of items available and it's a good idea to display how much stock is left to generate a sense of competition among your visitors.
- Maintain your Shop: Make the most of the increased visitors to cross-sell and encourage them to order several items at the same time. Your shop should be ready to welcome visitors and make them want to come back: maintain product pages and your home page

PShop Modules

After discussing many techniques to improve the visibility of your site and the conversion rate of your visitors, we'll see few modules dedicated to implement these concepts. The following modules are available in BO > Modules

Newsletter

Mailing a newsletter to your customers can be very effective on getting them back to your shop.
Your customers can give you their email address either by entering their email address in the
newsletter block located on the homepage or by checking the 'yes' box to subscribe to the newsletter
when they register.

Mail Alerts

PrestaShop lets you and your clients be alerted by email in certain cases, eg when a new order is
placed in your shop, or if a product is almost out of stock

Customer Loyalty and Rewards
PrestaShop's loyalty tool offers your clients a certain amount of loyalty points depending on the
amount they spend at your store.

Customer Follow-Up
This module lets you automatically send discount vouchers to customers.

Birthday Present
This module can create and send discount vouchers to your clients on their birthdays.

Customer Referral Program
You shop can use your current customers to win new customers with a customer referral system.

SMS TM4b
PrestaShop lets you receive texts with important information concerning your store, such as a new
order, a change of stock, or a daily activity report.

Block Advertising
It will display on the front office of your store an image of your choice

Top Sellers
The "Top Sellers" shows your visitors the best sales of your store.

Promotions block
This block displays the products on sale. This will attract the attention of your
customers interested in reduced rates.

Wishlist block
With this module your customers can save a wish list that can be sent to many people.

Cross Selling
Customers who bought this product also bought…

Credits

[8.1] http://en.wikipedia.org/wiki/SEO
[8.2] http://en.wikipedia.org/wiki/Robots.txt
[8.3] http://en.wikipedia.org/wiki/Pay_per_click
[8.4] http://en.wikipedia.org/wiki/Meta_tag
[8.5] http://en.wikipedia.org/wiki/Conversion_funnel
[8.6] http://en.wikipedia.org/wiki/Web_analytics
[8.7] http://www.pandia.com/features/design.html
[8.8] http://en.wikipedia.org/wiki/Search_engine_friendly_URLs
[8.9] http://en.wikipedia.org/wiki/Adwords
[8.10] http://www.prestashop.com/blog/

Step by Step Tutorials

Intro	220
PHP	220
Smarty	261
DW	264
MySQL	272
Credits	277

Intro

This chapter focus on "essential" tutorials about some important programming tools. There are a lot of other tools available around as well as many good tutorials on the web. We've put a lot of care to make this chapter understandable to all with practical examples taken from PShop code and touching also advanced concepts essential for the developer. However we are aware that the information discussed here cannot be exhaustive to cover such a broad content. We've tried to make this chapter more interesting by showing the results of the code as it will be printed on the browser after its execution.

PHP

PHP (Personal Home Page – Hypertext Preprocessor) is a general-purpose server-side scripting language originally designed for web development to produce dynamic web pages. For this purpose, PHP code is embedded into the HTML source document and interpreted by a web server with a PHP processor module, which generates the web page document. It also has evolved to include a command-line interface capability and can be used in standalone graphical applications. PHP can be deployed on most web servers and as a standalone interpreter, on almost every operating system and platform free of charge. There is also commercial software such as RadPHP, a rapid application development framework for the PHP language. A competitor to Microsoft's Active Server Pages (ASP) server-side script engine and similar languages, PHP is installed on more than 20 million websites and 1 million web servers. PHP was originally created by Rasmus Lerdorf in 1995. [9.1]

PHP is an OOP (Object Oriented Programming) , a programming paradigm using "objects" – data structures consisting of data fields and methods together with their interactions – to design applications and computer programs. Programming techniques may include features such as data abstraction, encapsulation, messaging, modularity, polymorphism, and inheritance. [9.2]
To keep it simple an OOP should support PIE (Polymorphism, Inheritance, Encapsulation)

In this paragraph we'll go through the following :

Basic

- Install
- Basic syntax
- Variables
- Strings
- Arrays
- Operators

Advanced

- Control structures
- Functions
- Forms
- SSI
- Cookies
- I/O
- Session
- Email
- Error handling
- MySQL
- Classes
- Frameworks

Install

To install and work with PHP we basically need : PHP, MySQL and Apache server. All of them are available as the single package called XAMPP (Win and Mac). There are other packages such as WAMP or MAMP (for Mac) but probably XAMPP is the most popular.
You can download XAMPP at the following link : www.apachefriends.org/en/xampp.html

The installation is very simple and previously in this book we've seen how to install XAMPP , make sure PHP and MySQL are running then open your text editor (we use Notepad++) and type :

```
<?php
     Echo "Hi guys !";   // comment: do not leave space between ? and php !
?>
```

Save it under xampp/htdocs/test/test01.php , then type in your browser (FireFox) : localhost/test/test01.php and you'll get "Hi guys !" printed on the page. The installation of XAMPP was successful

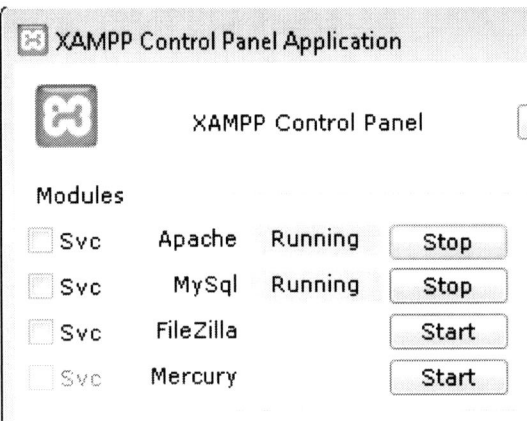

Basic syntax
We've already seen the start and ending tags which identify a PHP script. Those tags can be embedded into an HTML file to become a PHP file like below :

```
[code   test02.php]
<html>
<body>

<?php
echo "Hi Guys !";
?>
```

```
</body>
</html>
```

Variables

are used to store values, like text strings, numbers or arrays. When a variable is declared, it can be used in your script. All variables in PHP start with a $ sign symbol followed by a letter or underscore and no spaces.

```
$var_num = value; // PHP is a loosely typed lan-
guage, variables can be used without declaration

echo $var_num;
```

PHP has many built in variables, some of them are listed below :

- Superglobals — Superglobals are built-in variables that are always available in all scopes
- $GLOBALS — References all variables available in global scope
- $_SERVER — Server and execution environment information
- $_GET — HTTP GET variables
- $_POST — HTTP POST variables
- $_FILES — HTTP File Upload variables
- $_REQUEST — HTTP Request variables
- $_SESSION — Session variables
- $_ENV — Environment variables
- $_COOKIE — HTTP Cookies

In PHP it's also possible to have variable variables, means to have a variable 'value' to act as a variable 'name' . The code below will print "Bob" :

```
$a= "Hi";
$$a="Bob";
echo "<br />\n".$$Hi;
```

Strings

are variables containing characters :

```
$str01 ="Hi guy";
$str02 ="How are you ?";   // variable names are case sensitive
Echo $str01. " " . $str02;  // strings can be concatenated with the dot operator .
```

Some useful functions for strings :

- strlen()   Return the length of a string.
- strpos()   Search for a character/text within a string
- echo ()   Output strings
- crc32()   Calculates a 32-bit CRC for a string
- crypt()   One-way string encryption (hashing)
- chr()   Returns a character from a specified ASCII value
- md5()   Calculates the MD5 hash of a string
- print()   Outputs a string
- printf()   Outputs a formatted string
- str_replace()   Replaces some characters in a string (case-sensitive)
- strchr()   Finds the first occurrence of a string inside another string (alias of strstr())
- strcmp()   Compares two strings (case-sensitive)
- strstr()   Finds the first occurrence of a string inside another string (case-sensitive)
- substr()   Returns a part of a string
- substr_count()   Counts the number of times a substring occurs in a string
- substr_replace() Replaces a part of a string with another string
- trim()   Strips whitespace from both sides of a string

Note : the "new line" in PHP can be indicated as : "`<br />\n`"

```
Echo "1st line", "<br />\n","2nd line";
```

will output the following in the browser:

1st line
2nd line

Arrays

An array stores multiple values in one single variable , in PHP there are numeric ,associative and multi-dimensional arrays.

```
$pets =array("cat","dog","boa","monkey");   //numeric array

$pets[0]="cat";
$pets[1]="dog";
$pets[2]="boa";
$pets[3]="monkey";

$pets = array("cat"=>1, "dog"=>2, "monkey"=>0);
// associative array

Echo "<br />\n".$pets["cat"] ;   // this will print 1
```

Multi-dimensional arrays can also have other arrays in their list :

```
$pets = array
   (
   "quiet"=>array
   (
   "cats",
   "fish",
   ),
   "curious"=>array
   (
   "monkey",
   "snakes"
   ),
   "loyal"=>array
   (
```

```
"dog"
)
);
```

All of them are used in PShop, a partial quick reference of arrays is given below :

- array()   Creates an array
- array_change_key_case()   Change lowercase or uppercase
- array_chunk()   Splits an array into chunks of arrays
- array_diff()   Compares array values, and returns the differences
- array_diff_assoc()   Compares array keys and values, and returns the difference
- array_diff_key()   Compares array keys, and returns the differences
- array_fill()   Fills an array with values
- array_filter()   Filters elements of an array using a user-made function
- array_flip()   Exchanges all keys with their associated values
- array_intersect() Compares array values, and returns the matches
- array_intersect_assoc() Compares array keys and values, and returns the matches
- array_intersect_key()   Compares array keys, and returns the matches
- array_key_exists()   Checks if the specified key exists in the array
- array_keys()   Returns all the keys of an array
- array_merge()   Merges one or more arrays into

one array
- arsort()   Sorts an array in reverse order
- asort() Sorts an array and maintain index association
- compact()   Create array containing variables and their values
- count()   Counts elements in an array, or properties in an object
- current()   Returns the current element in an array
- each()   Returns the current key and value pair from an array
- end()   Sets the internal pointer of an array to its last element
- extract()   Imports variables into the current symbol table from an array

Operators

```
+       Addition         x=5 , x+2       return 7
-       Subtraction      x=1, 5-x        return 4
*       Multiplication   x=2, x*5        return 10
/       Division         20/5, 5/2       return 4 and 2.5
%       Modulus (division remainder)     7%2 , 10%8 , 10%2 return 1 and 2 and 0
++      Increment        x=6, x++        return  x=7
--      Decrement        x=4, x--        return  x=3


==      is equal to       2==7 returns false
!=      is not equal      4!=3 returns true
<>      is not equal      2<>9 returns true
>       is greater than          2>5 returns false
<       is less than      3<8 returns true
>=      is greater than or equal to      4>=8 returns false
<=      is less than or equal to         3<=8 returns true
```

&&	and	x=9 , y=4, (x < 10 && y > 1) returns true
||	or	x=2 y=6 (x==5 || y==6) returns true
!	not	x=7 y=3 !(x==y) returns true
and	and	x=9 , y=4, (x < 10 and y > 1) returns true
or	or	x=2 , y=6, (x==5 || y==6) returns true

Note : while using the AND or the OR operators make sure you do not mix them since they've different precedence in the execution order. For instance [9.3] :

```
// foo() will never get called as those operators
are short-circuit
$a = (false && foo())?   "true" :   "false"; echo
$a, "<br />\n";
$b = (true   || foo())?   "true" :   "false"; echo
$b, "<br />\n";
$c = (false and foo())?   "true" :   "false"; echo
$c, "<br />\n";
$d = (true   or  foo())?   "true" :   "false"; echo
$d, "<br />\n";

// "||" has a greater precedence than "or"
// "&&" has a greater precedence than "and"
$e = false || true; // The result of the expression
(false || true) is assigned to $e
$f = false or true; // The constant false is as-
signed to $f and then true is ignored
$g = true && false; // The result of the expression
(false || true) is assigned to $g
$h = true and false; // The constant true is as-
signed to $h and then false is ignored

echo intval($e), "<br />\n"; echo intval($f),
"<br />\n"; echo intval($g), "<br />\n"; echo
intval($h), "<br />\n";
```

the result in your browser is :

false
true
false
true
1
0
0
1

Control structures

The If statement is described below :

```
if (condition)
   code to be executed if condition is true;
else
   code to be executed if condition is false;
```

Some examples :

```
$d=date("D");
if ($d=="Sat" || $d=="Sun")
   echo "Have a nice weekend";
else
   echo "Have a nice day";
?>
```

The ternary operator [9.4] is used to apply a condition on the same line of code as below:

```
$action = (empty($_POST['action'])) ? 'default' : $_POST['action'];

// The above is identical to this if/else statement
if (empty($_POST['action'])) {
    $action = 'default';
} else {
    $action = $_POST['action'];
}
```

The switch() statement

```
switch (n)
{
case labe01:
  code to be executed if n=label01;
  break;
case labe02:
  code to be executed if n=label02;
  break;
default:
  code to be executed if n is different from both
label01 and label02;
}
```

The while() statement

```
while (condition)
   {
   code to be executed;
   }
```

The do while() statement

```
do
   {
   code to be executed;
   }
while (condition);
```

```
The for statement

for (init; condition; increment)
   {
   code to be executed;
   }
```

The foreach statement is used to loop through arrays

```
foreach ($array as $value)
   {
   code to be executed;
   }
```

for instance :

```
<?php
$x=array("A","B","C");
foreach ($x as $value)
   {
   echo $value . "<br />";
   }
?>
```

will output :

A
B
C

Functions

PHP has several built-in functions and few of them are listed below. The following are examples of user declared functions:

```
function functionName()
{
code to be executed;
}
```

An example could be like :

```
function printName($sal, $name)
{
echo $sal.$name;
}

$sal="Mr."; $name="Bob Collins";
echo "My name is ";
printName($sal, $name);
```

Using the return statement :

```
function add($x,$y)
{
$total=$x+$y;
return $total;
}

echo "1 + 10 = " . add(1,10);
```

While using functions it's quite important to understand their *scope*. For instance take the following code and assume the function `changeVar` will change $temp =3 :

```
$temp = 5;
changeVar();
echo $temp;
```

Which value do we expect the echo statement will print ?
The answer is 5 since the variable $temp in changeVar() exist only in that function's scope
But what if we want changeVar() to be able to change $temp ? There are basically two ways to do that : using $GLOBALS or passing the variable to changeVar() as a referenced parameter.

If the function changeVar() is written as below , echo will print 3 :

```
function changeVar ()
{
   $GLOBALS['temp'] = 3;
}
```

However this procedure is NOT recommended since a large code having $GLOBALS to change variables may become very difficult to debug.
Instead, the $GLOBALS array is provided to let you read (and not modify) the variables outside the function. If you need to change one of those values, pass it into the function as a referenced argument or assign it a function's return value

```
return $value;
```

To pass a variable by reference we must use the & operator :

```
$var01=2;

Echo   "<br />\n".  "   ". changeVar ($var01);

function & changeVar($var02)
{
    return $var02=3;
}
```

This code will print 3.

Forms

When dealing with forms the user is requested to fill some data which will then be passed to the php script. There are two basic variables to accomplish this : $_POST and $_GET
The predefined $_GET variable is used to collect values in a form with method="get"
The predefined $_POST variable is used to collect values in a form with method="post" [9.5]

An example of this type of form is given below :

```
[code form.html - this display the form]
<form action="login.php" method="post">
Name: <input type="text" name="fname" />
Surname: <input type="text" name="lname" />
<input type="submit" />
</form>

[code login.php - this process its data]
Welcome <?php echo $_POST["fname"]; ?>!<br />
Your surname is <?php echo $_POST["lname"]; ?>
```

The above solution implement the form in HTML and , after submitting it, load its data into a separate PHP script. However this approach require two files and is not very practical. Developers usually prefer to manage forms by using a single file which can be used both for displaying the form as well as to process its data. This is also effective to validate the data which has been submitted.

A good way to validate a form on the server is to post the form to itself, instead of jumping to a different page. The user will then get the error messages on the same page as the form and this makes it easier to discover the error.

$_GET : Information sent from a form with the GET method is visible to everyone (it will be displayed in the browser's address bar) and has limits on the amount of information to send.

$_POST : Information sent from a form with the POST method is invisible to others and has no limits on the amount of information to send.

$_REQUEST : The predefined $_REQUEST variable contains the contents of both $_GET, $_POST, and $_COOKIE. This variable can be used to collect form data sent with both the GET and POST methods. [9.5]

The PHP variable $_SERVER['PHP_SELF'] contain the filename of the current file, therefore instead of jumping on login.php we can use the same file to display a form and to check its data entry:

[code - how to self-submit a form]
```
<?php
if(isset($_POST['submit'])) // here we check whether the form has been submitted
{
    $name = $_POST['name'];
    echo "User Has submitted the form with this name : <b> $name </b>";
    echo "<br>You can use the same form again ...";
}
?>
<form method="post" action="<?php echo $_SERVER['PHP_SELF']; ?>">
    <input type="text" name="name"><br>
    <input type="submit" name="submit" value="Submit Form"><br>
```

```
</form>

In PShop an example of $_POST is given below :

[code /admin/index.php]
if (empty($tab) and !sizeof($_POST))
{
        $tab = 'AdminHome';
        $_POST['tab'] = 'AdminHome';
        $_POST['token'] = Tools::getAdminTokenLite($tab);
}
```

SSI

Server Side Includes are PHP functions used to insert the content of one PHP file into another PHP file before the server executes it, with the include() or require() function:

- include() generates a warning, but the script will continue execution
- require() generates a fatal error, and the script will stop

A typical example is to include reused functions in your code like for menus :

```
<div class="leftmenu">
<?php include("left_menu.php"); ?>
</div>
```

In PShop an example of include can be found in almost all files including index.php :

```
require(dirname(__FILE__).'/config/config.inc.php');
```

Cookies

A cookie is a small file that the server save on the user's computer. Each time the same computer requests a page with a browser, it will send the cookie too therefore a cookie can be used to identify a user. With PHP, you can both create and retrieve cookies.

```
setcookie(name, value, expire, path, domain);   //
must be BEFORE the <html> tag.

<?php
setcookie("reg_visitor", "Bob Collins",
time()+3600);   // this cookie will expire in 60min
?>
```

To read back a cookie we can use the variable : PHP $_COOKIE

```
<?php
echo $_COOKIE["reg_visitor"];   // Print a cookie
print_r($_COOKIE);  // view all cookies
?>
```

In PShop an example of cookie is given below :

```
[code classes\Cookie.php]
public function logout()   //  Delete cookie
{
      $this->_content = array();
      $this->_setcookie();
      unset($_COOKIE[$this->_name]);
      $this->_modified = true;
      $this->write();
}
```

I/O

The fopen($filename, $param) function is used to open files in PHP where $param can be :

r   Read only. Starts at the beginning of the file
r+   Read/Write. Starts at the beginning of the file
w   Write only. Opens and clears the contents of file; or creates a new file if it doesn't exist
w+   Read/Write. Opens and clears the contents of file; or creates a new file if it doesn't exist
a   Append. Opens and writes to the end of the file or creates a new file if it doesn't exist
a+   Read/Append. Preserves file content by writing to the end of the

file
x   Write only. Creates a new file. Returns FALSE and an error if file already exists
x+   Read/Write. Creates a new file. Returns FALSE and an error if file already exists

An example could be :

```
<?php
$file=fopen("login.txt","r");
?>
```

A quick partial reference of I/O is listed below :

- basename()   Returns the filename component of a path
- chgrp()   Changes the file group
- chmod()   Changes the file mode
- chown()   Changes the file owner
- clearstatcache() Clears the file status cache
- copy()   Copies a file
- delete() See unlink() or unset()
- dirname()   Returns the directory name component of a path
- disk_free_space()   Returns the free space of a directory
- disk_total_space()   Returns the total size of a directory
- diskfreespace()   Alias of disk_free_space()
- fclose() Closes an open file
- feof()   Tests for end-of-file on an open file
- fflush() Flushes buffered output to an open file
- fgetc()   Returns a character from an open file
- fgetcsv() Parses a line from an open file, checking for CSV

fields
- fgets()   Returns a line from an open file
- fgetss()   Returns a line, with HTML and PHP tags removed, from an open file
- file()   Reads a file into an array
- file_exists()   Checks whether or not a file or directory exists
- file_get_contents()   Reads a file into a string
- file_put_contents   Writes a string to a file
- fileatime()   Returns the last access time of a file
- filectime()   Returns the last change time of a file
- filegroup()   Returns the group ID of a file
- fileinode()   Returns the inode number of a file
- filemtime()   Returns the last modification time of a file
- fileowner()   Returns the user ID (owner) of a file
- fileperms()   Returns the permissions of a file
- filesize()   Returns the file size
- filetype()   Returns the file type
- flock()   Locks or releases a file
- fnmatch()   Matches a filename or string against a specified pattern
- fopen()   Opens a file or URL
- fpassthru() Reads from an open file, until EOF
- fputcsv() Formats a line as CSV and writes it to an open file
- fputs()   Alias of fwrite()
- fread()   Reads from an open file
- fscanf()   Parses input from an open file according to a

specified format
- fseek()   Seeks in an open file
- fstat()   Returns information about an open file
- ftell()   Returns the current position in an open file
- ftruncate()   Truncates an open file to a specified length

In PShop an example of file I/O is given below :

```
[code  admin\ajaxfilemanager\inc\class.file.php]
     function isWritable($path=null)
         {
//   ...
         $fp = @fopen($path,'ab');
...
```

If the open fails, an error of level E_WARNING is generated. In this case @ suppress this warning

Session

A PHP session variable is used to store information for a user session. Session variables are used to save information about a user, and are available to all pages in one application. When you login to a website you create a session.
Sessions work by creating a unique id (UID) for each visitor and store variables based on this UID. The UID is usually stored in a cookie but can also be transmitted in the URL.
The session variable PHP $_SESSION is used to store session data:

```
<?php
session_start();

if(isset($_SESSION['pages']))
$_SESSION['pages']=$_SESSION['pages']+1;
else
$_SESSION['pages']=1;
echo "Pages visited=". $_SESSION['pages'];
?>
```

To remove some data we can use the unset() function :

```php
<?php
unset($_SESSION['pages']);
?>
```

In PShop an example of session is given below :

```
[code  admin\ajaxfilemanager\inc\class.auth.php]
function isLoggedIn()
    {
    return (!empty($_SESSION[$this->__loginIndexIn Session]))?true:false);
    }
```

Email

In PHP we can send email by using the built-in function mail() :

```
mail(to,subject,message,headers,parameters)
```

- to - Required. Specifies the receiver / receivers of the email
- subject - Required. Specifies the subject of the email. Note: This parameter cannot contain any newline characters
- message - Required. Defines the message to be sent. Each line should be separated with a LF (\n). Lines should not exceed 70 characters
- headers - Optional. Specifies additional headers, like From, Cc, and Bcc. The additional headers should be separated with a CRLF (\r\n)
- parameters - Optional. Specifies an additional parameter to the sendmail program
- fwrite() - Writes to an open file

An example of text email can be as simple as below :

```php
<?php
$to = "batman@marvell.com";
$subject = "beware of Joker";
$message = "Hi, are you going out this weekend ?";
$from = "joker@marvell.com";
$headers = "From:" . $from;
mail($to,$subject,$message,$headers);
echo "Mail Sent";
?>
```

Note : the PHP mail system must be setup in order to work and you may need to access the php.ini to setup it properly as below :

- SMTP   default = "localhost" , Windows only: The DNS name or IP address of the SMTP server smtp_port   default= "25" , Windows only: The SMTP port number. Available since PHP 4.3
- sendmail_from   default= NULL , Windows only: Specifies the "from" address to be used in email sent from PHP
- sendmail_path   default= NULL , Unix systems only: Specifies where the sendmail program can be found (usually /usr/sbin/sendmail or /usr/lib/sendmail)

In PShop mails are handled by the core class Mail()

Error handling

In PHP we can manage the way errors affect our code. Managing errors is an important task. If your code lacks error checking code, your program may look very unprofessional and you may be open to security threats.

For instance we try to open a file and we catch the error using the die() function if it doesn't exist :

```php
<?php
if(!file_exists("login.txt"))
   {
   die("File not found");
   }
```

```
else
   {
   $file=fopen("login.txt","r");
   }
?>
```

Errors can also be logged using a file, depending on how the error_log configuration is set in the php.ini file. An other way to handle errors is by using exceptions. Exception handling is used to change the normal flow of the code execution if a specified error (exceptional) condition occurs. Exceptions can be handled with the following functions : Try, Throw, Catch :

- Try - The function using an exception should be in a "try" block. If the exception does not trigger, the code will continue as normal. However if the exception triggers, an exception is "thrown"
- Throw - This is where you trigger an exception. Each "throw" must have at least one "catch"
- Catch - A "catch" block retrieves an exception and creates an object containing the exception

An example can clarify the statements above where the object ($e) contain the exception information:

```
<?php
function checkVal($value)   //function with an exception
   {
   if($value>3)
      {
      throw new Exception("Value must be less or equal to 3 ");
      }
   return true;
   }

try  // "try" block
{
   checkVal(4);
```

```
      echo 'The value is less or equal to 3';
}

catch(Exception $e)   //catch exception
{
   echo "Message: " .$e->getMessage();
}
?>
```

In PShop an example of error handling is given below :

```
[code /classes/Cookie.php]
      public function __set($key, $value)
      {
          if (is_array($value))
              die(Tools::displayError());
          if (preg_match('/¤|\|/', $key.$value))
              throw new Exception('Forbidden chars in cookie');
...
```

MySQL

MySQL is a relational database management system (RDBMS) that runs as a server providing multi-user access to a number of databases [9.11]

MySQL is the de-facto standard database for web sites that support huge volumes of both data and end users (like Friendster, Yahoo, Google). PHP uses MySQL to store database objects called tables. A table is a collection of related data entries and it consists of columns and rows.

PHP connect to MySQL through the following statement :

```
mysql_connect(servername,username,password);

$conn = mysql_connect("localhost","bob","password");
if (!$conn)
```

```
{
    die('Could not connect: ' . mysql_error());
}
mysql_close($conn);
```

To run a query we can use the following :

```
mysql_query($strQuery,$connection)

mysql_query("CREATE DATABASE my_database",$conn));
```

MySQL has a web interface called phpMyAdmin from where you can create databases and tables and import/export data. For instance the fields supported in a table are listed below (partial):

- CHAR(size) Holds a fixed length string up to 255 characters
- VARCHAR(size) Holds a variable length string up to 255 characters.
- TINYTEXT Holds a string with a maximum length of 255 characters
- TEXT Holds a string with a maximum length of 65,535 characters
- BLOB (Binary Large OBjects). Holds up to 65,535 bytes of data
- MEDIUMTEXT Holds a string with a maximum length of 16,777,215 characters
- MEDIUMBLOB For BLOBs (Binary Large OBjects). Holds up to 16,777,215 bytes of data
- LONGTEXT Holds a string with a maximum length of 4,294,967,295 characters
- LONGBLOB (Binary Large OBjects). Holds up to 4,294,967,295 bytes of data
- TINYINT(size)   -128 to 127 normal. 0 to 255 UNSIGNED*.
- SMALLINT(size) -32768 to 32767 normal. 0 to 65535

UNSIGNED*.
- MEDIUMINT(size) -8388608 to 8388607 normal. 0 to 16777215 UNSIGNED*.
- INT(size) -2147483648 to 2147483647 normal. 0 to 4294967295 UNSIGNED*.
- BIGINT(size) -9223372036854775808 to 9223372036854775807 normal.
- FLOAT(size,d) A small number with a floating decimal point.
- DOUBLE(size,d) A large number with a floating decimal point.
- DECIMAL(size,d) A DOUBLE stored as a string , allowing for a fixed decimal point.
- DATE() A date. Format: YYYY-MM-DD from '1000-01-01' to '9999-12-31'
- DATETIME() A date and time combination. Format: YYYY-MM-DD HH:MM:SS
- TIME() A time. Format: HH:MM:SS
- YEAR() A year in two-digit or four-digit format.
- TIMESTAMP() values are stored as the number of seconds since the Unix epoch ('1970-01-01 00:00:00' UTC). Format: YYYY-MM-DD HH:MM:SS

- AVG() - Returns the average value
- COUNT() - Returns the number of rows
- FIRST() - Returns the first value
- LAST() - Returns the last value
- MAX() - Returns the largest value
- MIN() - Returns the smallest value
- SUM() - Returns the sum
- UCASE() - Converts a field to upper case
- LCASE() - Converts a field to lower case
- MID() - Extract characters from a text field
- LEN() - Returns the length of a text field
- ROUND() - Rounds a numeric field to the number of decimals specified
- NOW() - Returns the current system date and time
- FORMAT() - Formats how a field is to be displayed

In MySQL the INSERT INTO statement is described below :

```
INSERT INTO table_name (column1, column2, column3,...)
VALUES (value1, value2, value3,...)

mysql_query("INSERT INTO Animals (Name, Age)
VALUES ('Titty', '5')");
```

To retrieve data from a table :

```
$result = mysql_query("SELECT * FROM Animals");
```

The Update statement :

```
UPDATE table_name
SET column1=value, column2=value2,...
WHERE some_column=some_value

mysql_query("UPDATE Animals SET Age = '6'
WHERE Name = 'Titty' AND Name = 'Minny'");
```

To Delete records :

```
DELETE FROM table_name
WHERE some_column = some_value

mysql_query("DELETE FROM Animals WHERE
Name='Titty'");
```

When dealing with a database we should be careful to clean the query before submitting it . This will avoid possible threats like the SQL-Injection. In PShop the function pSQL has been designed to sanitize the query before executing it:

```
[code   classes/Db.php]
function pSQL($string, $htmlOK = false)
{
     if (_PS_MAGIC_QUOTES_GPC_)
          $string = stripslashes($string);
     if (!is_numeric($string))
     {
          $link = Db::getInstance()->getRessource();
          $string = _PS_MYSQL_REAL_ESCAPE_STRING_ ? mysql_real_escape_string($string, $link) : addslashes($string);
          if (!$htmlOK)
               $string = strip_tags(nl2br2($string));
     }

     return $string;
}
```

Classes

PHP is an OOP and classes are a convenient tool to manage your code.
In object-oriented programming, a class is a construct that is used as a blueprint to create instances of itself – referred to as class instances,

class objects, instance objects or simply objects. A class defines constituent members which enable these class instances to have state and behaviour. Data field members (member variables or instance variables) enable a class object to maintain its state. [9.6]

Shortly a class is used to define a collection of variables and functions that work together. A class can be seen as a new type of variable which is fully customizable, therefore classes are also known as abstract data types (ADTs) . After the class (a data type) is defined, an *instance* of that type must be created. An instance is just a variable that embed the structure of a class and is called *object*.

Variables and functions belonging to a class are called member variables and member functions (or methods) and a function associated with a class is *binded* to it.

```
class my_class
{
var variable1, variable2;   // it's good practice to declare class variables
var variable3;
function function1(argument_list)
{
// function1_body
}

function function2(argument_list)
{
// function2_body
}
}
```

In order to use a class we need to create the object which embed its structure, this is done with the keyword *new* and object members become accessible as its class members. To access both variables and functions we use the operator ->

```
$myobject= new myclass;


class cat
{
```

```
var $name;   // member var
function Miao() // member function
{
echo 'Miauu!';
}
}

// Create a cat and let him talk
$objcat = new cat;
$objcat->name = 'Minny';
echo $objcat->name . ' says : ';
$objcat->Miao();
```

There is a special object called *$this* which can be used to access an object from within its member functions. For instance to modify a variable from within a member function definition, you can use $this->my_var , where my_var is one of the class's member variables. In the above example the function Miao can access $name as below:

```
function Miao() // member function
{
echo 'Miauu!';
$this->$name='Minny';
}
```

Now try to execute the following :

```
class cat
{
var $pname;
function Miao()
{
echo 'Miauu!';
$this->pname="Titty";
}
}
// Create a cat and let him talk
$objcat = new cat;
$objcat->pname = 'Minny';
echo "<br />\n".$objcat->pname . ' says : ';
$objcat->Miao();
```

```
echo "<br />\n".$objcat->pname;
echo "<br />\n".$this->pname;   // Error, not in object context
```

the following will be printed in your browser, why ?

Minny says : Miauu!
Titty

Because Minny get saved before calling Miao() whereas after executing Miao() $pname changed into Titty. Note : be careful not to confuse the way we address arrays => with the way we address objects ->

A class can be initialized with a special function called Constructor which must have the same name of the class. PHP executes a constructor function automatically whenever an object of a class is instantiated. A class might or might not have a constructor function, but if it does, it must have the same name as the class.

```
class cat
{
var $pname;
function cat() // this is the constructor
{
echo 'Miauu!';
}
}
```

However we can also have a constructor defined explicitly with the function __construct() :

```
class BaseClass {
    function __construct() {  // constructor of the BaseClass
        print "In BaseClass constructor\n";
    }
}

class SubClass extends BaseClass {
    function __construct() {  // constructor of the
```

```
SubClass
        parent::__construct();   // constructor of the BaseClass
        print "In SubClass constructor\n";
    }
}
```

Public, Private, Protected

These are keywords used to restrict the access to the member functions of a class. They define the scope of those member functions.

Public members can be accessed from outside an object ($obj->publicMember) or by accessing it from inside method via the special $this variable ($this->publicMember). If another class inherits a public member, the same rules apply, and it can be accessed both from outside the derived class's objects and from within its methods.

Protected members can be accessed only from within an object's method ($this->protectedMember). If another class inherits a protected member, the same rules apply, and it can be accessed from within the derived object's methods via the special $this variable.

Private members are similar to protected members but they are inaccessible from a derived object's methods.

PIE : Encapsulation

With Encapsulation we can see a class as a black box and hide to the programmer some of its inner workings not relevant for the higher-level results we expect from it. An example could be to hide the error checking of the class or to avoid that the age of our cat could be changed outside its class by mistake. It's used to wrap data into an object :

```
<?php

class App {
    private static $_user;

    public function User( ) {
        if( $this->_user == null ) {
```

```
                $this->_user = new User();
            }
            return $this->_user;
      }

}

class User {
      private $_name;

      public function __construct() {
            $this->_name = "Bob Collins";
      }

      public function GetName() {
            return $this->_name;
      }
}

$app = new App();

echo $app->User()->GetName();

?>
```

PIE : Inheritance

In object-oriented programming (OOP), inheritance is a way to reuse code of existing objects, establish a subtype from an existing object, or both, depending upon programming language support. In classical inheritance where objects are defined by classes, classes can inherit attributes and behaviour (i.e., previously coded algorithms associated with a class) from pre-existing classes called base classes or superclasses or parent classes or ancestor classes. The new classes are known as derived classes or subclasses or child classes. The relationships of classes through inheritance gives rise to a hierarchy. [9.7]
In PHP a child class is defined with the keyword *extends* :

```
class child_class extends base_class
{
```

```
    // class definition
}
```

A small example is listed below where `$dblNum` get changed in the child class:

```
// Demonstrate Inheritance
$objNum = new Number;
$objNum->dblNum = 4.5;
$objFrac = new Fraction;   // Declare a Fraction

$objFrac->setNum(2, 7); // This makes the fraction = 2/7

echo 'The Number is: ' . $objNum->getNum() . '<br>';
echo 'The Fraction is: ' . $objFrac->getNum() . ' which is equal to ' . $objFrac->getString() . '<br>';

class Number
{
var $dblNum;
function getNum()
{
return $this->dblNum;
}
}

class Fraction extends Number
{
var $intNumerator, $intDenominator;
function setNum($intNumerator, $intDenominator)
{
$this->intNumerator = $intNumerator;
$this->intDenominator = $intDenominator;
$this->dblNum = $intNumerator/$intDenominator;
}

function getString()
```

```
{
return $this->intNumerator . '/' . $this-
>intDenominator;
}
}
```

In PShop an example of child class is given below :

```
[code /classes/contact.php]
class ContactCore extends ObjectModel
```

PIE : Polymorphism
In computer science, polymorphism is a programming language feature that allows values of different data types to be handled using a uniform interface. The concept of parametric polymorphism applies to both data types and functions. A function that can evaluate to or be applied to values of different types is known as a polymorphic function. A data type that can appear to be of a generalized type (e.g., a list with elements of arbitrary type) is designated polymorphic data type like the generalized type from which such specializations are made. [9.8]

PHP applies this by allowing you to give the same name to methods and properties that play similar roles in different classes. Please have a look at the **Interface** paragraph before trying the example below:

```
<?
    interface Surface
    {
        public function area();
        public function areaUnit();
    }

    class Rectangle implements Surface
    {
        private $w;
        private $h;
```

```php
        public function __construct( $w, $h )
        {
            $this->w = $w;
            $this->h = $h;
        }

        public function area()
        {
            return ($this->w * $this->h);
        }

        public function areaUnit()
        {
                return "sqm";
        }
    }

class Triangle implements Surface
{
    private $w;
    private $h;

    public function __construct( $w, $h )
    {
        $this->w = $w;
        $this->h = $h;
    }

    public function area()
    {
        return ($this->w * $this->h /2);
    }

    public function areaUnit()
    {
            return "sqm";
    }

}
```

```
        function outputArea( Surface $ha )
        {
                echo get_class($ha). ": the area is "
                        . " {$ha->area()} {$ha->areaUnit()} <Br
/>\n";
        }

        $Sur = array(
                new Rectangle(2,4),
                new Triangle(3,6)
        );

        foreach( $Sur as $S )
        {
                outputArea( $S );
        }
?>
```

Rectangle & Triangle implements the interface Surface.
The last three lines of code make a call to the function OutputArea which in turn call the derived classes of Surface. The right class is executed depending on the class_parameter passed to Surface.

the output on your browser is :

Rectangle: the area is 8 sqm
Triangle: the area is 9 sqm

Interface

An interface defines which methods a class should have but leaves the actual implementation up to the individual class. An interface is similar to a class except that it cannot contain code. An interface can define method names and arguments, but not the contents of the methods. Any classes implementing an interface must implement all methods defined by the interface. Such class must be declared with the keyword *implements*.

```
interface MyInterface {
        public function pfun1();
```

```
        public function pfun2();
        public function setName($name);
}


class MyClass implements MyInterface {
    protected $name;
    public function pfun1() {
        // some code ...
    }
    public function pfun2() {
        // some code ...
    }
    public function setName($name) {
        $this->name = $name;
    }
}
```

Abstract Class

An abstract class defines the basic structure of its child classes but cannot be instantiated on its own. Classes extending an abstract class must implement all of the abstract methods defined in the abstract class. An abstract class is declared the same way as classes with the addition of the keyword *abstract*:

```
abstract class MyAbstract {
    public $name;
    public function doThis() {
        // do this
    }
    abstract public function doThat();
    abstract public function setName($name);
}
```

In PShop an example of abstract class is given below :

```
[code /classes/ObjectModel.php]
abstract class ObjectModelCore
```

Type hinting:

Functions are able to force parameters to be objects by specifying the name of the class in the function prototype:

```
class MyClass
{
    /**
     * A test function
     *
     * First parameter must be an object of type OtherClass
     */
    public function test(OtherClass $otherclass) {
        echo $otherclass->var;
    }

    /**
     * Another test function
     *
     * First parameter must be an array
     */
    public function test_array(array $input_array) {
        print_r($input_array);
    }
}
```

Static :

Declaring class properties or methods as static makes them accessible without needing an instantiation of the class. A static method of a class can be called with the scope resolution operator ::

```
class Foo {
    public static function aStaticMethod() {   //
```

```
         example of static member function
            // ...
      }
}

Foo::aStaticMethod();
$classname = 'Foo';
$classname::aStaticMethod(); // As of PHP 5.3.0
```

Self :

Use self to refer to the current class. Use $this to refer to the current object. In other words, use $this->member for non-static members, use self::$member for static members.

Global keyword : The script below will output 3. By declaring *$a* and *$b* global within the function, all references to either variable will refer to the global version. There is no limit to the number of global variables that can be manipulated by a function.

```
$a = 1;
$b = 2;

function Sum()
{
    global $a, $b; // reference to global variables
    $b = $a + $b;
}

Sum();
echo $b;    // b=3
```

In PShop global is used frequently to recall the object cookie as in the code below :

```
[code   classes\Category.php]
public function getProducts($id_lang, $p, $n, $orderBy = NULL, $orderWay = NULL, $getTotal = false, $active = true, $random = false, $randomNumberProducts = 1, $checkAccess = true)
      {
        global $cookie;
```

...

Function signature

A function prototype is the declaration of a function name and parameters prior to its use— this is also called the function signature. (PHP does not require function prototyping)

Overloading:

In PHP, you can overload methods using the magic method __call and you can overload properties with the magic methods __set, __get. For instance if you call an undefined method like $class->NonExist() , PHP will execute __call instead. The same occurr if you try to access a nonExistent member variable. PHP in this case will execute __get or _set member functions.

Override:

Overriding is pertinent to derived classes, where the parent class has defined a method and the derived class wishes to override that function.

Magic Methods

The function names __construct(), __destruct(), __call(), __callStatic(), __get(), __set(), __isset(), __unset(), __sleep(), __wakeup(), __toString(), __invoke(), __set_state() and __clone() are magical in PHP classes. You cannot have functions with these names in any of your classes unless you want the magic functionality associated with them.

.htacces :

when using PHP as an Apache module, you can also change the configuration settings using directives in Apache configuration files (e.g. *httpd.conf*) and *.htaccess* files. There is a huge range of things .htaccess can do including: password protecting folders, redirecting users automatically, custom error pages, changing your file extensions, banning users with certain IP addresses, only allowing users with certain IP addresses, stopping directory listings and using a different file as the index file.

Frameworks

In computer programming, a software framework is an abstraction in which software providing generic functionality can be selectively changed by user code, thus providing application specific software. It is a collection of software libraries providing a defined application programming interface (API). [9.9]

PShop use a commercial 'template' framework called Smarty which is a template /presentation framework (see later in this chapter). There are other popular frameworks around including Zend Framework , Prado CakePHP or the high-performance Yii Framework.

Smarty

Smarty is a web template system written in PHP. Smarty is primarily promoted as a tool for separation of concerns. Smarty is intended to simplify compartmentalization, allowing the presentation of a web page to change separately from the back-end. Ideally, this eases the costs and efforts associated with software maintenance. Smarty generates web content by the placement of special Smarty tags within a document. These tags are processed and substituted with other code. [9.10]

When doing web application development, it is important to make the separation between presentation and application. PShop achieve this using the Smarty Framework.

Install

Install is pretty simple, do the following :

1. download Smarty from the official website : http://www.smarty.net/
2. make a folder in your Apache sever named Smarty
3. unzip Smarty there and create two more folders : template and template_c (compiled)

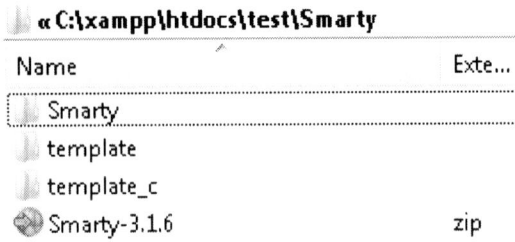

Basics

Using the class Smarty we'll prepare our first template. To do this we'll create two files :

Test01.tpl - the template
Test01.php - the main script

```
[code test01.tpl]
<html>
   <head>
      <title>{$title}</title>
   </head>
   <body>
      {$hello}
   </body>
</html>
```

```
[code test01.php]
<?php
require '../Smarty/libs/Smarty.class.php';

$smarty = new Smarty;

$smarty->assign('title','Page Title');
$smarty->assign('hello','Hi guys');
$smarty->display('test01.tpl');
?>
```

Open your browser and type the following in the address bar (depending on your server) :

http://localhost/test/Smarty/template/test01.php

You should get the following : Hi guys

In PShop there are number of templates available, let's look at the following files :

```
[code /modules/blockmyaccount.tpl]
<div class="block myaccount">
      <h4><a href="{$link->getPageLink('my-account.php', true)}">{l s='My account' mod='blockmyaccount'}</a></h4>
      <div class="block_content">
            <ul class="bullet">
                  <li><a href="{$link->getPageLink('history.php', true)}" title="">{l s='My orders' mod='blockmyaccount'}</a></li>
                  {if $returnAllowed}<li><a href="{$link->getPageLink('order-follow.php', true)}" title="">{l s='My merchandise returns' mod='blockmyaccount'}</a></li>{/if}
                  <li><a href="{$link->getPageLink('order-slip.php', true)}" title="">{l s='My credit slips' mod='blockmyaccount'}</a></li>
                  <li><a href="{$link->getPageLink('addresses.php', true)}" title="">{l s='My addresses' mod='blockmyaccount'}</a></li>
                  <li><a href="{$link->getPageLink('identity.php', true)}" title="">{l s='My personal info' mod='blockmyaccount'}</a></li>
                  {if $voucherAllowed}<li><a href="{$link->getPageLink('discount.php', true)}" title="">{l s='My voucers' mod='blockmyaccount'}</a></li>{/if}

                  <li><a href="{$AdminPath}index.php" title="">{l s='My products' mod='blockmyaccount'}</a></li>

                  {$HOOK_BLOCK_MY_ACCOUNT}
            </ul>
            <p class="logout"><a href="{$link->getPageLink('index.php')}?mylogout" title="{l s='Sign out' mod='blockmyaccount'}">{l s='Sign out' mod='blockmyaccount'}</a></p>
      </div>
```

```
</div>
```

```
[code /modules/blockmyaccount.php]
      $smarty->assign(array(
         'voucherAllowed' => (int)(Configuration::get('PS_
VOUCHERS')),
         'returnAllowed' => (int)(Configuration::get('PS_OR-
DER_RETURN')),
         'HOOK_BLOCK_MY_ACCOUNT' => Module::hookExec('myAcco
untBlock')
         ));
...
```

As we can see Smarty's command are embedded in the tpl file inside curley brackets {}
For instance in the BO we setup whether Vouchers or Return are allowed, then in `blockmyaccount.php` we save these settings in the Smarty array (above).
Finally we call back these values in the template and , programmatically, we display the final template selecting the portion to display with the { if } statement :

```
{if $returnAllowed}<li><a href="{$link-
>getPageLink('order-follow.php', true)}"
title="">{l s='My merchandise returns'
mod='blockmyaccount'}</a></li>{/if}
```

DW

DW is the short of DreamWeaver one of the most popular web development application.
This paragraph is dedicated to it, not on how to make a website with DW (we'll download one ready-made from the web) but how DW can help the developer doing his work especially with PShop. The examples shown here refer to DW CS5.

- Download a Template
- Getting Started
- Widget Browser
- Manage CSS

- Live View & Live Code
- PShop in DW
  - Site Specific Code Completion
  - Clean Up HTML (and CSS)

Download a Template

From the following link download bizsolutions.zip :
http://www.csstemplatesfree.org/

Unzip the file in the folder *DW_demo* , you'll get a folder structure as below :

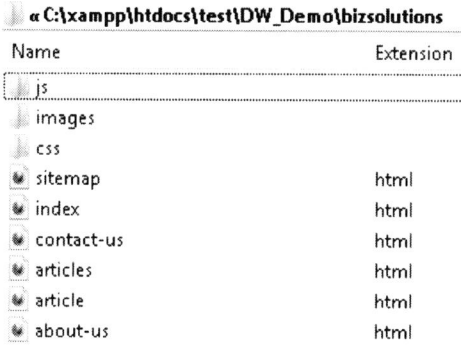

We've already seen how to create a Site while discussing about themes in a previous chapter.
Run DW and in the main menu select Site > New Site and enter the site name *DW_Demo* .
Your configuration in DW should look as below :

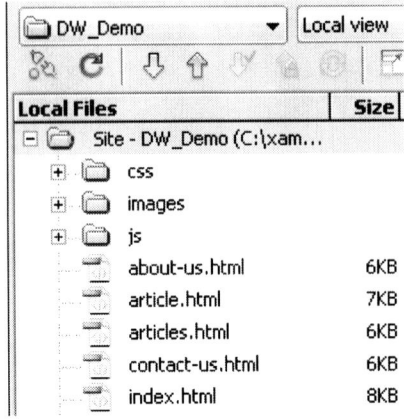

Getting Started

If you wish you can setup the FTP access to upload your files directly on the server.
Goto Site > Manage Sites > Server > and click on the icon + (add a new server) :

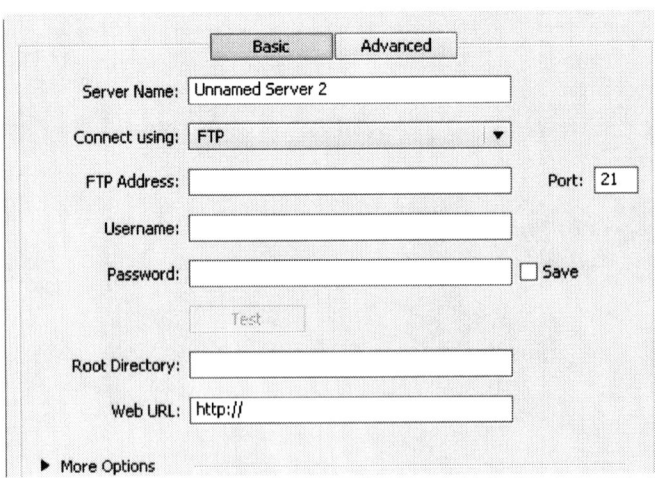

Open an HTML template with 2 columns : select New > HTML > 2 Columns, liquid, left sidebar, header and footer.

Liquid layouts are designed to expand and contract depending on the size of the browser window. Fixed layouts are centered within the browser and set to a width of 960 pixels. Liquids layouts looks more flexibility but you'll probably have more design control with fixed layouts Note that by default the CSS is internal (embedded in the HTML script) , but you can choose to have an external style sheet in the same page where you selected the HTML template.

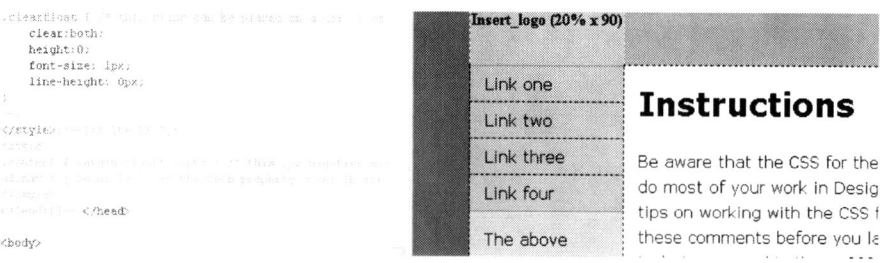

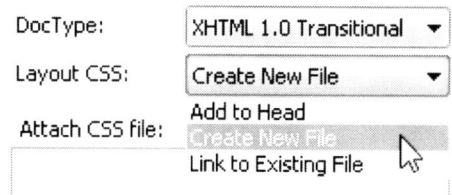

Widget Browser

In computer programming, a widget (or control) is an element of a graphical user interface (GUI) that displays an information arrangement changeable by the user, such as a window or a text box. [9.12]
Adobe Dreamweaver Widget Browser is an Adobe AIR® application that lets you preview, configure the widgets using a visual interface, and then insert them in your site with Dreamweaver.. You need Adobe AIR to be installed on your system (in CS5 is already installed otherwise you can download it from the Adobe website).

From the top bar of DW select Widget Browser and download it from Adobe website . After installing it you need to login before using this tool :

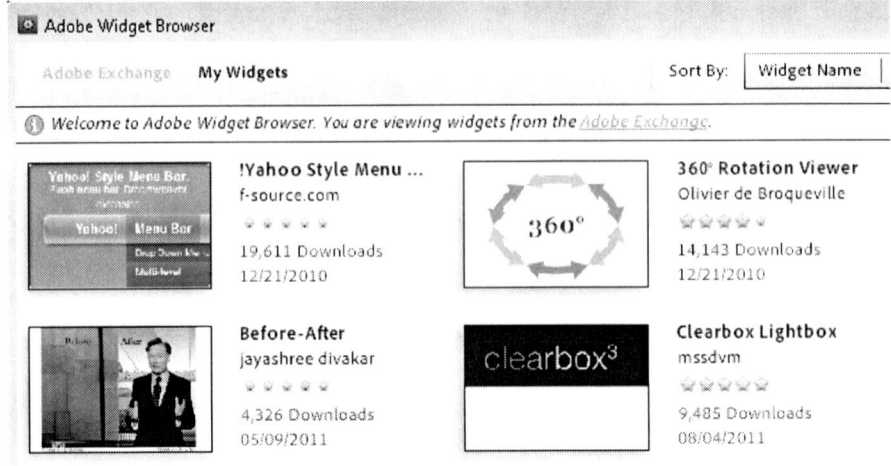

Select !Yahoo Style Menu and add it to *My Widgets*
Now if you want to use it in DW just goto Insert > Widget and select the !Yahoo widget.
Now your page should look like below with the new widget added on the top of your page (as a Flash) :

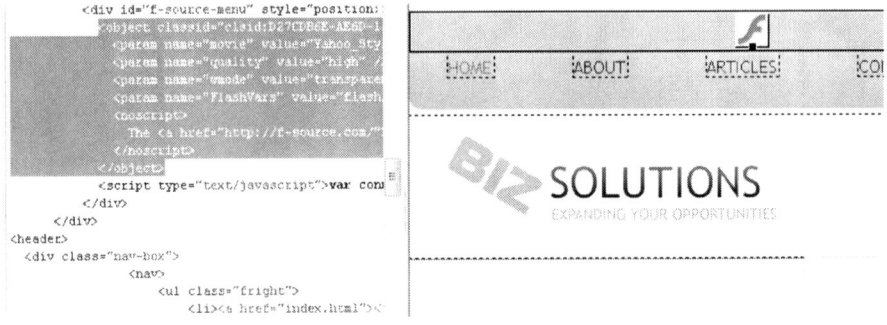

Press F12 to preview this page in Firefox

Manage CSS
In the bizsolution template select the menu item ABOUT
In the right CSS pane select Current , you'll see the properties for this element :

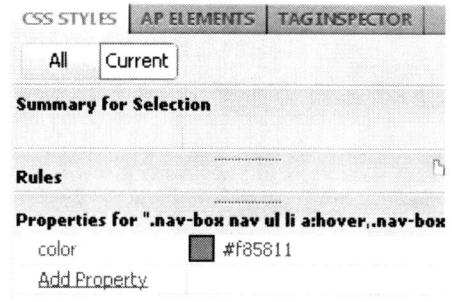

Click on All on the CSS pane and you'll get the list of all CSS used in that page (index.html). To edit a CSS rule just double click on it and a new dialog will open :

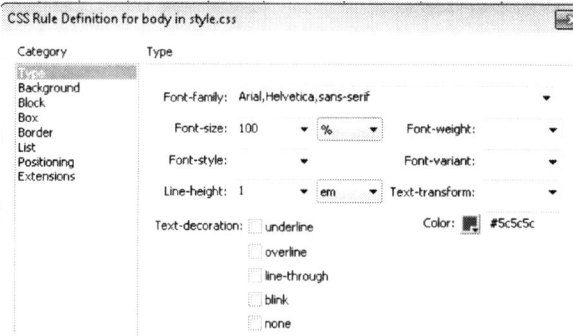

CSS Inspect is a special feature which allow you to view the style information in any part of the page.
Click the Inspect button and (in case) switch to the optimized workspace settings.

As soon as you hover the mouse over an element both the HTML and the CSS info will be highlighted.

Live View & Live Code

This option allows you to interact with your page as if it were loaded in your browser. If you push the button *Live View* on the top and you hover the mouse on the top menu you'll get the same look and feel as in your browser. More interesting with *Live Code* you can change on the fly the CSS rule of any element.
For instance put your mouse over the menu item About and click the right-mouse while holding Ctrl + Alt.

The following dialog will pop-up :

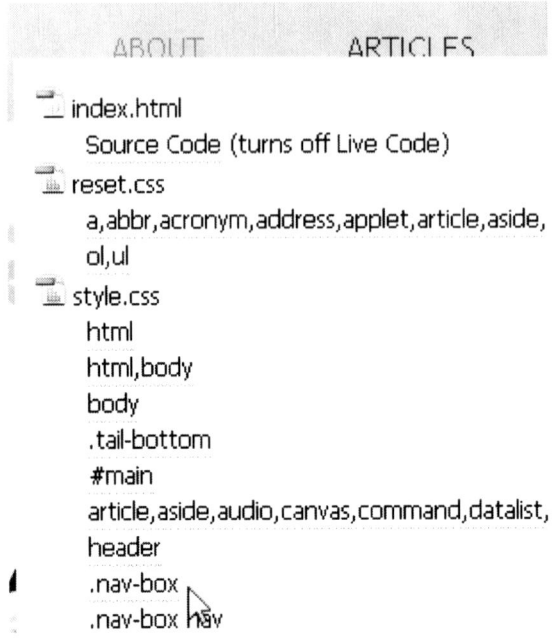

Click on the rule .nav-box and the style.css will open pointing directly to this rule. We're working with an HTML template but the same apply exactly even to a PHP file providing you've an Apache server (XAMPP) installed on your PC.

PShop in DW

In the previous paragraphs we've seen some HTML examples , now we'll switch to PShop by opening the index.html.php directly in DW. Do the following : Site > Manage Sites > New
Enter the sitename *pshop144* and point to that folder : *C:\xampp\htdocs\pshop144*
On the Advanced Settings > Local Folders > select the image folder *pshop144\img*

Now Select Server , click + (add new server) then *Advanced* and as *Testing server* > *Server Model* select *PHP MySQL*. Go back to *Basic* options and select *Connect using* > *Local network*
As local server put : *C:\xampp\htdocs\pshop144*
As Web URL put : *localhost/pshop144* , click *Save* then in the next

window (Site setup) check the checkbox *Testing* .

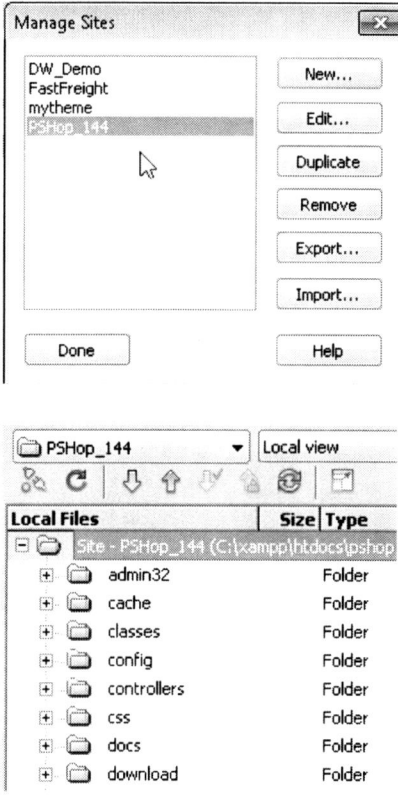

Start MySQL and PHP from your XAMPP control panel, then dbl click index.php Click on Live View and you'll see the main page of your shop in the *Design View* of DW as below :

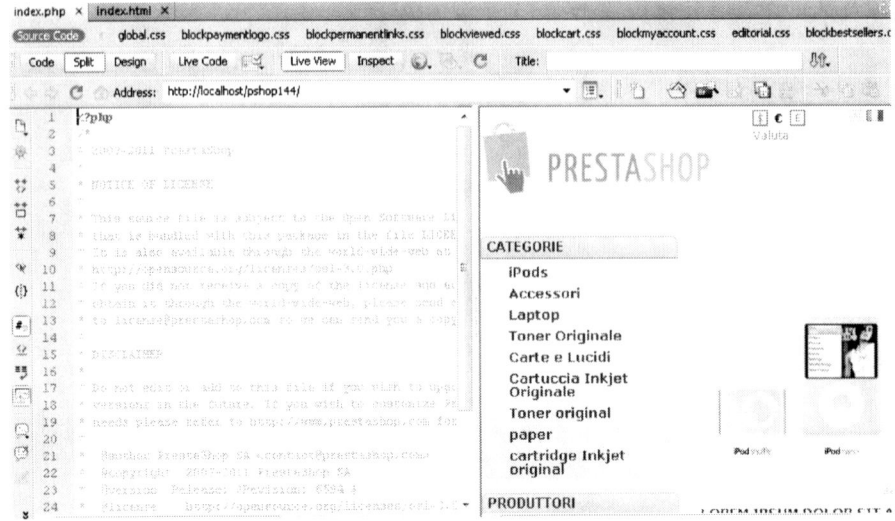

Site Specific Code Completion

Under Site > Site Specific Code Hints you can select code hints for a specific package like Wordpress or Joomla. Unfortunately this option is not yet available for PShop…

Clean Up HTML (and CSS)

Goto Commands > Clean up Word HTML..
From there you can also check to clean the associated CSS file

MySQL

Using this database is quite simple, make sure you've installed XAMPP on your PC or just download MySQL from the official website.

- XAMPP
- Create a Database
- Tables
- Backup
- SQL queries

XAMPP

Make sure MySQL is running in the XAMPP control panel (on the tray bar)

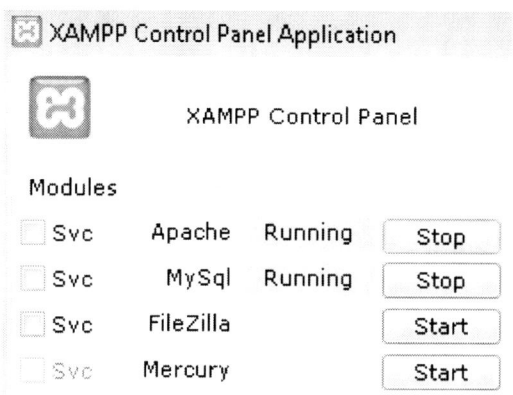

then type the following in your browser : localhost/xampp
The main page of XAMPP will open.

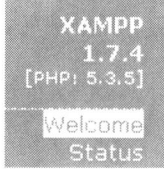

Create a database

This is very simple, goto the main page of XAMPP and click on phpMyAdmin on the left sidebar.

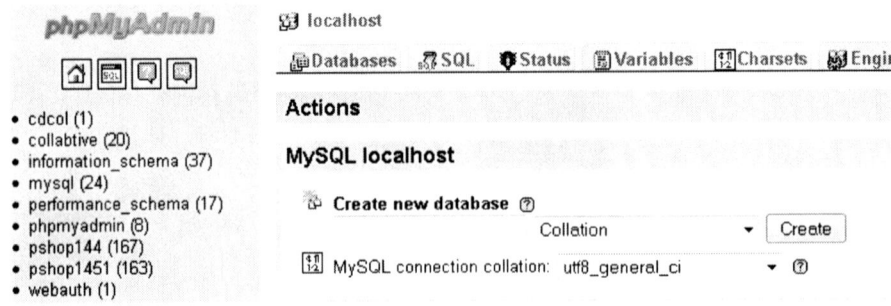

Enter a name in the textbox named *Create new database*. The newly created database will appear in the left sidebar.

To setup a password do the following :

- Goto http://localhost/xampp/
- Click Security in the left sidebar

The following will appear on the page indicating that both PHP , MySQL and XAMPP are unsecure:

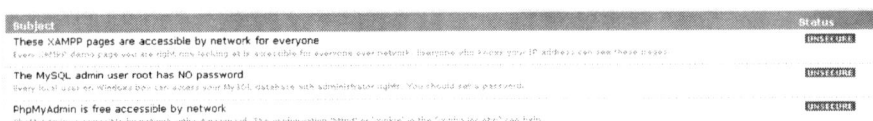

To secure them from unauthorized access click on the link below :

http://localhost/security/xamppsecurity.php

Tables
Tables are the core of every database. Open the phpMyAdmin interface and select the database pshop144. Then select the table ps_customer on the left sidebar .

By default the tab Browse on the page-top is selected :

Change the size of this field as above and click Save

SQL Queries

We'll do a query by joining two different tables. Click on the link phpMyAdmin on the left sidebar.
On the top of the window find the SQL tab from which you can run several queries on your tables. For instance select the database pshop144 on the left sidebar (there are 167 tables in that), then on under the SQL tab enter the following query and click Go:

```
Select * from ps_customer
```

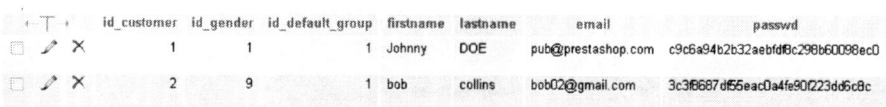

Using the SQL language we can also make complex queries involving more than one table.
Suppose we want to get all the customers who have placed valid orders

We want to list the following fields:

Table ps_customer :

- id_customer
- firstname
- lastname
- email

Table ps_orders :

- id_customer
- id_order
- total_paid
- total_products

Step by Step Tutorials - Pag. 275

In our query we'll check the total amount to see whether a valid order has been placed. We can run the following SQL query :

```
SELECT
A1.id_customer , A1.firstname, A1.lastname, A1.email ,
A2.id_customer, A2.id_order, A2.total_paid, A2.total_
products
FROM ps_customer A1 , ps_orders A2
WHERE A1.id_customer = A2.id_customer and A2.total_paid
>0
```

Backup

A database backup can be saved in the .sql format which is a text file containing the whole data tables of the selected database. In phpMyAdmin it's also possible to backup multiple databases. We can make a backup of our database (advisable) by doing the following steps :

- Select the database you want to export
- Select the .sql format on the left sidebar
- Under Structure check : Add DROP TABLE / VIEW / PROCEDURE / FUNCTION / EVENT
- Click Go

You can also export a query by running it , then scrolling down the window and selecting *Export* under the *Query results operations*

Credits

[9.1] http://en.wikipedia.org/wiki/PHP
[9.2] http://en.wikipedia.org/wiki/Object-oriented_programming
[9.3] http://php.net/manual/en/language.operators.logical.php
[9.4] http://it.php.net/ternary
[9.5] http://www.w3schools.com/php/php_get.asp
[9.6] http://en.wikipedia.org/wiki/Classes_(computer_science)
[9.7] http://en.wikipedia.org/wiki/Inheritance_(object-oriented_programming)
[9.8] http://en.wikipedia.org/wiki/Polymorphism_(computer_science)
[9.9] http://en.wikipedia.org/wiki/Software_framework
[9.10] http://en.wikipedia.org/wiki/Smarty
[9.11] http://en.wikipedia.org/wiki/MySQL
[9.12] http://en.wikipedia.org/wiki/Widget_(computing)

NuSphere PhpED

Intro	279
Configuration	280
Setup the Server	282
NuSoap	284
Profiler	287
Editor	289
Debugging PShop	296
Credits	299

Intro

PhpED is the Integrated Development Environment of NuSphere. PhpED is very convenient to debug large projects and we'll see in this chapter how to debug PShop using this tool.

PhpED is the Integrated Development Environment for PHP (PHP IDE), HTML, CSS, XML, SMARTY, XHTML and other. Balanced combination of advanced code editor, reliable dbg debugger, productive database connectivity client and fast and secure deployment abilities make PhpED a complete solution for most sophisticated developer needs. Ajax, PHP and Database make a great combination for producing Web based ecommerce applications. Ajax based asynchronous calls to PHP scripts on the back end implement Model View Controller architecture and allow the developer to separate the presentation layer from the business logic. Ajax PHP Database template files are located in plugins folder of PhpED installation [10.1]

As in any complicated process, in php development a great deal of effectiveness depends on your choice of production tools. According to our customers, PhpED 6.2 saves up to 75% of development time. With PhpED you can: [10.1]

Create : Code creation with our PHP IDE got a lot easier with the new PhpED 6.2 editing features. With PhpED's new highlighting abilities you can now navigate through your code easily and save the precious developing time. PHP Code Folding sets NuSphere PHP IDE apart from all others.

Debug : Powerful PHP Debugger is one of the best features in PhpED. Debug your code locally or remotely.

Profiler: Introduced by NuSphere, PHP Profiler helps you find and eliminate all the bottlenecks in the code.

Deploy: Secure, fast and flexible publishing of your PHP scripts to a remote server right from PHP IDE. All major protocols such as FTP, FTPS, SSH/SFTP, and WebDAV are supported.

Integrate: New extensibility scope allows to integrate PhpED with

3rd party tools like php encoders, formatters or html validators. Pre-configured tools already include php documentor, html tidy, cvs client and html validator.

Configuration

Let's have a look at the main options from Tools > Settings :

Run & Debug > SRV web server : you don't need to use this if you setup the external server Apache
Editor > Appearance : here you can setup the colouring view you prefer to use
Editor > Shortcuts : useful to speed up recurrent actions. The Editor has many great features like :

- Full support for PHP versions from 4.2 to 5.3
  in IDE and the Editor - from functions and local
  variables to namespaces and aliases

- Dynamic Syntax Highlighting
  The editor will automatically switch the syntax highlighting dependant on the position in the file. The strength of PHP is in ability to embed it in the other documents, like HTML. However, sometimes the document becomes too crowded with the lines of code from multiple languages. Auto-switch feature will let you focus on the code and the language that you are currently working on. It will only highlight those parts of the document, which are written in the same language as the current position of the cursor and deem the rest of the text. The editor will switch between php, html, smarty, css and javascript, depending on the type of the file.

- Multiple Language Syntax Highlighting
  Code sensitive syntax color highlighter gives you the ability to have separate highlighting for different languages in the same file. Highlighting for each language is of course fully configurable in PhpED's settings.

- Auto Highlight variable
  System highlights all occurrences of a variable in the Editor, when PHP variable is selected. Also highlighted are open/close HTML tags

IDE Settings : useful settings to configure like auto save workspace
Code Insight > Code Explorer (on the left sidebar) is a file manager from where we can pick up our scripts
Code Insight > Code Navigation (on the right sidebar) is an insight of the current script (classes, member functions, member variables..)
Code Insight > Settings : here you can enable the autocomplete option of PhpED Editor. Code Insight has many great features like : [10.1]

- Code Completion. Dynamically provides the available properties and methods for a given variable or class, and automatically concludes partially typed keywords. Code completion works for JavaScript, HTML and CSS too.
  It shows properties for tags, classes and attributes.

- Tool tips and Instant error analysis for Php, JavaScript, HTML and CSS make coding an easy task - no more simple mistakes and typos.

- Full control over different versions - select which parser to use for any PHP version or HTML and CSS - including PHP 5.3, HTML5 and CSS3

- Project-wide code explorer in PhpED IDE shows all php, javascript classes, methods, properties, functions and variables in every detail and facilitates object-oriented programming. Also supported: HTML and CSS.

- Hints show you arguments and returning value for a just typed function, as well as a short description for them.

- Fast functions reference shows you all the PHP functions as they are available from PHP extensions. Nested calls are supported with unlimited nesting level.

- Code intellisense HTML Tags - IDE automatically adds closing bracket when you type in HTML tag

- Auto Add HTML attributes - IDE automatically displays required attributes when the tag is entered

- Code intellisense CSS - with support for CSS3 features

- PHP, HTML, and CSS code Validator
  PhpED's built-in code Validator checks out the syntax in PHP, HTML and CSS code and displays the error
  - both in the PHP editor and error bar. PHP IDE finds all errors that will cause problems during execution

- e.g. missing semicolons, open brackets, missing quotes etc. HTML sections of the code are checked for unmatched tags and/or attributes, which are not supported in the corresponding version of HTML standard, missing required attributes, open quotes etc.

PhpED main debugging capabilities are reported below [10.1] :

- Commercial versions of PHP DBG Debugger - the most powerful debugger currently available provides unmatched debugging productivity and safety in both local and remote debugging modes.
- PhpED advanced php profiler shows executing time for each line, function or module of the code with tenth millisecond's precision. You can locate all the bottlenecks quickly and efficiently. Profiler saves all the timings among multiple sessions so your can compare them and evaluate the improvements.
- Triggering debugger on errors or exceptions.
- Remote and local debugging setup with easy to follow wizard

To configure the internal browser goto Tools > Default Browser and select Embedded Mozilla Browser

Setup the Server

PhpED runs your scripts using two basic servers : the local server of PhpED and a local web server (Apache). To debug complex applications it's advisable to run on the Apache server which comes with XAMPP. We'll setup PhpED using Apache ; goto Tools > Settings > Run & Debug and select HTTP mode (3rd party web server) as below:

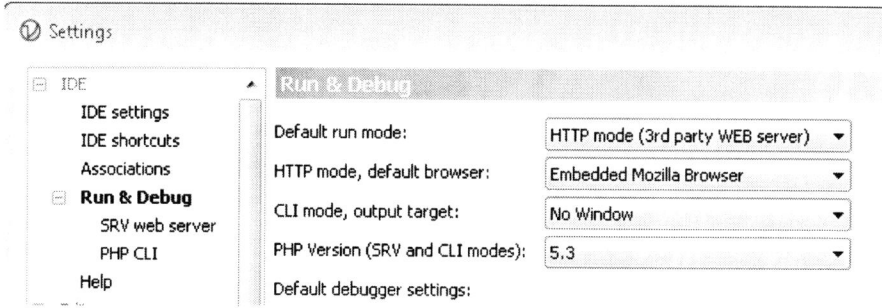

Next File > New Workspace, then right mouse on the new workspace (left sidebar) and select New Project. In the next window you need to specify the path of your project, in our case it's the folder pshop144 as below :

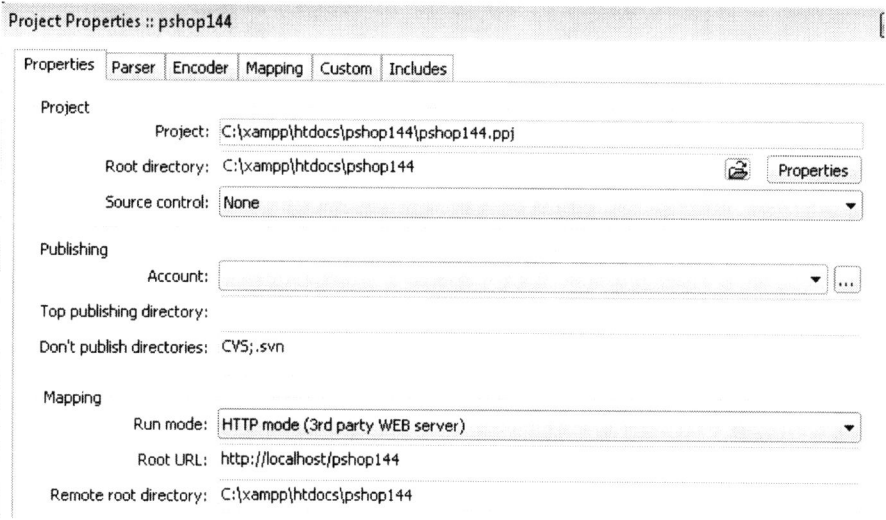

On the bottom of the above window click on the button *Settings Wizard* This is quite useful to verify whether the server and the debugger has been properly installed.
Finally you'll get a working IDE having :

Central area : your scripts opens here
Left area : the workspace and the Code Explorer sliding-tab
Bottom area : logs, breakpoints details…
Right area : Code navigator plus other sliding-tabs

NuSoap

NuSOAP is a rewrite of SOAPx4, provided by NuSphere and Dietrich Ayala. It is a set of PHP classes - no PHP extensions required - that allow developers to create and consume web services based on SOAP 1.1, WSDL 1.1 and HTTP 1.0/1.1. NuSOAP PHP Web Services implementation is tightly integrated with PhpED [10.2]

The NuSOAP Wizard allows you to create PHP scripts for calling remote SOAP services.
Simple Object Access Protocol (SOAP) is a standard lightweight protocol for exchanging information in decentralized, distributed environment. It uses XML to encode remote procedure calls and typically uses HTTP as a communications protocol.
The wizard will automatically generate the PHP script for calling a SOAP object and operation that you specify, and will automatically insert into this code into your file. You can then modify this code as desired. [10.5]

- SOAP (Simple Object Access Protocol) is a simple XML-based protocol to let applications exchange information over HTTP. SOAP became a W3C Recommendation 24. June 2003. [10.6]
- WSDL (Web Services Description Language) is an XML-based language for describing Web services and how to access them. [10.7]

PhpED can generate SOAP and WSDL code using Tools > NuSoap wizard as well as using the sliding-tab nuSoap Client (on the right sidebar). Do the following :

Open a new project under C:\xampp\htdocs\test :

```
Project Properties :: Test

Properties | Parser | Encoder | Mapping | Custom | Includes
  Project
              Project:  C:\xampp\htdocs\test\Test.ppj
       Root directory:  C:\xampp\htdocs\test
       Source control:  None

  Publishing
              Account:
  Top publishing directory:
  Don't publish directories:  CVS;.svn

  Mapping
             Run mode:  System Default
             Root URL:  http://localhost/test
  Remote root directory:  C:\xampp\htdocs\test
```

Copy C:\Program Files\NuSphere\PhpED\include_lib\nusoap.php under /test

Right mouse on the new project Test > New File and type the following code [10.8] :

```
[code converter.php]
<?php
// include NuSoap.php
require_once('nusoap.php');


?>
```

Save the file as converter.php.
Open the tab nuSoap Client and right-mouse on Custom WSDL > Add..

In the capture textbox type *Capture* and in the URL textbox type : http://www.webservicex.com/CurrencyConvertor.asmx?wsdl , you'll get the following :

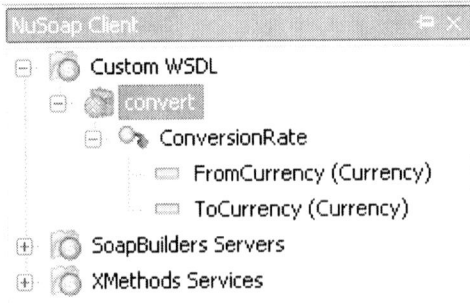

Now copy the item convert in the above window and paste it into the code above, you'll get:

[code converter.php]
```php
<?php
// include NuSoap.php
require_once('nusoap.php');

//convert
$wsdlURL = "http://www.webservicex.com/CurrencyConvertor.asmx?wsdl";
$soap = new soapclient($wsdlURL, "wsdl");
...
```

Finally drag & drop the item ConversionRate from the nuSoap window into the code :

[code converter.php]
```php
<?php
// include NuSoap.php
require_once('nusoap.php');

//convert
$wsdlURL = "http://www.webservicex.com/CurrencyConvertor.asmx?wsdl";
$soap = new soapclient($wsdlURL, "wsdl");

$parameters['parameters']['FromCurrency'] = "USD";
$parameters['parameters']['ToCurrency'] = "EUR";
$result = $soap->call("ConversionRate", $parame-
```

```
ters);
if($error = $soap->getError()){ die($error);}

?>
```

The line `$soap->call` will do the conversion between USD and EUR

Profiler

PhpED profiler can help finding code coverage and other issues related to the script. Below you'll find the main features : [10.3]

- Which PHP scripts take the longest time to run
- What are the particular lines of code, function calls and class methods where most of the time is spent by the application
- What are the lines of code, function calls and class methods which are visited the most - in other words get the biggest number of hits
- How does the data above changes when you run through the application multiple times

Open the file index.php and press Alt-F9 or click the icon *Run Profiler* After few seconds the homepage of your shop will be displayed. Click on the tab *Profiler* and sort the column *Chart*

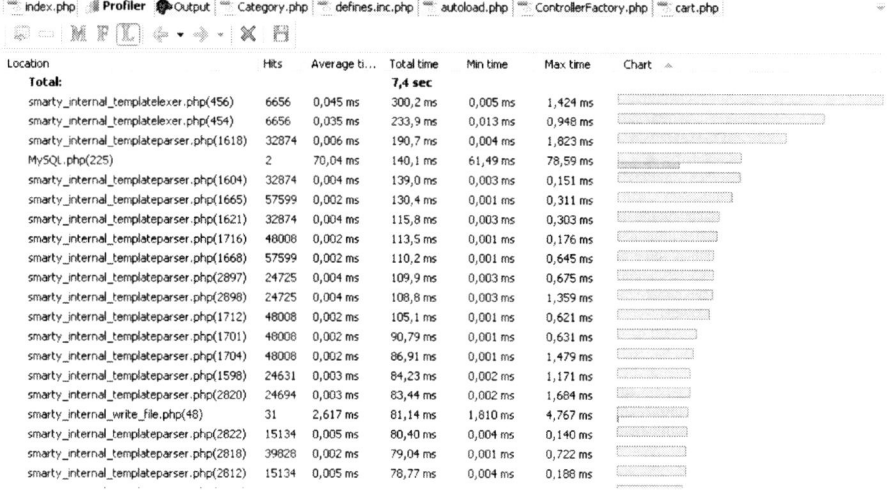

From the picture we can see that Smarty is taking most of the CPU time to execute as well as the access to the MySQL database. Above is listed the total time and the average time for each script to be executed.

In the profiler window you will see the following information: [10.5]

- Location. Shows the code lines executed. You can select to show code lines grouped by modules or by routine.
- Hits. Shows how many times the line was executed.
- Average time. Shows the average time of code line execution (in milliseconds).
- Hits. Shows how many times an object was executed.
- Total time. Shows the total time of execution.
- Minimum time. Show the maximum time of item execution.
- Maximum time. Show the minimum time of item execution.
- Chart. Shows the relative execution time of every object. The object consumed most processing time is taken for 100%, while others are shown as against to this one. Note that the upper part of each chart reflects the total time of object execution while the lower chart part shows a hit time.

In the top bar the following buttons are also available :

- Show source for selected item. Use this button or press Enter to show the source of the item in the Editor area.
- Exclude from analyzing. Removes from the table the selected item (Del). You may want to exclude an item from the table of profiling results in case it consumed too much/little time, and it is difficult to evaluate other items' performance on the

chart.
- M button. Group data by module.
- F button. Group data by routine.
- L button. Show all lines ungrouped.
- Back button. Use to see the previous profiling session results or choose the particular session from the selection list.
- Forward button. Use to see the next profiling session results or choose a particular session from the selection list.
- Floppy disk button. Use to export profiler data to .xml file. You can analyze profiling results using 3rd party tools that work with data in xml format.

By default the L button is selected.

Editor

Open /classes/Category.php and dblClick on the variable id_category from the Code Navigator. PhpED will jump on the variable directly on the script. (line 33).
Now scroll down and put the cursor inside the public function getFields().
Similarly on the Code Navigator you'll get a list of the variables used here : $fields and $this

Put your cursor on return and press F1, PhpED will open a context-sensitive window displaying the usage of the return keyword :

declare	Control Structures
	PHP Manual

return

If called from within a function, the **return()** statement immed of the current function, and returns its argument as the value o **return()** will also end the execution of an eval() statement or

Now after return type : mysql(
Before you finish typing a popup dialog will open suggesting the syntax for this statement :

```
$field mysql(string $database, string $query [, resource $link_identifier])
return   Send a MySQL query
   mysql()
}
```

Using autocorrect

The autocorrect function allows defining short text strings, the same way as while adding, deleting, or modifying the autocompletion list. It can be used for expanding a short sequence of symbols into longer items while typing on a regular basis. When you type the predefined text string followed by space, PhpED will automatically complete the string, replacing it with the "autocorrected" text.

For example, if 'fx' is defined as a shortcut for 'function ()', and the autocorrection is on, when you type 'fx' and press the space bar, it is automatically expanded to 'function ()'.

You can further enhance this feature by using a pipe character (|) to specify the cursor position within the expanded text. This way, the cursor will then be properly positioned for your work once the expansion is complete. [10.5]

This feature is available in Tools > Editor > Autocorrection

Code Cues

Code cues are displayed in the code completion popup for HTML and CSS file types.

There are two types of code cues. [10.5]
- Tags. While coding in HTML and entering an open angle bracket (<), brief pausing will bring up a popup window near the cursor. This popup displays the tags you can enter at this point in your syntax. You can scroll up and down the list of available tags, and select the one you want. If you enter one or more characters when the popup is displayed, PhpED highlights the first word that begins with the letter or letters you typed.
- Tag Attributes. When your current cursor location is within the boundaries of a HTML code tag, the popup list gives you the Tag parameters that are appropriate for that tag. Select an item in the list to insert it in your code.

Using code completion
In the editor, code completion displays a resizable popup box that lists valid elements that can be selected and added to your code. Upon typing the name of a variable that represents a class instance followed by -> and pressing Ctrl+Space (or if you simply pause for several seconds) Code completion displays the properties and methods available in the class. This includes inherited properties and methods derived from the ancessor class(es). [10.5]

PhpED has code completion for
- Functions
- Methods
- Classes
- Global and local variables
- Standard functions
- Standard classes
- Standard variables.

There is a wide list of predefined functions comes with PhpED by default. When you begin to enter a variable name and pause, PhpED displays a popup which suggests variable names for the current context. When pausing while entering a function name, PhpED displays a popup which suggests commonly-used PHP functions.

In addition, PhpED keeps track of the variable and function names used in the current project. While entering a function or variable name, previously used names appear in the Code Completion list. If a dollar sign ($) is entered, PhpED displays a popup list of all the variables that have been defined in the currently opened file.
Please use Reserved Words tab to edit the list of standard functions showed in code completion popup. Code completion can be enabled/disabled for various objects on Code Insight tab.

If you move your mouse on the right over the sliding tab Help you'll see the help topics available in PhpED.

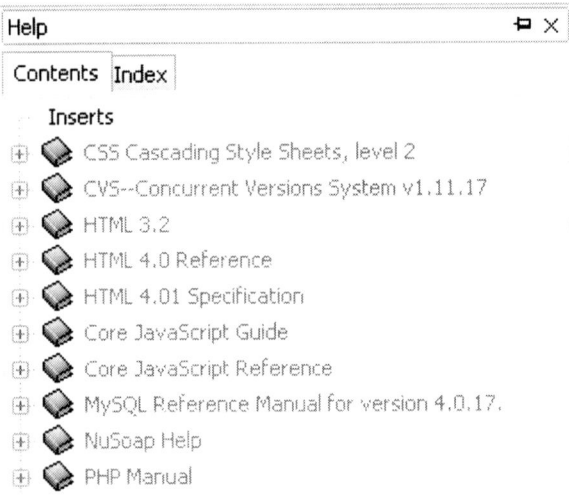

The same will happen for PHP functions if you hover over the sliding tab Functions

```
Functions

PHP 5.x functions
  Apache-specific Functions (apache)
  Array Functions (array)
  BBCode Functions (bbcode)
  BCMath Arbitrary Precision Mathematics Function
  PHP bytecode Compiler (bcompiler)
  Bzip2 Compression Functions (bzip2)
  Calendar Functions (calendar)
  CCVS API Functions [deprecated] (ccvs)
  Classkit Functions (classkit)
  Class/Object Functions (classobj)
```

Now try to move your mouse over the sliding-tab Code Explorer on the left sidebar. All constants, variables, classes ecc.. are listed there. For instance dblClick on the constant _PS_IMG_DIR_ and PhpED will open the file where it has been defined (pointing at the exact line- 78):

```
[code   /config/defines.inc.php]
define('_PS_IMG_DIR_',              _PS_ROOT_DIR_.'/img/');
...
```

In the top bar of Code Explorer is also possible to view the same information in three different modes and in each one filter public, protected and private members :

Project List

PrestaShop for Developers © Alex Manfield

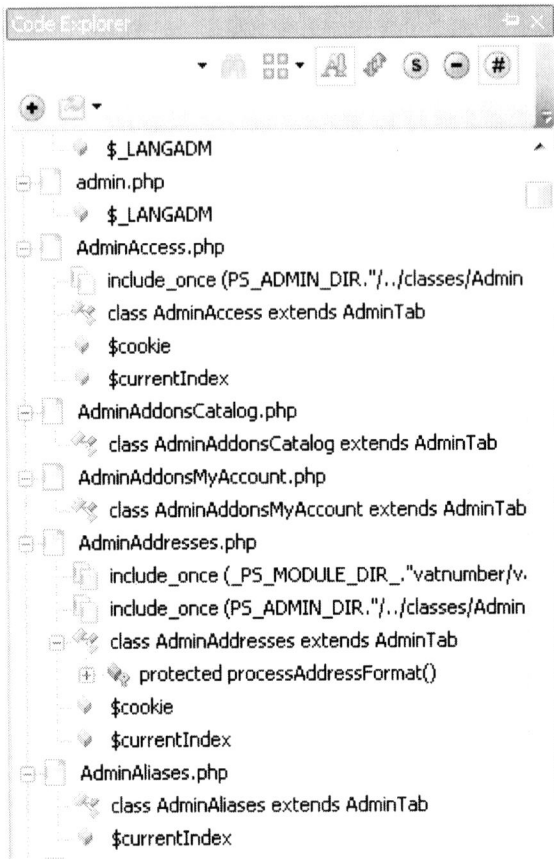

Project Tree

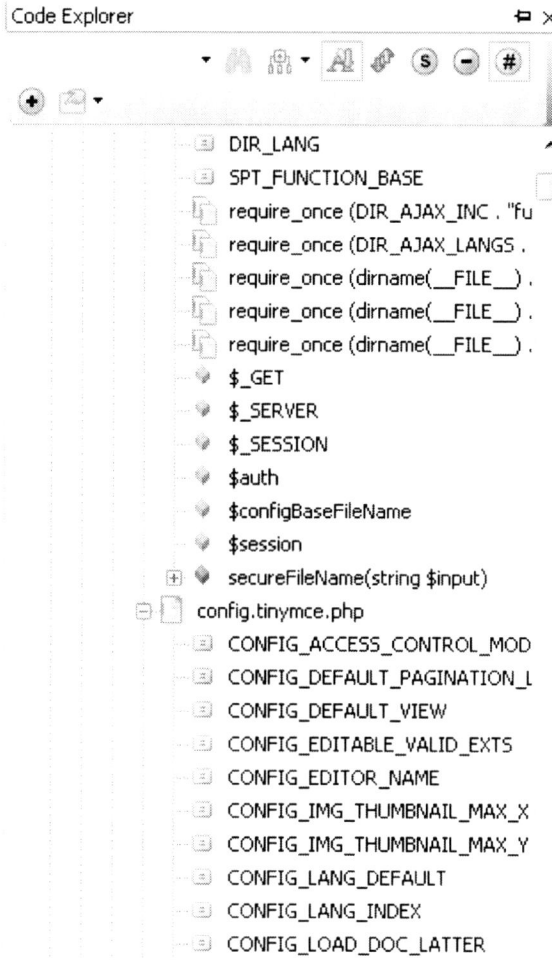

Class View

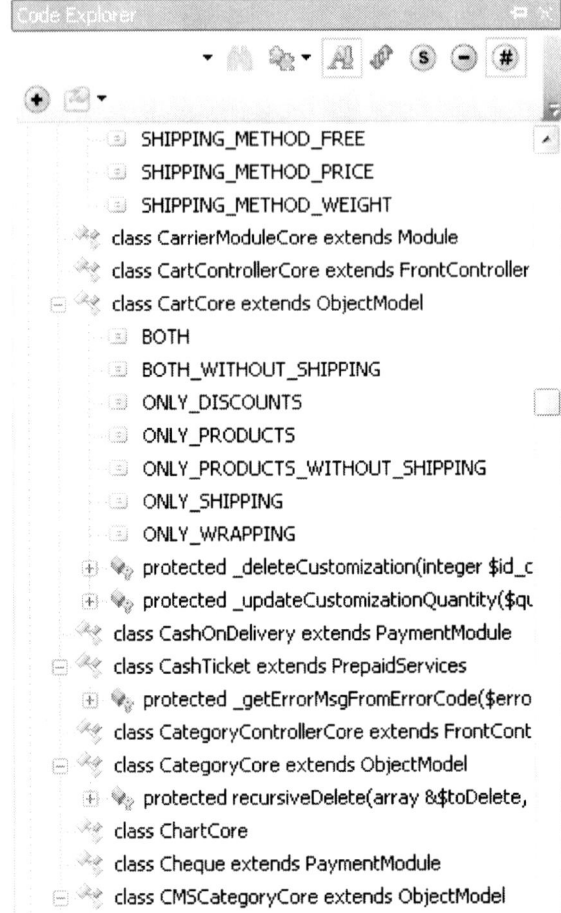

Debugging PShop

In this chapter we'll start debugging some code in PShop using PhpED. Assuming you've created a new PShop project as described before, locate the file pshop144/index.php and double click it.
You'll get the script open in the main workarea as below :

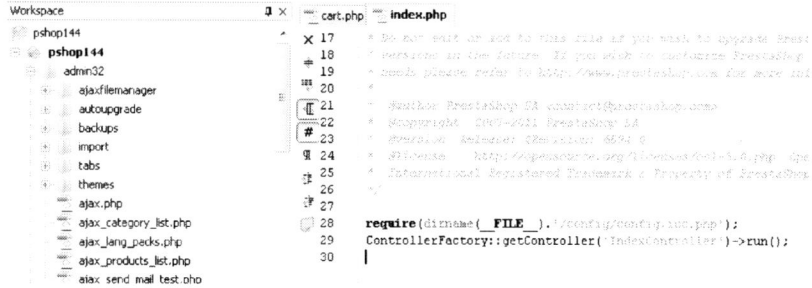

Setup a breakpoint on line 29 (just dbl click that line) and press F9 to run the debugger :

```
28  *   require(dirname(__FILE__).'/config/conf
29 *•  ControllerFactory::getController('Index
30
```

A small blue arrow will soon appear on line 29 indicating that this line will be executed as soon as we proceed to debug this script.
While stepping through your code in PhpED you can select basically 5 types of stepping :

- Step Into (F7) – this will step into the selected code
- Step Over (F8) – this will step over the selected code
- Step Out (Shift-F8) – this will run until execution returns from the current function
- Run to cursor (F4) – this will run upto the cursor
- Run In debugger (F9) – this will run the debugger on the selected script

Note that the bottom window has now changed to display useful informations about watches and breakpoints :

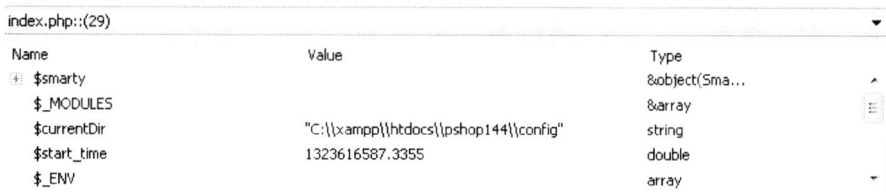

On the right area of the bottom window is also available the system log .

Now press F7 to step into ControllerFactory::getController('IndexController')->run();
PhpED will show us the __autoload() function , why ?
In PShop each class has its own file named as the class itself.
Many developers writing object-oriented applications create one PHP source file per-class definition. One of the biggest annoyances is having to write a long list of needed includes at the beginning of each script (one for each class). In PHP 5, this is no longer necessary. You may define an __autoload function which is automatically called in case you are trying to use a class/interface which hasn't been defined yet. By calling this function the scripting engine is given a last chance to load the class before PHP fails with an error. [10.4]

```
[code /config/__autoload.php]
function __autoload($className)
{
    if (function_exists('smartyAutoload') AND smartyAutoload($className))
          return true;

    $className = str_replace(chr(0), '', $className);
    $classDir = dirname(__FILE__).'/../classes/';
    $overrideDir = dirname(__FILE__).'/../override/classes/';
    $file_in_override = file_exists($overrideDir.$className.'.php');
    $file_in_classes = file_exists($classDir.$className.'.php');
...
```

In this function we can also see the mechanism to override classes as described before in this book.

Press F9 to continue debugging.
The control will come back to index.php, press F9 again and you'll get the FO of your shop on the workarea (red tab Output) as below :

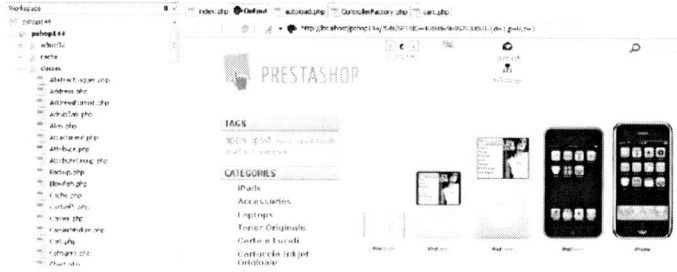

Credits

[10.1] http://www.nusphere.com/products/phped_features.htm?
[10.2] http://www.nusphere.com/php_script/nusoap.htm
[10.3] http://www.nusphere.com/products/php_profiler.htm
[10.4] http://php.net/manual/en/language.oop5.autoload.php
[10.5] PhpED Help
[10.6] http://www.w3schools.com/soap/soap_intro.asp
[10.7] http://www.w3schools.com/wsdl/default.asp
[10.8] http://www.nusphere.com/flash_files/NuSoap.html

Developer's Tools

Intro	301
Agent Ransak	301
Buttons	302
Clean AJAX	302
Codango	303
CSS framework Blueprint	303
CSS Sprite generator	304
DoxyGen	305
FileZilla	305
FireBug	306
Firephp	307
Google Sitemap Generator	308
Javascript debugger	308
Logic CSS framework	308
Notepad ++	309
Photos (Yahoo)	310
PHP and Javascript	311
PHP classes	311
Pingdom Tools	312
Sajax	312
Swish	313
Test plugin for JavaScriptMVC	313
XAMPP	314
Xplorer²	314
Yahoo Design Patterns	315

Intro

There are surely tons of good tools around which can help the developer, most of them are also freeware. It's difficult to list all of them since many excellent tools will probably remain hidden to most of us. There is a limitation of time to discover all of them therefore I tried to be realistic by highlighting those I came across.

Agent Ransak

http://mythicsoft.com

This is a free File Searching Utility . It's not exactly a web developer tool but quite useful to have it. Google Desktop create an index for the searchable items whereas Ransak doesn't but I found it still quite smart and fast especially because I can run the search on specific folders applying many filters to restrict the search. Once installed it's available in the Windows right-mouse menu

Buttons

http://free-web-buttons.com/

Many free buttons can be found in the following sites:
www.freebuttons.com – download ready made buttons

Clean AJAX

http://clean-ajax.sourceforge.net

Clean is an open source engine for AJAX, that provides a high level interface to work with the AJAX technology. This open source engine speeds up Ajax development by cutting down the amount of code you have to write, giving you access to common design patterns used in Ajax applications

- Server side technology agnostic, you can use it with any server side language;
- Simple to install, to configure and to use;
- Small learning curve solution;
- Full based on client side JavaScript.

Codango

http://www.codango.com

A review and guide to PHP web applications, libraries, scripts, hosting, tutorials, and much more.

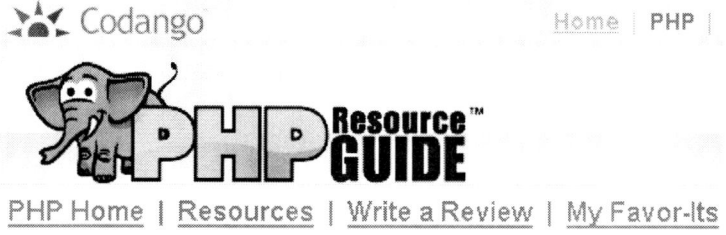

CSS framework Blueprint

http://www.blueprintcss.org/

Blueprint reduces the amount of CSS code you have to write by including common styles that developers typically use. Blueprint is a CSS framework, which aims to cut down on your development time. It gives you a solid foundation to build your project on top of, with an easy-to-use grid, sensible typography, useful plugins, and even a stylesheet for printing.

CSS Sprite generator
http://spritegen.website-performance.org/

CSS sprites are a way to reduce the number of HTTP requests made for image resources referenced by your site. Images are combined into one larger image at defined X and Y coordinates. Having assigned this generated image to relevant page elements the background-position CSS property can then be used to shift the visible area to the required component image.

This technique can be very effective for improving site performance, particularly in situations where many small images, such as menu icons, are used. The Yahoo! home page, for example, employs this technique.

This software works online but you can also download the code and run on your local server. Upload your zipped images and fill up the form in the home page, the software can also generate the CSS for you.

Source Files

Upload Images (ZIP):

Browse... Max Upload Size: 0.5MB

Image Duplicates

- Ignore duplicate images
- Remove duplicate images but merge CSS rules

DoxyGen

www.doxygen.org/index.html

Doxygen is a documentation system for C++, C, Java, Objective-C, Python, IDL (Corba and Microsoft flavors), Fortran, VHDL, PHP, C#, and to some extent D.

This tool can help you in three ways:

- It can generate an on-line documentation browser (in HTML) and/or an off-line reference manual from a set of documented source files. There is also support for generating output in RTF (MS-Word), PostScript, hyperlinked PDF, compressed HTML, and Unix man pages. The documentation is extracted directly from the sources, which makes it much easier to keep the documentation consistent with the source code.
- You can configure doxygen to extract the code structure from undocumented source files. This is very useful to quickly find your way in large source distributions. You can also visualize the relations between the various elements by means of include dependency graphs, inheritance diagrams, and collaboration diagrams, which are all generated automatically.
- You can even `abuse' doxygen for creating normal documentation

Doxygen Documentation

FileZilla

http://filezilla-project.org/

FileZilla Client is a fast and reliable cross-platform FTP, FTPS and SFTP client with lots of useful features and an intuitive graphical user interface.

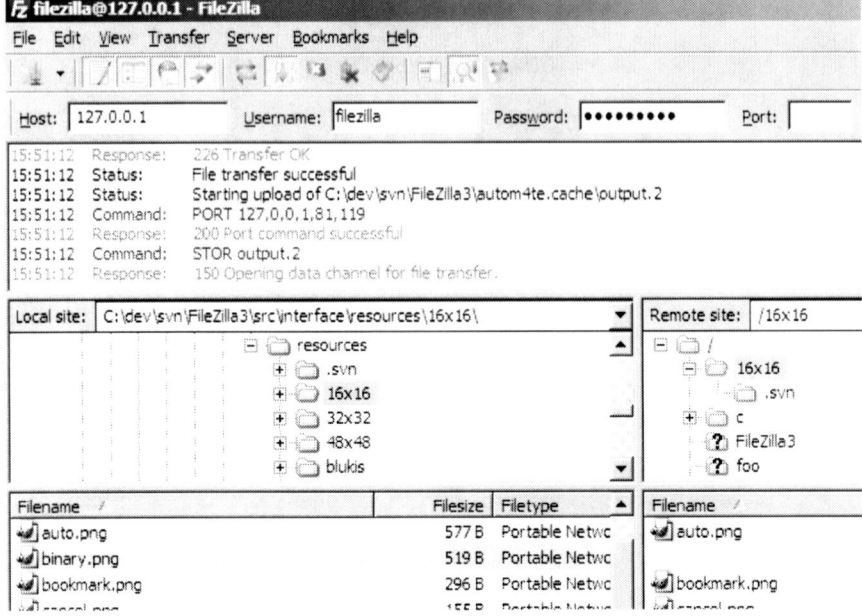

FireBug

http://getfirebug.com/

This add-on for Firefox is able to inspect and debug your HTML

- Inspect HTML and modify style and layout in real-time
- Use the most advanced JavaScript debugger available for any browser
- Accurately analyze network usage and performance
- Extend Firebug and add features to make Firebug even more powerful
- Get the information you need to get it done with Firebug

Firephp
http://www.firephp.org/

FirePHP enables you to log to your Firebug Console using a simple PHP method call. All data is sent via response headers and will not interfere with the content on your page. FirePHP is ideally suited for AJAX development where clean JSON and XML responses are required.

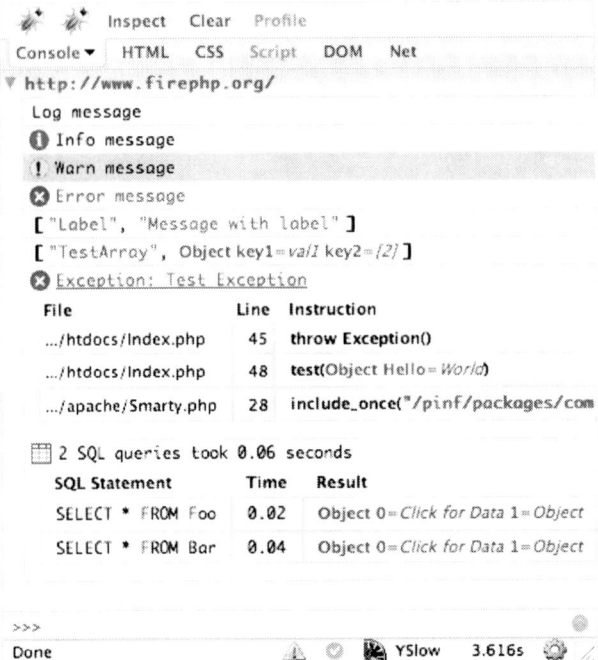

Google Sitemap Generator

http://sourceforge.net/projects/goog-sitemapgen/files/sitemapgen/

Quickly generate a sitemap file based on the Sitemap XML protocol without having to write it yourself.

Javascript debugger

There are many available , please look at FireFox > Add-on

Logic CSS framework

http://code.google.com/p/logicss/

a collection of CSS files and a toolset designed to cut development times for web-standards compliant web layouts and templates.

- Common cross-browser rendering behaviour approach (not

a reset).
- Beautiful font stacks.
- Typography with text resizing capabilities and vertical baseline/rhythm.
- Three totally flexible layout grid templates, customizable with the toolset.
- Elastic layout using EMs.
- Liquid layout with percentages.
- Fixed layout using pixel dimensions.

Notepad ++
notepad-plus-plus.org

Notepad++ is a free source code editor and Notepad replacement that supports several languages. Running in the MS Windows environment, its use is governed by GPL License.

Based on the powerful editing component Scintilla, Notepad++ is written in C++ and uses pure Win32 API and STL which ensures a higher execution speed and smaller program size. By optimizing as many routines as possible without losing user friendliness, Notepad++ is trying to reduce the world carbon dioxide emissions. When using less CPU power, the PC can throttle down and reduce power consumption, resulting in a greener environment.

```
33              $this->setName($name);
34          }
35          public function speak(){
36              return "Hi I'm " . $this->name;
37          }
38      }
39
40      $animal = new animal();  // Generic Animal
41      $bird = new bird('Titty');  // Bird named Titty
42      $cat = new cat('Tommy');  // Cat named Tommy
43      $human = new human('Bob');  // Human named Bob
44
45      echo "<br />\n".$animal->speak();
46      echo "<br />\n".$bird->speak();
47      echo "<br />\n".$cat->speak();
48      echo "<br />\n".$human->speak();
49
50
51      $a= "hello";
52      $$a=" world";
53      echo "<br />\n".$hello;
54
```

Photos (Yahoo)
http://www.flickr.com

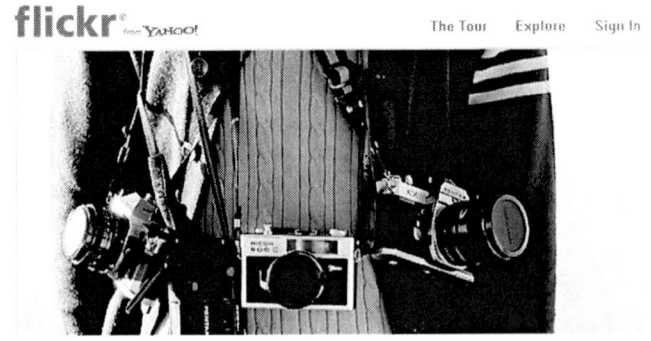

PHP and Javascript
jcay.com

Tons of code available here :

Categories

- ASP (2477)
- ASP.NET (1519)
- Ajax (290)
- C and C++ (487)
- CFML (272)
- CGI and Perl (4576)
- Flash (2126)
- HTML5 (1)
- Java (1507)
- JavaScript (2956)
- PHP (16057)
- Python (128)
- Remotely Hosted (2495)
- Ruby on Rails (82)
- Tools and Utilities (4426)
- Web Hosting (24)
- XML (269)

PHP classes
www.phpclasses.org

An other interesting site for developers :

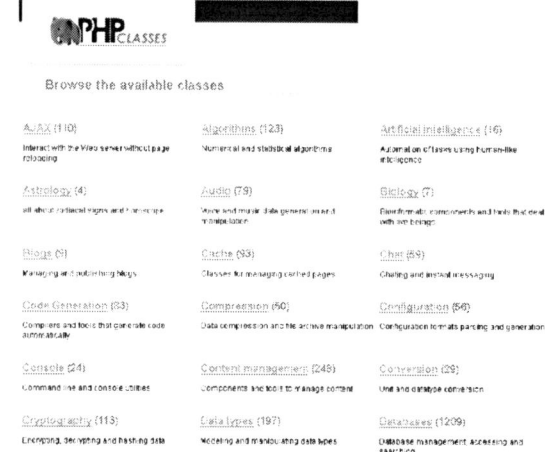

Pingdom Tools
http://tools.pingdom.com/fpt/

Web-based application that you can use for easily testing the performance of your web pages. It can give you information on the total loading time of a web page and the total number of objects required to render the page to give you insights on things you can leave out or combine.

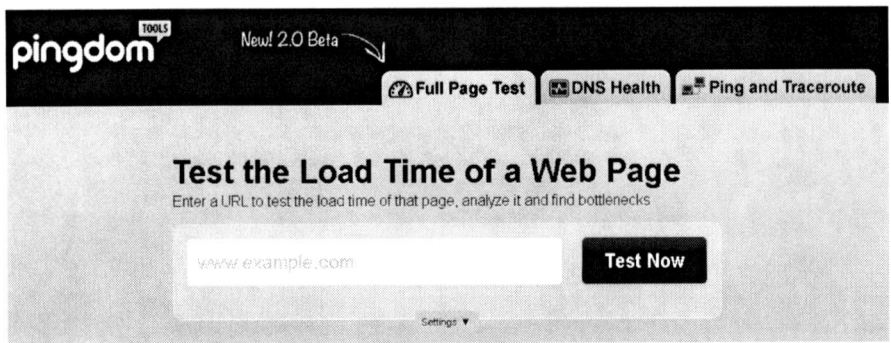

Sajax
www.modernmethod.com/sajax/index.phtml

Simple Ajax Toolkit is an open source framework developed to speed up the creation of Ajax applications. It supports major sever-side technologies such as ASP, Cold Fusion, PHP, Perl, Python, and Ruby. Sajax has a fairly large community of over 39,000 registered users on their forums

Swish

www.swishzone.com

Advanced Flash creation tool for the graphic artist or web professional. Advanced drawing tools, scripting, Flash video - everything you need for a dynamic Flash animation.

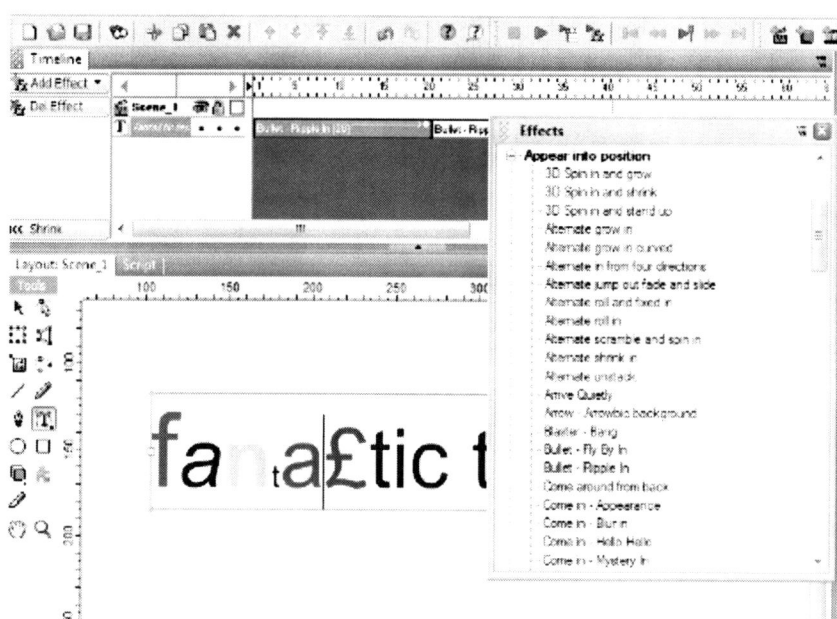

Test plugin for JavaScriptMVC

http://javascriptmvc.com

JavaScript testing framework to help speed up Javascript development

Let JavaScriptMVC do the heavy lifting

XAMPP

www.apachefriends.org/en/xampp.html

An easy to install Apache distribution containing MySQL, PHP and Perl. XAMPP is really very easy to install and to use - just download, extract and start.

Many people know from their own experience that it's not easy to install an Apache web server and it gets harder if you want to add MySQL, PHP and Perl.

XAMPP is an easy to install Apache distribution containing MySQL, PHP and Perl. XAMPP is really very easy to install and to use - just download, extract and start.

Xplorer²

http://zabkat.com/

Desktop file manager combining the simplicity of windows explorer with the speed and efficiency of traditional dual pane orthodox file managers, helping you be productive with your documents, pictures, music, source code and other files.

Yahoo Design Patterns

http://developer.yahoo.com/ypatterns

The *Yahoo! Design Pattern Library* is a large collection of proven optimal web design patterns to save you time in creating highly-sophisticated design solutions.

Yahoo! Design Pattern Library

Welcome! This library shares user interface patterns with the web design and development community. We've got 59 patterns today and more on the way, and we welcome your feedback.

Get Started   Browse All Patterns   About the Library   Join the Community

PShop Upgrades

Intro	317
System Requirements	317
Backup	317
Update PShop (auto)	317
Update PShop (manual)	319

Intro

As any software PShop is also releasing regular updates and a lot of activity is recently going on with meetings held around the world. In this chapter we'll discuss how to Upgrade PShop to the latest version (currently 1.4.6.2 but the procedure is the same for 1.4.7 too). The full documentation on how to upgrade can be found on the official Wiki of PShop :
http://www.prestashop.com/wiki/Installing_and_Updating_PrestaShop_software/

System Requirements

To run properly PShop need the following :

- Linux, Unix, or Windows
- Apache Web server
- PHP 5.0 or later. (you may have to activate PHP 5 on your hosting service.)
- MySQL 4.1.14 or later

You can have all of the above installed in your PC using XAMPP or alternatively you can install PShop in a web space (hosting) provided by your ISP.

Backup

It's essential to backup your data before proceeding with the upgrade. You can see how to backup your database in the previous chapter dealing with MySQL. Do not proceed to the next step without having a valid backup of your database.

Update PShop (auto)

In this paragraph we'll see how to upgrade PShop from version 1.4.4 upto version 1.4.6.2 although this procedure will probably be the same also for any future version.

- Open BO > Tools > Upgrade
- Check that your current configuration is valid as below :

Your current configuration

Root directory : C:\xampp\htdocs\pshop144

Root directory status : fully writable

Autoupgrade allowed : This release allow autoupgrade..

Shop status : Active

PHP time limit : disabled

Root directory : writable recursively.

- Locate the Update dialog and click : Upgrade PrestaShop Now!

Update

Your current prestashop version : 1.4.4.0

Last version is 1.4.6.2 final (1.4.6.2)

- Latest Prestashop version available is: **1.4.6.2 final**

Upgrade PrestaShop now !

PShop will deactivate and will start to download the upgrade..
During this process PShop will :

Provide a RollBack functionality (this will probably be fully functional only in the next releases)
Backup (again) your files

At the end you should get the following message :

Currently processing :

Upgrade process done. Congratulations! You can now reactivate your shop.

- Goto BO > Preferences > Enable Shop

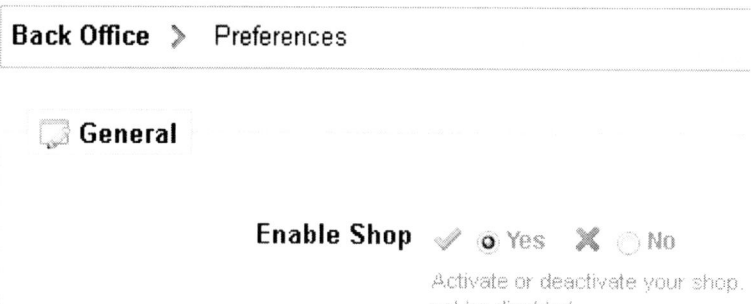

Scroll down the window to the footer, you should now see the new version in the bottom-left corner as below :

Update PShop (manual)

In this paragraph we'll see how to upgrade manually PShop from version 1.4.4 upto version 1.4.6.2
You can run this procedure in case you had problems with the automatic update described above.

- Download the latest PrestaShop release from the official

website
- Unzip it in your hard drive.
- Upload the contents of the /prestashop folder to the root folder of your site via FTP.
- Make sure the following PrestaShop folders have 'write' permissions (CHMOD 755) but do not apply these permissions recursively to their subfolders. Then make sure the following folders have 'write' permissions and apply these permissions recursively to their subfolders : /img, /mails, /modules, /themes/prestashop/lang, /translations . You can do this with the FTP client FileZilla
- In case you've modified the contents of the /mails folder, copy the contents of your backup copy of /mails to the new build's /mails folder.
- Copy the contents of your backup copy of the /img folder to the new build's /img folder.
- In case you added any extra modules to your default version of PrestaShop, copy the added modules from the backup copy of /modules to the new build's /modules folder.
- In case you installed some modules having their configuration inside a file (instead of the database) such as the "editorial" module you will have to copy them from your backup to your current module folder (e.g., "/modules/editorial/").
- In case you've modified the .htaccess file, merge the contents of the old and new .htaccess files, deleting any duplicate information. Do not replace one with the other.
- If applicable, copy your customized themes subfolder (e.g., /themes/mythemes) from the backup /themes folder to the new build's /themes parent folder.
- In case you made changes to the default theme itself, running the updater will therefore erase your changes. To recover the changes you had made to the default theme, create a new customized themes folder (for example, /themes/mythemes) in the new build and then transfer into it the contents of the old default theme folder located in your backup copy of PrestaShop.
- Copy the settings.inc.php file from the backup folder /config to the new /config folder.

- In your Web browser, launch the Installer by adding /install to your shop's URL (e.g., http://www.mysite.com/prestashop/install) and select 'update' at the beginning of the process.

Index

Symbols

$_SERVER 19, 20, 21, 22
.htacces : 260

A

Abstract Class 257
Access MySQL database 17
Agent Ransak 301
ASP 220
autocorrect 290
Autoload 91

B

Back Office 9
Backup 272, 276
Birthday Present 217
BO. *See* Back Office

C

Cache 9, 13, 23
Carriers 31
Classes 221, 247, 257, 277
Clean AJAX 302
Codango 303
code completion 290, 291, 292
Code Cues 290
Contact Form 28
Cookies 89
Copyright 27
Cross Selling 215, 217
CSS 104, 106, 107, 108, 109, 110, 111, 114, 120, 123, 125, 126, 132
CSS framework Blueprint 303
CSS Sprite generator 304
Customer Follow-Up 217
Customer Referral Program 217

D

database 8, 17, 18

Database Locking 46
Data Import 56
DB class 69
Debugging PShop 296
Domain Name Selection 202, 203
DoxyGen 305
DW 165, 166, 167, 168, 190, 192, 193, 194

E

eCommerce 4, 5, 8
Editor 280, 281, 288, 289, 290
Email notifications 27
Employee class 80
Error handling 221, 241

F

Favicon 25
FileZilla 305
FireBug 306
Firephp 307
Flash 25
FO. *See also* Front Office
Forein keys 45
Frameworks 221, 261
Front Office 9
Function signature : 260

G

GET 18, 22, 23
Google Sitemap Generator 308

H

Homepage 25
Homepage logo. *See* Homepage
hook 137, 138
Hooks 94, 95, 99
HTML , 13, 18, 20, 21, 22, 23, 104, 105, 112, 113, 114, 115, 120, 124, 127, 128

I

Image Sprite 111
Indexing 46
Information Blocks 29
InnoDB 45, 46, 47

J

Javascript 114, 125
Javascript debugger 308
JQuery 120, 122, 123, 125
jQuery AJAX Methods , 123
JQuery CSS methods , 123
JQuery Effects , 122
JSON , 124, 126

L

Language 140
Link Popularity 202, 204
Live Edit 125
Logic CSS framework 308
logo 25, 28, 29, 31

M

Magic Methods : 260
Mail Alerts 216
MD5 21
Meta Tags 202, 203
Module class 85
Modules 8, 11
MVC 9, 11
MyISAM 45, 46, 47
MySQL 8, 14, 15, 17
MySQL class 82
MySQL Workbench 47

N

Namespaces 87, 88
Newsletter 216
Notepad ++ 309
NuSoap 284, 285, 286, 299

O

ObjectModel class 83
OOP 69, 92
Orders 27
Overloading: 260
Override 92
Override: 260

P

Page Title 26
PEAR 127, 128, 132
PhotoShop 164, 165, 189, 190, 191, 193
Photos (Yahoo) 310
PHP 5, 8, 14, 15, 16, 17, 18, 19, 20, 21, 22, 23
PHP and Javascript 311
PHP classes 311
PHP_SELF 19, 20, 21, 22
PIE 220, 251, 252, 254
Positions 137
POST 18, 19, 20, 21, 22, 23
Preferences 33, 34
PrestaShop 1, 2, 3, 4, 5, 7, 8, 9
products 8, 10, 11, 12
Profiler 279, 282, 287
Promotions block 217
PShop 4, 104, 8, 9, 10, 11, 13, 14, 17, 18, 22, 125, 101, 103, 296, 298, 124, 125, 126, 127, 130, 131, 279, 294, 296, 316, 317, 318, 319

R

Retrieve Data 61
Robots Exclusion File 202, 204

S

Sajax 312
SEO 200, 201, 202, 205, 208, 209, 212, 218
Session 221, 223, 239
Site Map 202
Smarty 261, 262, 263, 264, 277
SMS TM4b 217
SQL 101, 102, 104, 132
SQL Injection 64, 66
SQL queries 55
Structure 43, 45
Swift Mailer 129, 130
Swish 313

T

templates 8
Test plugin for JavaScriptMVC 313
Themes 8
Tips 162

Tod for MySQL 47, 49
Tokens 17, 18, 23
Tools 25, 26, 37
Tools class 72
Top Sellers 217
Transactions 46

U

Units 106
Update Data 63
Update PShop 316, 317, 319

V

Validate class 77
Vouchers and Coupons 29

W

web server 8, 14, 15
Web Service 59
Web Site Content 202, 203
Wishlist block 217

X

XAMPP 8, 14, 15, 16, 17
Xplorer² 314

Y

Yahoo Design Patterns 315